Zhong Nanshan: People above Everything

Xiong Yuqun
Translated by Haiwang Yuan

Prunus Press USA

Original Title: 《钟南山：苍生在上》

Original book published by
Guangdong Flower City Publishing House Co., Ltd

This edition is published by arrangement with Prunus Press USA, through the agency of China National Publications Import and Export (Group) Co., Ltd.

All rights reserved.

Zhong Nanshan: People above Everything

Copyright © Prunus Press USA

Written by Xiong Yuqun

Translated by Haiwang Yuan

Designed by Wu Yanfeng & Brandy Ding

First edition: 2023
ISBN: 978-1-61612-163-1

It's a political task of prime importance for one to do his best in his post.

—Zhong Nanshan

Xiong Yuqun is the dean of the Guangdong Institute of Arts, Adjunct Professor of Tongji University, of which he is an outstanding alumnus. He is a winner of the 5th Award of the Lu Xun Literary Award, the 18th Hundred Flowers Awards, and the 13th Award of the Bingxin Literary Award. He has been selected as one of the national "Four Batch of Talents," one of Guangdong Province's leading talents in literature, and a writer reputed for moral integrity and literary skills.

He is a prolific author of over two dozen literary works. His poetry collections include *Sanzhi yanjing* (*Three Eyes*) and *Wo de yisheng zai wo zhi wai* (*My Life Is Beyond Myself*). His full-length novels are represented by *Lian'erju* and *Jimao nian yu xue* (*Rain and Snow of 1939*). His essays collections and full-length documentary writings include *Chuntian de shi'er tiao heliu* (*Twelve Rivers in Spring*), *Xizang de gandong* (*The Touching Tibet*), *Zou bu wan de Xizang* (*The Boundless Tibet*), *Luoma de shiguang youxi* (*Rome's Game of Time*), *Lu shang de zuxian* (*Traveling Ancestors*), and *Yi ji heshan: dadi shang de qianxi* (*Sojourners: Migration on the Great Land*). His *Rain and Snow of 1939*, *The Touching Tibet*, *Wu chao* (*No Nest*), *Shengming dakai de chuangkou* (*A Life-Opened Window*), and *My Life Is Beyond Myself* have been translated and published in Germany, Russia, Italy, Hungary, Egypt, Jordan, Japan, and the UK.

Midnight

(As an Introduction)

Tonight,
Rain has ceased.
Tears hit and pained the land muddy.
The snow in the north is like a beast,
Piercing through the wind gusty.

A city lying by the Yangtze
Never sees its street lamps dimmed
On its empty boulevards.
The last month of 2019 and the next two
Witnessed farewells as eternal as the river
Bid to the nameless and ageless people,
Who journeyed back to their ancestors
In a continuous stream.
Death
Was unstoppable.

That midnight was lengthy
Because the day was short.
It saw a man at over eighty
Setting off in a hurry.
The tears in his eyes
Mingled with those of many a family,
Or rather, those of the country.
In early 2020, who cared about birds' twitter?
In the city by the Yangtze River,
Curtain walls couldn't keep spring's rainwater.
Illusionary voices sounded like from the Tang.
That night, darkness burned severely.
The night continued to linger,
And who alone had to forego slumber?
Those in white, hand in hand,
Like helping angles, hustle hither and thither.

Written on the midnight of March 6, 2020

Contents

Chapter One
Mourning of the "Coronaviruses'" Victims in 2020 7

Chapter Two
The Pain of SARS in 2003 83

Chapter Three
The Best Doctors Are Those Who Care about Ordinary People 169

Chapter Four
Setbacks Are a Man's Stepping Stone to Becoming Strong 189

Chapter Five
A Studying Tour in the UK 225

Chapter Six
A Man of Strict Moral Principles 247

Afterword 253

Appendix
A Biographical Timeline of Zhong Nanshan's Life 275

Chapter One

Mourning of the "Coronaviruses" Victims in 2020

He felt he was traveling in a dreamland instead of actual space. Time also became fuzzy.... He was 67 when he was called to fight the severe acute respiratory syndrome (SARS), but today he was 84. Seventeen years seemed to have fleeted away in the blink of an eye, leaving its trace only on his hair, as gray as the autumn dew. He had never imagined that he would still have been at war with the coronavirus.

- 1 -

It looked much darker as the sun submerged itself in the grayish twilight that appeared like mist or fog. The winter of 2019 felt warm. He already forgot when it last rained. However, the land in the south of the Nanling Mountains was still covered with lush vegetation. The low-hanging horizon was as hazy as frosted glass. Only the patch of the sky above his head appeared light blue. His car left the urban area under the starry sky and turned to the Outer Ring and into the Guangzhou West Line Expressway. A plain journey soon took him to the Guangzhou South Railway Station.

Zhong Nanshan and his assistant Su Yueming got off the car at the platform on the second floor. People who had long been waiting at the door came up to greet them.

Built the earliest in China, this large-scale high-speed rail station appeared like a razor clam from the bird's-eye view and a light tent when looked up. Long lines of passengers with bulky luggage moved in the super-large space like flying dragons or a waving sea in slow motion. The setting sun gave way to street lamps. Zhong Nanshan arrived at the departing hall and was instantly engulfed by the sea of passengers.

Jiao Yahui, ombudswoman of the National Health Commission's Bureau of Medical Administration, called Su Yueming, who was fixing his lunch at the time. Jiao said on the phone that the epidemic situation in Wuhan was urgent and asked that Zhong Nanshan get to the city that day. Simultaneously, Zhong Nanshan was at a meeting to discuss the novel coronavirus epidemic with other experts. Suspected cases of the disease had appeared in Shenzhen. Soon after he treated two such patients in Shenzhen yesterday, the health department of Guangdong held a meeting. The Guangdong Health Commission would convene another special meeting that afternoon to discuss the epidemic. In the past few days, Zhong Nanshan had paid close attention to the situation in Wuhan while treating patients in Shenzhen. He had been worried and obsessed with the novel coronavirus.

Su Yueming hung up the phone and glanced at his watch. It was 11:00 a.m. sharp. He called Academician Zhong immediately. Zhong Nanshan paused a little on the other end of the phone and said, "I have a meeting in the afternoon. It's impossible to get there today. See if it will work tomorrow."

Su Yueming called the ombudswoman of the National Health Commission's Bureau of Medical Administration back and asked if they could get to Wuhan the next day. Jiao Yahui responded that she had to consult the other administrators.

Su Yueming felt that things were unusual, so he quickly checked the plane tickets for that day, but all were sold out. He then checked the high-speed train tickets, but they were all gone. Not even a standing ticket was available.

Jiao Yahui phoned back and said they insisted that Academician Zhong arrive in Wuhan that day after consultation. After Su Yueming told her that none of the plane and train tickets were available, Jiao Yahui said she would contact the Railway Bureau so that Academician Zhong could come by high-speed train.

Still unassured, Jiao Yahui called Zhong Nanshan directly. She told him that the Health Commission had set up a team of senior experts. Director Ma Xiaowei wanted him to study the details of the epidemic in Wuhan and see if it was a human-to-human transmitted disease.

Zhong Nanshan said there were such cases in Shenzhen as well, and those cases revealed that the disease was transmissible from person to person. He added that an elderly woman, who had never been to Wuhan, was stricken with the condition when a family member who had returned from Wuhan also fell ill.

Jiao Yahui said, "Please come to Wuhan as soon as possible."

Zhong Nanshan asked if he could go on the 19th, saying that he was treating acutely sick patients in consultation with his colleagues.

The outspoken Jiao Yahui responded, "You certainly can't. You must get to Wuhan on the 18th so that we can consult with one another to ascertain the epidemic." Jiao Yahui's tone was anxious.

Zhong Nanshan said he would hurry to Wuhan after treating the patients with other consultant physicians. Jiao Yahui responded, "You must come to Wuhan overnight today, and we'll help with your transportation."

Zhong Nanshan had anticipated the suddenness and usualness of the happening. He had felt that he might be called on to get involved in its solution. But he had never expected it to be so compelling. Knowing that the country was in dire need of his help, he responded as soon as Jiao finished, "I'll leave after the afternoon's meeting and reach Wuhan tonight."

It was the Spring Festival travel rush. Therefore, the National Health Commission contacted the newly established State Council Joint

Prevention and Control Mechanism, asking to get train tickets for Zhong Nanshan. The solution was that Zhong Nanshan and his assistant would be led into a car of the train by the railway station's staff member. If they couldn't find their seats, they would be offered a small stool each.

As soon as he finished lunch, Zhong Nanshan went to the meeting convened by the Guangdong Health Commission. He even had no time to pack for his journey. Su Yueming helped with the packing in the afternoon and rushed to the Health Commission's meeting venue. The Guangdong experts analyzed and discussed various countermeasures for the novel coronavirus epidemic. At this time, the staff of Guangzhou South Railway Station called, telling Su Yueming that the station staff could send them to the high-speed train.

Zhong Nanshan hurried out of the venue at 4:30 p.m. Su Yueming rose from his seat quickly and rushed downstairs with Zhong Nanshan. The two scrambled straight to the high-speed railway station.

A young woman in her dark-blue uniform led them to the ticket-checking entrance in haste at the station. The long queue outside the gate had disappeared, and the electronic screen displayed that the G1022 train from Guangzhou South to Wuhan leaves at 17:51.

It was the only train that would leave the station soon, starting from Shenzhen and stopping at the Guangzhou South Railway Station. The entrance was closed as quickly as they entered. All the cars were packed. The young woman found the train-crew captain and told him about the emergency and its significance. The captain led Zhong Nanshan to the dining car and found two seats for him and his assistant.

Zhong Nanshan wore a coffee suit that he had put on in the morning when leaving for the meeting. With his shirt, it was alright for the warm weather in Guangzhou. But it was much colder in Wuhan. Su Yueming asked if he would like to add his woolen sweater, and he reached out for the luggage as he spoke. Zhong Nanshan signaled him not to bother. He was thinly clad even in winter anyway. When packing for him, Su Yueming had placed a change of clothes, a sweater, and a down-filled coat. He had thought that they would stay in Wuhan just for a day.

Taking out his laptop, Zhong Nanshan started working.

During his investigation in Shenzhen yesterday, Zhong Nanshan found a family who had just returned from Wuhan and its members falling ill one by one. They were hospitalized at the University of Hong Kong-Shenzhen Hospital. One of the patients had never been to Wuhan. It was an alarming sign! The National Health Commission had arranged for experts to fly to Wuhan, with some joining them one after another later. This second assembly of the experts didn't bode well. Zhong Nanshan called the doctors in Wuhan to learn about the epidemic. The one who answered his phone was his former student.

He hurriedly went through the relevant data on his computer to sort things out and analyze them. He worked so attentively that he seemed to have forgotten that he was on a high-speed rail. Su Yueming knew that Zhong Nanshan hated to be interrupted at the moment like this.

The train-crew captain rushed over to return the money paid for the meal, saying since Academician Zhong was going to Wuhan for the country, they were not supposed to charge him. Su Yueming tried to decline, but after a few trials, he gave up, and he had to take the cash.

Zhong Nanshan felt sleepy at 9:00 p.m. and closed his eyes, leaning his head against the seat's low back. He had been stricken by an illness not long before, coughing and feeling feeble and tired. The scene touched Su

Yueming, who took a candid photo of Zhong Nanshan nodding off. The time print was 9:15 p.m. Later, the picture became viral. It showed rows of red seats, with passengers looking at the cellphones in their hands. Zhong Nanshan was the only senior citizen.

Zhong Nanshan opened his eyes about a quarter later. He asked Su Yueming to record his judgment on the epidemic on the laptop. He believed that 1) the novel coronavirus disease was bound to be transmitted from human to human, and 2) attention must be paid to early discovery and isolation, and the public must be warned against going to Wuhan and refrain from going out or gathering....

The information disclosed on the Internet showed that 59 newly confirmed cases of novel coronavirus patients with pneumonia infection were reported in Wuhan on January 18, 2020.

– 2 –

The first person to report unexplained pneumonia was Dr. Zhang Jixian from the Hubei Provincial Hospital of Integrated Chinese and Western Medicine (HPHICWM). During this warm winter, she lived a life of traveling back and forth between her home and her hospital. She lived on Hong Kong Road, a 20-minute walk to the hospital or one subway station. After graduating from the Medicine Department of the Wuhan University School of Medicine, she worked in the hospital for three decades. Working had become life's focus, treating outpatients as an expert in the morning twice a week and dealing with the problems in the wards the rest of the week. She had been so busy that she had repeatedly given up the chance to visit foreign countries. This short-statured woman from Huilongshan Town of Huanggang City, Hubei Province, did everything efficiently and orderly. She also spoke fast and expressively, characteristic of the Hubei natives' dauntlessness and tenaciousness.

Outpatients came in increasing numbers on the afternoon of December 26, 2019. Zhang Jixian came to work at 2:00 p.m. and treated a woman in her seventies in consultation with other physicians at 4:00 p.m. The patient Du had a high fever and breathed hard. Zhang Jixian found the X-ray film of the patient's lungs, whose frosted-glass appearance struck her unusual.

The patient was to be hospitalized. As usual, hospitals receive more patients in winter. Because the inpatient department was filled with them, Ms. Du's sickbed was set in the corridor. When Zhang Jixian saw her condition worsen and nothing but an oxygen cylinder available, she swapped No. 22 patient, whose condition was milder, out of his ward to accommodate Ms. Du. She was worried that something terrible might happen to her at night. Zhang Jixian concluded that Mr. Du was infected with some virus and asked the doctor on duty to pay attention to her breathing frequency and oxygen saturation.

Ms. Du's condition was stable the following day. A patient with the family name Zhang hospitalized in the Neurology Department also showed abnormality in his lungs. He has been admitted for a problem in his right eye that caused it to be blurry. The Neurology Department called the Respiratory and Critical Care Department (RCCD) to ask for a consultation. The doctors from the RCCD went to see the patient and asked Zhang Jixian for advice. She decided to transfer him to the RCCD.

While going through the paperwork for the transfer, the patient Zhang asked that he share the same ward with Ms. Du. They turned out to be husband and wife. A relative had driven them to the hospital the day before. Ms. Du had just returned from Guizhou with a tour group. She had coughed a little before the trip and had a fever on the tour bus. She felt lethargic and coughed more severely with short breaths when she came back. High fever dominated the evening. She had been to the Central Hospital of Wuhan's OPD before being transferred to the HPHICWM.

Hearing that they were a couple, Zhang Jixian became alert, sensing something was wrong. She compared the CT scans and found similar symptoms. Zhang Jixian realized the severity of the problem. She had participated in identifying SARS patients during its prevention and control campaign. Now, something reminded her of that experience.

The young man who hurried here and there to help Mr. Zhang with his transfer procedures told Zhang Jixian he was the couple's son when she asked him who he was. This 5.9-foot young man looked healthy and strong. Zhang Jixian suggested giving him a checkup. His wife encouraged him to comply, considering the conditions of her parents-in-law.

The young man had a CT scan, and Zhang Jixian was shocked to see its similarity to his parents'. She also performed influenza-related tests for the family of three, including Influenza A and B, RSV (respiratory syncytial virus), adenoviruses, rhinovirus, chlamydia, and mycoplasma. All the tests turned out to be negative, which meant that the possibility of their infection with influenza was excluded. It was noon now, time to get off work.

As soon as she got to the hospital at 2:00 p.m., Zhang Jixian first called the director of her hospital's Public Health Department, but no one picked up the phone. She rushed to the office and saw it vacant. She went to the director of the Medical Department and told him everything about the three patients. The director called the Public Health Department, but no one answered. Zhang Jixian couldn't wait. She dialed the phone number of Xia Wenguang, the associate head of the hospital in charge of the hospital's day-to-day operation, but he was unexpectedly unavailable, either.

While getting someone to send for the Xia Wenguang, the associate head, he called back. He was at the year-end summary meeting at the Jianghan District Center for Disease Control and Prevention. Upon hearing this, he immediately reported it to the center and arranged for his hospital to discuss the matter. The Jianghan District Center for Disease Control and Prevention dispatched two experts to the hospital, and they arrived a little past 4:00 p.m. They sampled the patients and did an epidemiological investigation. Zhang Jixian isolated the family of three and asked all the doctors and nurses to wear masks when in close contact with the patients.

It was already odd for a whole family to suffer from the same disease. Then, there came a middle-aged man name Fang on the same day. He was dumpy and coughed with short breaths as the family of three did. The condition of his lungs also resembled theirs. The patient had a shop in the Huanan Seafood Wholesale Market. He sold frozen animals and fowls like ducks and pork. He was also hospitalized.

Zhang Jixian transferred all the other patients in her department to other departments.

Three more patients came to the outpatient service on the 28th and 29th with the same symptoms. They all worked at the Huanan Seafood

Wholesale Market and knew one another. The two patients who came to the ER on the afternoon of the 29th were Mr. Fang's cousins. They helped him move the frozen meat in his shop. The patients' conditions were so acute that they were almost breathless in the wheelchairs after getting off the ambulance. After examining their CT scans, Zhang Jixian immediately sent them to the Wuhan Jinyintan Hospital, which specializes in treating infectious diseases.

The HPHICWM held a consultation involving ten experts from the Respiratory Department, the Hospital Infection Control Office, the Cardiovascular Department, the ICU, the Radiology Department, the Pharmaceutical Department, the Clinical Test Department, the Infectious Disease Department, and the Medical Department. When they asked about how the patients were related, they found out that the Zhang family did not know anyone who came later. Neither did they visit the Huanan Seafood Wholesale Market. The patient Fang revealed that two other people who suffered from the same disease had gone to the Wuhan Tongji Hospital and Wuhan Union Hospital. They both had businesses in the Huanan Seafood Wholesale Market.

All those with infectious diseases must be transferred to the Wuhan Jinyintan Hospital. But none of the Zhang family believed they had gotten the disease and worried that they would be infected once in the Jinyintan Hospital. Eventually, they insisted that one of them must remain in the HPHICWM. After repeated persuasion, the parents of the Zhang family asked that their son stay where he was. Zhang Jixian promised that she would keep him if he showed signs of recovery and insisted he go with them if the test result proved otherwise. She finally allowed the son to remain in the hospital for further treatment when she found his lungs improved.

The Wuhan Health Commission issued the "Urgent Notice on Reporting or Sending Patients with Pneumonia of Unknown Causes for Treatment" on December 30. The "Notice" explained that patients with pneumonia of unknown causes appeared one after another in the Huanan Seafood Wholesale Market in Wuhan. It requested all clinics and hospitals to immediately check and count the patients with similar symptoms of pneumonia of unknown causes that they had received in the past week to better respond to the situation. It also required them to report the statistics to the Municipal Health Commission's Medical Administration and Management Office before 4 p.m. on the same day.

At 11:00 p.m. that day, Gao Fu, director of the Chinese Center for Disease Control and Prevention, read the news on WeChat. After verifying it, he reported it to Ma Xiaowei, the National Health Commission director, and three other associate directors. The National Health Commission Expert Team was set up at 3:00 a.m. on December 31. The expert team took the first flight from Beijing to Wuhan at 6:50 a.m. and arrived in Wuhan in the morning.

The Wuhan Health Commission issued the "Wuhan Municipal Health Commission's Bulletin on the Current Novel Coronavirus Epidemic in Our City" on December 31. The bulletin read, "Recently, some medical institutions have found that many novel coronavirus cases they received are related to the Huanan Seafood Wholesale Market.... So far, 27 cases have been found, of which seven are in serious condition. The remaining cases are stable and controllable, and two cases have improved and are scheduled to be discharged shortly. The clinical manifestations of the cases are primarily fever. A few patients have difficulty breathing, and chest

X-rays show infiltrative lesions in both lungs. At present, all cases have been isolated and treated while the follow-up investigation and medical observation of close contacts are in progress. Hygienic investigation and sanitary treatment of the Huanan Seafood Wholesale Market is being conducted.... So far, the investigation has found no obvious human-to-human transmission, and no medical staff infection has been found. The detection of the pathogen and the investigation of the cause of infection are currently underway.... The disease can be prevented and controlled. In terms of prevention, keep indoor air circulated; avoid visiting poorly ventilated public places and crowded venues, and wear masks when going out."

Many media reported the news of Wuhan issuing a bulletin on the novel coronavirus epidemic situation, highlighting the wording: "27 cases have been found" and "the investigation has found no obvious human-to-human transmission."

As soon as the National Health Commission Expert Team, led by the commission's deputy director Yu Xuejun arrived in Wuhan on December 31, it divided itself into two groups. One went to the Huanan Seafood Wholesale Market for an epidemiological investigation. The other group, composed of clinical experts, headed for the Jinyintan Hospital to analyze the cases and determine the diagnostic and treatment plan. They worked through the night on New Year's Day and issued nine documents the following morning. The documents covered designated hospitals, fever clinics, doctor protection, hospital infection management, and hospital transfer. The documents were distributed in Wuhan.

After the Chinese Center for Disease Control and Prevention received the specimens from Wuhan on January 2, 2020, the scientific research team, led by the center's director Gao Fu, obtained a positive result from the fluorescence quantitative RT-PCR process in three hours. They completed the genome sequence determination of the first novel coronavirus in 24 hours. They successfully developed a high-specific and high-sensitive nucleic acid antigen test kit in 48 hours. They successfully isolated and cultured the novel coronavirus and observed the typical coronavirus particle morphology under the electron microscope on January 7, providing critical etiological evidence for scientific understanding of the epidemic. The center released the whole genome sequence and electron microscope photos of the novel coronavirus to the world for the first time, which the WHO highly praised.

– 3 –

The train entered the boundary of Hunan Province after passing through the Dayaoshan Tunnel at Shaoguan City, Guangdong Province. The high-speed train zoomed like lightning into winter under the Nanling Mountains. The villages flashed back like a memory thrown to the other side of time and space.

The train's cars were full of passengers returning home for the Chinese New Year. The festive atmosphere got increasingly tense as the Year of the Rat drew near day by day. After busying themselves for a year, they were all planning their New Year celebrations.

The passengers hung their heads down with their eyes fixed on their mobile phones. They were recounting their travel experiences, sharing what they had seen, arranging and planning the New Year celebration activities with their loved ones with whom they would soon reunite, or simply idling away the unbearable time on their journey. At the sight of the young people's joyful expressions and eager looks, Zhong Nanshan felt more uneasy. Probably none of them was aware of the quietly looming epidemic.

Zhong Nanshan concluded that SARS had not been rooted out after its outbreak in 2003. Its resurgence was highly possible. Others might be convinced that everything was fine after the SARS eruption in 2003. But Zhong Nanshan was fully aware that the danger was still there. Therefore, he had never given up tracking the coronavirus.

In September 2003, some scholars initially determined that "SARS" was related to civet cats, badgers, and raccoon dogs and that civet cats were the primary, intermediate host of the SARS coronavirus. Cooperating with microbiology experts in Hong Kong, Zhong Nanshan immediately got to the bottom of the situation. Sure enough, four SARS patients appeared in Guangzhou in the following spring, the same season as the first SARS outbreak.

Zhong Nanshan was super alert and asked to meet the province governor at once. Huang Hua called a meeting that night attended by the various departments and bureaus heads to listen to Zhong Nanshan's report. Zhong told them that two of the four cases had had contact with civet cats. Zhong Nanshan and his colleagues had isolated coronaviruses from them and civet cats. All four cases shared the same source. As the wildlife markets are essential carriers of infectious viruses, he asked that civet cats be eliminated from them.

More than 10,000 civet cats in Guangdong were destroyed five days later, and SARS was curbed before it broke out. Little attention was paid to this close call. Though stamped out timely, this resurgence of SARS still scared Zhong Nanshan when he thought back of it. He couldn't take similar events lightly anymore.

At the end of 2019, the initial cases in Wuhan came from the Huanan Seafood Wholesale Market. The pathogen was preliminarily determined to be a new type of coronavirus similar to that of SARS. Was it true that this new coronavirus was untransmissible from human to human? The expert team might have gone, but why was the information they had released so dubious? The ambiguity was faintly unsettling. It was revealing for the National Health Commission to invite Zhong Nanshan at the moment like this. He shuddered slightly, not because it was chilly in the train car. The images of those who had died of SARS under his nose had haunted his memory all these years. Their struggling postures for survival and their wrought faces caused by suffocation had been pounding his mind, making him mentally uncomfortable. It's common for doctors to see people die, but seeing them die in drones is another thing....

He seemed to be traveling in a dream instead of time and space. Time appeared blurry at the moment. Seventeen years ago, he was asked to serve as the Guangdong Provincial SARS Medical Rescue Expert Steering Team leader for the epidemic that left a deep impression on the Chinese people. It was also in spring and close to the Spring Festival. The timing was such a coincidence. There was only a few days' difference between the flare-up of SARS and the eruption of the first novel coronavirus case! SARS suddenly occurred in Guangdong and soon spread to Beijing. Then case reports also came from some other countries. The epidemic had threatened to become a pandemic.

He remembered that the first patient he had treated was Guo, a stout young taxi driver. He was the second confirmed SARS victim. He was transferred from the Guangdong Heyuan Hospital on December 22, 2002, and admitted to the Guangdong Institute of Respiratory Health (GIRH), where he worked.

All sorts of feelings still welled up in his mind when he recalled the completion of the first ICU in the GIRH, in line with advanced international medicine. The patient came on the fourth day of its establishment. This ICU became the most tragic and yet heroic battleground and a core bastion for combating the fatal SARS virus as if Henry Fok had anticipated the epidemic's coming when he donated his 10 million RMB yuan to the unit's founding.

On the first day of work after the New Year's Day holiday in 2003, Zhong Nanshan went to the ICU for the rounds as usual. The doctors on duty, Liu Xiaoqing, and He Weiqun, reported to him the condition of the patient in bed No. 10. The man's life was hanging in the balance. Since then, Zhong Nanshan has devoted himself to rescuing critically ill patients.

Then, he went to Zhongshan City to rescue patients, not one but a large number. Guangzhou received a steady stream of patients. People who came into contact with them fell ill. The doctors and nurses were no exceptions. They had a fever and suffered congestion in the face and neck. They then vomited and coughed dryly. Their lungs became "white" as they started experiencing shortness of breath. Death was caused mainly by the prostration of breathing or the failure of many organs.

Although the epidemic was highly severe, no one dared to tell the truth. They even cover it up instead of facing reality. At that time, Zhong

Nanshan had felt isolated, which tormented him and plunged him into anxiety and pain like calamity. Seventeen years had passed, and the innately optimistic old man still hated to recall those days. Would the same situation occur if the novel coronavirus disease proved to be as epidemical? He felt uneasy and couldn't help mumbling to himself....

Rumors had run rampant that spring. People scrambled to purchase roxithromycin, the indigowoad root medicine, and vinegar.... Though immaterial, when all was well, their prices skyrocketed. A package of indigowoad root medicine valued at eight RMB yuan was sold for 40. The originally 10-yuan antiviral oral liquid had increased to 130.

Zhong Nanshan was anxious. He immediately asked that all the severely ill patients be transferred to his GIRH. The cause of the difficult-to-treat disease was unknown, and what was worse, its transmission channels were unclear. He could understand when some doctors had concerns because it was a matter of life and death. Looking into their worried eyes, Zhong Nanshan said frankly, "Our job is to research respiratory diseases. If we didn't take the arduous work of rescue and treatment on us, who would?" Faced with the challenging situation, they had to take a solemn oath, "The hospital is the battlefield, and we are the soldiers. If we didn't fight bravely, who would? Now, it's the time for us to step up without hesitation because it's our duty as doctors!"

In 2020, the novel coronavirus patients in Wuhan were plagued by fever and fatigue. Some had a dry cough with little phlegm, a few had a runny nose and nasal congestion, and others showed gastrointestinal symptoms. Some even had problems with the heart muscle, digestive tract, and nervous system. These symptoms were similar and dissimilar to SARS at once because many did not have a high fever. Besides, they were mildly ill at first and had different lung problems. Zhong Nanshan decided that there might be many homologies between the two viruses, but they must be parallelly different. However, he had no idea how dangerous this new virus was and how it would mutate, and the information he could access was vague. The delay in coming to a definite conclusion worried him. He feared that something unexpected would happen again.

He was 67 when he had combated the SARS, but he was 84 now. Seventeen years had passed in the blink of an eye, leaving only the gray on his otherwise black hair. He had never expected that he would have to combat a similar virus at such an advanced age. (Later, some netizens commented, "He tried to persuade others not to go to Wuhan, but he went, though knowing that the elderly people are more vulnerable to the infection of the disease.)

The train sped forward as the land outside flashed back in different light shades. The flickering scene was depressing. Zhong Nanshan intuitively turned the corners of his lips down. The expression revealed more of his sadness and sympathy than fatigue. He had a foreboding that something terrible would happen. Between now, when he was worried, and later, when he shed tears, the epidemic grew into a pandemic, a situation much worse than he had expected. What role would he play in such a critical situation? But now, he had no time to ask questions like that. What was on his mind was nothing but to fathom the situation and take professional measures accordingly.

An earth-shattering event was about to take place! The modern high-speed train pierced through the chilly night and roared toward Wuhan, the "epicenter" of the epidemic spiraling out of control. The earth shook while the air whistled. The elderly man was tense even when he dozed, the corners of his lips turned further down. He was sad even in his drowsiness, feeling the dark clouds ahead pressing heavily upon him.... He might refuse to give in to his old age, but how much could he do as a senior citizen? Could the people be safe under the dark clouds?

Simultaneously, Zhong Nanshan tried to console himself, imagining that things might not be as bad as SARS. He believed that China had gained enough experience after the SARS epidemic. Besides, with rapid economic development, its medical and health services progressed by leaps and bounds, significantly improving its ability and quality of disease prevention and control. It boasted a good prevention and control system, including a safe prevention and control system for outpatients. Each province had designated hospitals for the treatment of patients due to public health incidents. Each hospital had a fever clinic with complete detection methods to screen out pathogens as soon as possible. A team of experts for epidemic control and treatment had been formed at the municipal, provincial, and national levels with a complete set of treatment and rescue measures. Besides, there was also the surveillance and isolation system. The national system ensured the effective establishment and operation of institutional mechanisms for epidemic control and prevention.

– 4 –

After traveling at high speed for four hours, the train arrived in Wuhan late at night. It was chilly and windy here and felt like a different season from Guangzhou. Zhong Nanshan added a sweater and followed his assistant out of the station. Zhang Zongjiu, director of the National Health Commission's Bureau of Medical Administration, was waiting to meet them at the station. Since arriving in Wuhan on December 31, Zhang Zongjiu had stayed in Wuhan with the experts except for returns to Beijing for urgent matters.

The Wuhan High-speed Railway Station is also a large depot. Connected to it was a broad boulevard. As they stepped out, a myriad of street and neon lamps greeted their eyes. Like bustling Guangzhou, Wuhan was also sleepless. Fragments of his past in the city flitted through his memory like the twinkling lights. One finds it harder to forget the olden days as one grows older, only that those things are still there, but people are no more the same ones with the fundamental changes taking place everywhere.

Wuhan was the first city he had visited, but he had no memory. His parents told him that he was about a year old when he followed them from Nanjing to Changsha and then Guiyang via Wuhan. The family disembarked from the pier by the Yangtze River and stopped briefly in

Wuhan. After the Battle of Shanghai against the Japanese aggressors, the Kuomintang government decided to relocate its central organs inland. As a result, his parents had taken him to start a life of displacement....

Zhong Nanshan and others reached the Wuhan Conference Center. It's a tranquil hotel in the heart of the city, with its modern and grand buildings hidden among the trees. Among the experts, Zhong Nanshan was the latest to arrive. Those who had gotten to Wuhan the same day were Gao Fu, academician of the Chinese Academy of Sciences and director of the Chinese Center for Disease Control and Prevention; Li Lanjuan, academician of the Chinese Academy of Engineering and director of the National Laboratory for Diagnosis and Treatment of Infectious Diseases; Yuan Guoyong, Academician of the Chinese Academy of Engineering and Docent of the Department of Microbiology, Faculty of Medicine, The University of Hong Kong; Zeng Guang, chief scientist of epidemiology at the Chinese Center for Disease Control and Prevention; and Du Bin, director of the ICU (Intensive Medicine Department) of Peking Union Medical College Hospital and an expert in critical care medicine. The National Health Commission held a meeting for the experts, where the convener briefed them on the situation in Wuhan.

It was late at night. Zhong Nanshan washed up and went to bed. But he couldn't calm down because it was hard for him to accept the reality of the novel coronavirus disease. The clouds of the SARS catastrophe flooded his mind like a deluge. He couldn't imagine experiencing the same tragedy again.

The vrooms of cars on the streets had died down, and the clanking of a train passing over the Yangtze River was vaguely audible. Ships and boats passed by from time to time. Wuhan had had a facelift since it had recently hosted the Military World Games. It's the old Jiang'an District, next to the section of the river overlooked by the Gui (Turtle) and She (Snake) mountains from either side. It's the site of the famed Hankow Customs House. The silent bell awaited the advent of a significant event before ringing. When it opened as a port in those years, the Greater Wuhan was "as good as the Tianjin port and gaining on Shanghai." Many European-style buildings rose in the riverside concessions. The opening of Hankou as a port is like a book recording over a century's volatile changes. The People's Republic of China's first railway bridge across the Yangtze River was built here. Many overpasses spanning the Yangtze River shone like silver snakes lying still. They reminded Zhong Nanshan of the line from Mao Zedong's poem, "A bridge will fly to span the north and south / Turning a deep chasm into a thoroughfare." They also brought back the line of a poem written by a Tang poet Cui Hao, "On a sunny day, trees on the Hanyang plain are visible / Aromatic grass grows luxuriantly all over the Parrot Isle."

Zhong Nanshan tossed and turned that night in Wuhan, profoundly saddened by the thought that China was again faced with a test and another plague threatened its people.

Day broke. Outside the windows, the lawns were browned, and the trees were bare. It was a scene strikingly different from the lush Lingnan. Swayed by the chilly wind, they were experiencing the cold of the north. The Chinese hackberry, loquat, southern magnolia, hall crabapple, and citron—the transplanted uncommon trees—still had some lingering green foliage. Under the overcast sky, the biting northwest wind blew toward the Yangtze River, bushing the streets. Dark clouds piled layer upon layer above forced Zhong Nanshan, who had a high tolerance for cold weather, to huddle himself a bit.

Zhong Nanshan had a full itinerary on January 19, 2020. The epidemic worsened day by day, and the situation was highly volatile. In two days, 136 cases were confirmed in Wuhan, and a total of 198 cases were reported on that day alone. By then, four people had died. Among the 169 cases in Wuhan's designated medical institutions receiving patients to be treated in isolation, 35 were severe, while nine were critical. Cross infection occurred in the Union Hospital affiliated with the Huazhong University of Science and Technology. A patient in the hospital's Neurosurgery Department suffered a fever after neurosurgery and was diagnosed with pneumonia caused by the novel coronavirus. The 14 doctors and nurses in the Neurosurgery Department were infected.

On this day, Greater Wuhan was permeated with a festive atmosphere to welcome the Spring Festival. Despite the occurrence of the epidemic, the residents initially had some hesitation. But after the public announcement that the disease had no obvious sign of human-to-human transmission and was preventable and controllable, they no longer took it to heart. On January 18, a "Ten-Thousand-Household Banquet" was in full swing in the Baibuting community, where 40,000 families gathered together. The 13,986 semi-finished dishes fixed by the residents were spread on the tables throughout the main venue and nine branches. The main venue was at the Community Service Center, a large glass house with rounded corners at a crossroads, with dishes spread over two floors. These dishes were meant to demonstrate the residents' culinary skills. After being displayed to crowds of enthusiastic viewers, they would be distributed to each subdivision, where they would be further prepared and served or donated to low-income families. In addition to the banquet, there was also a New Year purchases fair and a cultural fair.

Baibuting was a 20-year-old large community with multi-story buildings and overlapping trees. With a population of over 180,000, it had organized the banquet for two decades nonstop, involving a few hundred and then a few thousand households from the beginning to ten-thousand today. As the size grew, its reputation spread far and wide and had become the community's routine celebration.

The national team of senior experts listened to the reports on preventing and controlling the novel coronavirus epidemic in Wuhan City and Hubei Province. Accompanying the experts at the meeting were Yu Xuejun, deputy director of the National Health Commission; Yang Yunyan, vice governor of Hubei Province; Zhang Jin, secretary of the CPC Group of Hubei Health Commission; Chen Xiexin, deputy mayor of Wuhan; and Zhang Hongxing, secretary of the CPC Group and director of Wuhan Health Commission. Zhong Nanshan was surprised to see the word "leader" marking his name on the list of the senior expert team. Neither did he expect that no one should greet him, which gave him a sense of being entrusted with a mission in times of danger.

The team of senior experts was established on the 18th without delay. The member list was determined after the National Health Commission leaders communicated via telephone. As soon as they confirmed the members, they notified them by phone and asked them to rush to Wuhan on the same day.

Some experts who had come earlier for inspection told Zhong Nanshan that they felt the reports they had gotten weren't complete and found it hard to press for the rest. They had questioned the related leaders closely, but the leaders blamed them for having no trust in them. They had been to the hospitals for investigation but were given the same answers to their questions so that they couldn't proceed further.... What's more, his students coming to see him were depressed. Some of them were doctors working in the respiratory department. They told him that the actual situation of the epidemic was far more severe than what the public knew. Zhong Nanshan's heart was as heavy as a mountain of lead. How familiar it sounded! Some of his apprehensions would become a reality.

The administrator of the Wuhan Health Commission reported the epidemic situation in Wuhan: as of the 17th, there had been 62 cases, of which eight were severe and two dead. Close contacts reached 763, and no related cases were found among the close contacts.... They had concentrated their efforts on four areas recently: going all out to treat and rescue the patients, tightening the management of close contacts, implementing a joint prevention and control policy, and positively guiding the public opinion. The number of confirmed cases and close contacts that the Hubei Provincial Health Commission reported was the same, while their measures were more detailed. The eight steps to deal with the situation covered almost every aspect. As he took notes attentively, Zhong Nanshan pricked his ears, hoping to hear if the disease spread from human to human and if doctors or nurses were infected.

Zhong Nanshan was emotional after hearing the reports, so much so that he couldn't control his emotions. He no longer cared about considering the reporters' feelings and sprayed a barrage of incisive questions at their faces: *Are there any more cases? How many of you fell ill? How many have succumbed? Does the disease infect any medical professionals? Has it been transmitted from person to person?* He waved his hands and pounded the desk with his fist. He even took off his coat, making himself the only person at the meeting wearing a shirt only. His face turned livid with rage.

After a brief silence, Zeng Guang broke it and said, "It's the last chance for you to tell the truth today."

Under Zhong Nanshan's ruthless questioning, it was revealed that a patient in the Neurosurgery Department of Wuhan Union Medical College Hospital had infected 15 doctors and nurses. New epidemic statistical data was delivered to the meeting place twice. Someone explained that the patients were being tested and had not been diagnosed yet. The Hubei Provincial Center for Disease Control and Prevention didn't receive the state-issued test kit until January 16. Another person argued that all the unreported cases were undiagnosed and repeatedly emphasized that the test kits had just been distributed to Wuhan. There was no way to diagnose without a test....

Gao Fu retorted that the Chinese Center for Disease Control and Prevention had provided a small number of probes for testing before the kits were produced.

Zhong Nanshan felt sorrowful. Three teams of senior experts had come to investigate, but the situation dragged on until it was like this. The images of those who had died of SARS floated in his mind like the seaweed drifting toward him from the deep ocean of time. He heard the same argument to cover up the SARS epidemic seventeen years before and was even forced to repeat the same explanation. It was a nightmare hard to look back on!.

He was fully aware of their situation: people didn't take the disease seriously. Neither did they take enough measures. They were already standing on the cliff's edge without knowing the imminent peril.

A new type of coronavirus had long been discovered by pathogen detection, and the whole genome sequence of the virus had also been obtained. Even when doctors were infected, why were they still saying that "there is no clear evidence of human-to-human transmission?" Why did they state that limited human-to-human transmission couldn't be excluded without forgetting to emphasize that "the risk of continuous human-to-human transmission is low?"

After the epidemic was reported, the expert team went to the Jinyintan Hospital to investigate, check the inquiry and triage services in the outpatient hall, and learn about patients' centralized admission, diagnosis, and treatment. The Jinyintan hospital specializes in infectious diseases and is designated for medical treatment should public health emergencies occur in Wuhan. It has a history of nearly a hundred years. With a low-lying and yet wide gate, it has the imposing manner of a higher education institution. Although long been enclosed in the urban area due to Wuhan's expansion, the hospital still feels like a wild, vast suburb. It had been vacated with sickbeds added, totaling over 800. The experts watched the treatment of critically ill patients in the ICU through video surveillance. Zhong Nanshan looked carefully and put forward some suggestions for treatment.

It was a 48-year-old female patient with Yin as her family name. She fell ill on December 10, 2019. She had such underlying health conditions as diabetes, brain infarction, and gallstones. She started to have difficulty breathing on December 27 and was transferred to the Jinyintan Hospital. She suffered severe respiratory distress when she came. She was being rescued with multiple organ failures now. Unfortunately, she died the day after the expert team left. A patient with the family name Chen also died that day. He was found ill on January 13, 2020, and was admitted to the hospital on January 18 with acute dyspnea.

On their way to the Wuhan Center for Disease Control and Prevention, the experts passed the Huanan Seafood Wholesale Market. Their minibus drove around it a few times without letting them off. The market had been closed as early as January 1. Surrounded by tall buildings, the two-storied structures sprawling along the Xinhua Road were conspicuous. The first floor hosted a variety of seafood and meat shops, whereas the second floor accommodated mostly optical stores. On one side of the two-story houses was a huge banner sign with white characters on a blue background. Behind it was a transparent glass arcade, flanked inside with stalls that aligned the whole length of the gallery. These stores had already been shuttered. At a glance, the market was empty. Since the scene had been vandalized, the experts couldn't find a thing even if they had gotten out of their minivan.

Someone asked what the market had looked like in the past. Experts who had been to it told him that it was filthy, besieged by garbage and rats. In a word, the environment was horrible.

A block away from this foul place sits the bustling commercial center and stand the high-rise residential buildings. Yuan Guoyong, an expert from Hong Kong, said, "In addition to controlling the consumption and trade of wild animals, we must manage the environmental sanitation of the vegetable market. The wet and stinky markets in many big cities are likely to become hotbeds of infectious diseases and need to be changed in the future." Some experts were concerned that the wild animals sold before the market's closedown might have been shipped nationwide. Would the novel coronavirus be carried to other provinces by the wild animals?

The experts investigated the etiology laboratory to learn about the work related to specimen sampling and testing at the Wuhan Center for Disease Control and Prevention.

Zhong Nanshan was restless, his mood as gloomy as the sky outside the window. The places they had visited today behaved like "demonstration units" because they seemed to have prepared themselves for interviews: they wouldn't volunteer to say anything except answer their questions.

During a conversation at lunch, the deputy mayor, who ate at the same table with Zhong Nanshan, had a long face and a heavy heart. He knew that a catastrophe would occur to Wuhan.

Neither Zhong Nanshan had any appetite as his worries turned into a reality.

Gao Fu was sadder and tormented by mixed feelings. With his professional knowledge, the director of the Chinese Center for Disease Control and Prevention took immediate action after learning about the outbreak late at night on December 30, 2019, and began to simulate the isolation of the virus with normal saline the following day. The center instantly obtained live lung cells from a hospital in Wuxi. The person who got the lung slices rushed back to the center at 2:00 a.m. On the 6th, a probe for case detection was made, and the CDC's second-level response to major public health emergencies was activated simultaneously. He isolated the virus on the 7th. After returning from Wuhan on the 14th, he initiated the CDC's first-level response to major public health emergencies. He had known that the novel coronavirus was transmissible from humans to humans. However, though CDC enjoys a vantage point as a technical department, it can function as it should be because it has no right to release epidemic information to the outside world at critical moments. Having no administrative authority and being at the hierarchy's low level, the center can't lead in the effort to prevent and control an epidemic.

History once again pushed Zhong Nanshan into a position where he had been during the SARS outbreak. People say that he acquired fame from combat against the SARS, but he didn't want such fame. As a doctor in a situation like this, he listened to his conscience, telling him he had no choice. He merely told the truth, and he dares to do it because what he says is nothing but the truth. The public has the right to know what they should.

– 5 –

At 2:00 p.m. on January 19, 2020, the expert team returned to the Wuhan Conference Center for a closed-door meeting. They had drawn an obvious conclusion from the study of the Wuhan epidemic. The leaders of the National Health Commission's Bureau of Medical Administration immediately reported the "human-to-human transmission" judgment and the "management according to Class A infectious diseases" suggestion to the leaders of the National Health Commission. The leaders of the National Health Commission reported them to the State Council without delay. With the team of the senior experts, Zhong Nanshan left the venue of the meeting at 3:30 p.m. and rushed to the Wuhan Tianhe International Airport, where they took the HU7582 flight to Beijing. The State Council would convene its executive meeting on the morning of the 20th. The National Health Commission decided that Zhong Nanshan give their report to the executive session on behalf of the team of senior experts. The National Health Commission held an emergency meeting in Beijing that night.

There was heavy traffic on the streets, with cars and buses zooming in the howling northwest wind. The sidewalks were bustling with pedestrians. Among them were beaming sweethearts holding their hands, children frolicking and having fun, and residents chatting and laughing in their peppery Hubei accent in small groups. Passersby or travelers either carrying their bags or hauling their luggage of various sizes hurried on their way, some wearing their winter garments unbuttoned and all exhaling steam from their mouths.... The shops were all decorated festively, and spicy aromas whiffed from eateries from time to time. It was jubilantly festive everywhere.

Almost at the same time yesterday, he and his assistant had rushed to the Guangzhou South Railway Station. Compared with Guangzhou, the sky was gloomy, as if rain or snow were imminent. It was freezing, and there was nowhere to escape the cold. It was a challenge for people from Lingnan to adapt to it. Zhong Nanshan had a strange feeling that he wasn't firmly on the ground. There was such a difference in climate overnight, and he found himself like an unseasonable creature of a different species.

But Wuhan had become an epidemic-stricken city. It wasn't an illusion! From now on, brewing darkness would engulf one square and one street after another. The novel coronavirus would take over the city's life, forcing everything to move toward silence and emptiness. The hustle and bustle would disappear in the blink of an eye. The street lamps turned on earlier seemed so feeble. Zhong Nanshan was scared and confused, his eyes welling with tears. The heartbroken feeling he had during the SARS breakout hit him again. How much he wanted to shout out a warning to wake up the people on the streets! They were walking toward a cliff in a trance.

It was dusky when the airplane landed in Beijing. There were few people on the capital's streets in the freezing weather. The Spring Festival's atmosphere wasn't as manifest in metropolises. Only the files of vehicle tail lights on the streets gave a sense of warmth.

Zhong Nanshan checked into the No. 2 Guesthouse of the State Council, where a concierge delivered food to his room. Mao Xiaoguang, the National Health Commission director, came to see him, and they chatted for half an hour.

Subsequently, a meeting on the epidemic and its prevention and control was convened in the conference room of the National Health Commission's office building. The meeting lasted till midnight and beyond. The experts spoke, stating that the situation was grave and the disease must be human-to-human transmissible. They said that the window period for prevention and control left to the city was very small now, and the situation would worsen if drastic measures weren't taken in the following few days. Eating nonstandard food animals and trading wildlife must be managed and controlled. The experts also suggested that no one leave or enter Wuhan.

Zhong Nanshan stayed on after the meeting adjourned. The National Health Commission's leadership listened to his opinions on the report he was to give to the State Council and decided on the specific items to report. Zhong Nanshan didn't leave the venue until 1:30 a.m. The National Health Commission's staff began to write the report per Zhong Nanshan's ideas.

It was 2:00 a.m. when Zhong Nanshan returned to his hotel room. He slept only four hours that night. He couldn't lie in bed peacefully anymore, so he got up at six in the morning. The report written by the National Health Commission's staff overnight was delivered to him. He went over the manuscript, scrutinizing the wording and weighing what needed editing. The experts were to rush to the State Council at 7:30 a.m. to report to the state leaders.

None of the experts had gone to sleep because each had sorted out his judgment and suggestions on preventing and controlling the novel coronavirus epidemic. They had emailed their opinions to Zhong Nanshan by 4:00 a.m. when the latter synthesized them. The materials provided by the experts were much more detailed than their speeches at the meeting. They had sufficient information on the judgment of the epidemic. The Wuhan Municipal Health Commission also sent the latest number of confirmed cases early in the morning. Based on this, Zhong Nanshan came up with the most authoritative opinions on epidemic research, prevention, and control.

He had to factor in the approaching Spring Festival, the grand national holiday, and the massive crowds of passengers at the Guangzhou South Railway Station kept flashing back in front of his mind's eye…. Feeling a little numb in the head, Zhong Nanshan rubbed his forehead and temples vigorously and forced himself to think straight.

Though in the face of a similar crisis, he was in a different position from when he had participated in the combat against SARRS: he had the opportunity this time to report the epidemic directly to the national leaders as the head of a team of senior experts. His report would affect the national leaders' decision-making in fighting the novel coronavirus. So, he felt that he couldn't be over-cautious. He wanted to give a genuine and comprehensive report to the state leaders, including his thoughts on fighting the epidemic.

The morning wind in Beijing was dry and cold. Zhong Nanshan stepped out of the warm guesthouse and felt as if he had had nothing on in his thin clothes. The chill pierced through his entire body and gave him a shudder. No one around him was so thinly clad. The sky, however, was particularly blue that day, which was refreshing. Sensitive to the air, he felt his tense nerves relaxed somewhat by such pure azure.

At 8:30 a.m. on January 20, an expert symposium on epidemic prevention and control officially started in the State Council's Conference Room No. 2. Ma Xiaowei, director of the National Health Commission, convened the meeting and briefed the state leaders on the latest epidemic prevention and control situation. Then, the experts took the floor one by one. Three more experts, namely Liu Qingquan, Zhang Zhongde, and Qi Wensheng, joined the six senior expert team members. Speaking on behalf of the expert team, Zhong Nanshan said that the novel coronavirus had broken out locally in Wuhan. In view of the reports of confirmed and suspected cases coming from other cities and provinces, coupled with the peak of the massive flow of people during the Spring Festival travel rush, it was most likely that the grave situation of the 2003 SARS outbreak would repeat itself should they not take active and effective measures to put it under strict control. He said that the team of senior experts made the following suggestions. First, we should stick to a localized operation and management principle to reinforce local government leaders' responsibilities and establish an organizational structure led by local governments' leading officials. Especially in Wuhan, their leaders must prioritize commanding at the forefront and activate a joint prevention and control mechanism involving multiple departments. Second, we must list pneumonia caused by the novel coronavirus as a Class B notifiable disease as soon as possible and manage it as a Class A notifiable disease. Third, we must step up the effort to prevent and control the epidemic in Wuhan, implementing a policy of "no traveling in and out of Wuhan" to reduce exported cases. Fourth, we must implement an "early discovery, report, quarantine, and treatment" policy and strengthen the mechanism of public health workers' emergency duty and protection. Fifth, we must intensify the effort to inform and educate the public, enhancing the public's awareness of self-protection and healthcare, promoting the "civilized habit of wearing masks," and improving the transparency in information notification. Sixth, we must enhance scientific research and actively investigate the novel coronavirus's virulence, transmissibility, transmission routes, and mutation.

The other experts also shared the results from studying the epidemic and unanimously agreed that the situation was grave and clarified that it was already human-to-human transmissible, so the strictest prevention and control measures must be taken immediately.

After the reporting session, Zhong Nanshan and Li Lanjuan were invited to attend the subsequent State Council's executive meeting. There were only five minutes between the back-to-back conferences. They rushed to the next without further ado.

The State Council's executive meeting added preventing and controlling the novel coronavirus pneumonia to its agenda. After listening to the reports on the latest epidemic situation given by the director of the National Health Commission and the governor of Hubei Province, the top leader of the State Council asked Zhong Nanshan and Li Lanjuan to speak. They shared their opinions and suggestions on how to curb the spread of the epidemic and rescue and treat the infected patients. Zhong Nanshan explained the significant impact of the Spring Festival on the epidemic, emphasizing that information on the epidemic should be shared and transparent, and everyone should be aware of the situation's gravity.

He asked that strict prevention and control measures be taken as quickly as possible. It also demanded that the government timely and objectively inform the public of the epidemic, announce the result of prevention and control, and respond to social concerns....

The State Council leader approved their opinions and suggestions and thanked them, saying that the professional advice provided by the two experts was crucial for scientific decision-making in the next step.

When Zhong Nanshan and Li Lanjuan left the venue, the State Council leaders walked them out and bid farewell. The executive meeting immediately classified the novel coronavirus as a Class B notifiable disease.

Zhong Nanshan returned to the guesthouse for a simple lunch. At 1:30 p.m., he hurried to Zhongnanhai, the central headquarters for the CPC and the State Council, to attend the national video and telephone conference held by the State Council and the National Health Commission to make arrangements for joint epidemic prevention and control work nationwide.

At 5:00 p.m., the National Health Commission held a meet-and-greet event, where the National Health Commission's Team of Senior Experts gave a news briefing. Experts include Zhong Nanshan, Gao Fu, Li Lanjuan, Yuan Guoyong, Zeng Guang, and Du Bin. More than a dozen mass media participated in the meet-and-greet event, including Xinhua News Agency, the *People's Daily*, the *Guangming Daily*, China Global Television Network, Phoenix Television, *Health News*, Central Radio-Television General Station (merged into the present-day China Media Group), and China Central Television or CCTV (merged into present-day China Media Group). That day, Zhong Nanshan appeared for the first time in front of the world as the head of the National Health Commission's Team of Senior Experts.

The meet-and-greet event for the media was held in the National Health Commission's long and narrow conference room. The experts and the reports sat across the large conference table. Zhong Nanshan sat composed in the middle of the experts. After what had been going on that day, he knew that the state leaders attached great importance to the experts' advice and that corresponding measures would be taken soon. He felt relieved. The reporters' microphone and digital voice recorder were held in a tray, which would be brought to the expert who would answer their questions.

At the meet-and-greet event for the media, the reporters raised many grave and sensitive questions, making the atmosphere a little tense. A reporter asked Zhong Nanshan a straightforward question. Zhong Nanshan was prepared because dealing with the media for so many years had familiarized him with their nature. He never hides anything from the press and always tells the truth. He needed this opportunity to inform the public of what he knew, understanding that transparency was essential for the fight against the epidemic. He hoped that every Chinese citizen would grasp the characteristics of the virus and the know-how to prevent and control it. Only he who had experienced it would understand what he was doing and its significance.

A Central Radio-Television General Station reporter threw the media's first question at Zhong Nanshan, "A hundred and thirty-six confirmed cases popped up in two days in Wuhan, and the novel coronavirus cases also appeared in Beijing and Guangzhou. What's your take on the current epidemic situation, Academician Zhong?"

Zhong Nanshan watched the reporter placing the tray in front of him and a row of cameras and video cameras aiming at him. Instead of shying away, Zhong Nanshan responded frankly, "It is in its infancy where the epidemiological state is concerned. The six of us went to Wuhan yesterday. The situation there was different yesterday from the day before, and the day before was different from three days before. Human-to-human transmission has been confirmed, and It has also been confirmed that public health workers have been infected while treating and caring for patients. It is a significant mark."

In response to the question raised by a Xinhua News Agency reporter, Zhong Nanshan directly aired his opinion on preventing and controlling the epidemic in Wuhan: reducing exported cases, which meant the residents of Wuhan must refrain from exiting it as much as possible. Strict testing measures must be implemented at ports such as railway stations and airports. They must first and foremost measure body temperatures. Quarantine must be forced upon those with symptoms, especially those with abnormal body temperature. We must intensify the enforcement of prevention measures. Only persuasion isn't enough. No one should be allowed to enter Wuhan except on essential errands.

The suggestion that "no one leave or enter Wuhan" is as good as locking Wuhan down. Wuhan might be taking measures to gauge body temperature at railway stations, airports, and other entry or exit points, but they were merely persuasive. No compulsory quarantine measures had been in place.

He reminded them that the most effective way to prevent and control the epidemic was early detection, diagnosis, treatment, and quarantine. Though the most primitive, this method would be the most effective. Patients already diagnosed or highly suspected must be effectively quarantined. It was crucial because there was no specific for the disease. It was also imperative to wear masks.

He called on government leaders at all levels to take responsibility and emphasized that it wasn't the business of the National Health Commission. He said the central government, the public health workers, and society must be concerned. The local governments must take responsibility. We were now at a critical juncture since the number of sick people would increase during the Spring Festive season. But he didn't want to see chain reactions, saying that transmission must be prevented. The key to doing this was being vigilant against the appearance of super-spreaders....

The meet-and-greet event for the media lasted till 7:00 p.m. Zhong Nanshan was exhausted. He leaned against the back of his chair and closed his eyes at supper. He hung his head low, hearing ringing in his ears. He rubbed his temples hard, seemingly driving the fatigue out of his system.

At 9:30 p.m., Zhong Nanshan appeared as a special online guest on CCTV's News 1+1 program. He faced the camera, wearing a pair of mobile phone earplugs. There was a few-second delay in the dialog, but his remarks were crystal clear. Zhong Nanshan disclosed vital information on the epidemic in the live broadcast. While answering one of the host Bai Yansong's questions, Zhong Nanshan suddenly lost the thread of his thought: his mind went blank. That state of numbness and brief amnesia reoccurred. The audience has no way of knowing how much torment the old man went through when he appeared in front of the camera. The tense and tiring three days and nights had a toll on this aged man with good memory and thinking capacity: his brain was temporarily short-circuited.

Zhong Nanshan felt a little remorse afterward and laughed at himself. He had faced reporters many times, and this accident of memory loss was his first.

History seemed to repeat itself: what he had feared reappeared. Faced with efforts to conceal the epidemic and wrong conclusions arrived by authoritative departments during the SARS outbreak, Zhong Nanshan told the TV viewers about the "Face to Face" program hosted by Wang Zhi on China Central Television in 2003. Now, in Bai Yansong's "News 1+1" program from the same television station. He solemnly announced, "The novel coronavirus infection has just begun and is on the rise.... The disease is categorically human-to-human transmissible. For example, we have two cases in Guangdong. The man hasn't been to Wuhan, but his wife has and was infected with the novel coronavirus.... Now, it's fair to say that there is the phenomenon of definitely human-to-human transmission."

His remarks startled the Chinese awake and had magic power. They halted their bustling and hustling, disrupting their Chinese New Year celebration preparations. The memory of the 2003 SARS epidemic instantly returned to their minds.

The Baibuting community's "Ten-Thousand-Household Banquet" participants were shocked, some regretful, and some fearful. They were no longer at ease. Soon, Baibuting found itself at the heart of public opinion. Criticized by everyone, the organizers were faced with tremendous pressure.

Two days later, at 10:00 a.m. on January 23, Wuhan announced its lockdown. The tolling stations on the expressways were filled with police officers and cars flashing their lights and, from time to time, blaring their sirens, which pierced through the sky. The grim faces of the police officers could bounce back any doubtful looks. People couldn't believe what they saw was reality: all the roads leading out of the city were blocked. The cars going out of the city were packed like sardines. Eventually, they managed to turn around and headed back to the city one by one. Their Spring

Festival reunion plans that they had worked on for a month or two now vaporized into thin air. Many people were still suspicious on their way back, wondering if it was April Fool's Day. They might have sped out of town, but they found their cars now powered by a weak engine. But when they woke up to reality, they panicked. All means of public transportation, ranging from buses, subways, ferries, and long-distance coaches, stopped operation. Citizens were not allowed to leave Wuhan without special reasons. All airport and railway station passages of exit from Wuhan were closed.

Three days later, starting from 00:00 a.m. on January 26, all motor vehicles were prohibited from the central urban area of Wuhan. The bustling streets were suddenly deserted, a scene from a magic drama in real life. The microscopic, formless viruses halted everything in a clamorous world of humans who more than dwarfed them in size.

There has been no historical record in China and the world for a metropolis of 14 million residents to be put under lockdown. It caught everyone off guard. Catastrophes are always unpredictable, anyway.

It shocked Wuhan, China, and the world!

Huanggang, Ezhou, Xiantao, Qianjiang, and Jingmen cities in Hubei Province were also locked down immediately afterward. Even the county-level cities of Yueqing and Rui'an and Yongjia County of Wenzhou City, Zhejiang Province, which were hundreds of kilometers away, were also under lockdown. Streets were closed throughout the country. So were the roads leading to each village. Isolated "islands" of various sizes dotted the vast mainland of China.

China went into a heroic war against the novel coronavirus, with campaigns launched everywhere: the Battle to Defend Wuhan and Hubei and the blocking battles everywhere else in the country.

The novel coronavirus has become a public health emergency of grave concern spreading faster and wider than any other. It has proven to be the most difficult to contain since the founding of the PRC in 1949. On January 23, the same day that Wuhan was placed under lockdown, the provinces of Guangdong, Zhejiang, and Hunan activated their provincial first-level emergency response to the epidemic as a public health emergency of great concern. As of 24:00 on January 22, a total of 444 confirmed cases of novel coronavirus had been reported in Hubei, 32 in Guangdong, 27 in Zhejiang, and nine in Hunan. Then, the provinces of Hubei, Anhui, Jiangxi, Sichuan, and Yunan and the metropolises of Tianjin, Beijing, Shanghai, and Chongqing also activated their first-level response to the epidemic as a major public health emergency. They were soon followed by the rest of the 31 administrative provinces and regions on China's mainland.

On January 23, local time in Geneva, the World Health Organization (WHO) Emergency Committee held a meeting to decide on whether the current round of novel coronavirus in Wuhan constituted a "public health emergency of international concern (PHEIC)." (Then, the WHO declared the novel coronavirus outbreak in China as a PHEIC on January 30.)

The series of news filled Zhong Nanshan with mixed feelings. This 84-year-old man was all in tears.

– 6 –

No firework or firecracker was heard on the 2020 New Year's Day. Wang Anshi, a Chinese poet and politician of the Song Dynasty (960-1279), wrote in his poem, "Firecrackers are shouting goodbye to the last year / In warm spring breeze people drink wine with cheer." This thousand-year tradition suddenly paused on the land north and south of the Yangtze River. Instead of "Thousands of households greeting the bright morning sun/Replacing old couplets on their doors with new ones," the Chinese had to shut themselves up at home and could no longer pay New Year calls. The jubilant and auspicious atmosphere was washed clean by the epidemic. Not a soul could be seen on the streets of Chinese cities of various sizes.

The country entered a state of war, with the central leadership calmly in command. It convened the Politburo Standing Committee meeting on New Year's Day, leading the Chinese in a battle without the option to lose, for they must work against time to save lives.

A metropolis connecting nine provinces presented a scene of stark contrast. On the one hand, doctors and nurses were working like firefighters against the novel coronavirus that had infected so many people that they came to the hospitals wave upon wave. On the other hand, the streets were void of vehicles and pedestrians, with only the street lamps and traffic lights still on. Silence also reigned in train stations and airports. A street sweeper cried before a TV reporter's video camera. She said she was sad to see no one on the streets and in the alleys and missed the days when people swarmed them. She would rather work harder to clean a lot of trash than sweep nothing but fallen leaves every day. She was kept company only by the decorative plants and trees as she cleaned the streets. Wild boars and rabbits began to claim the streets.

One night, tens of thousands of households opened their windows in the skyscraping apartment buildings and shouted unanimously, "Go, Wuhan! Go, Wuhan!" The shout from everyone, old and young, merged into one voice, "Ah! Ah! Go, go, go!" It echoed, bounced, and churned in the streets as empty as mountain valleys. The voice increased its volume incrementally until it sounded like a gale. Some people shone their flashlights or spotlights on the opposite walls. They might not see each other, but they communicated with the constantly sweeping light beams and shouts, thus sharing their feelings and emotions.

Humans seemed to have gone back to the cave-dwelling ages. The thought of it brought tears to the eyes of many a citizen. Some of them faced death alone in a struggle between life and death. No one knew whom the vicious epidemic would hit next. But the enemy was nothing but the teeny viruses smaller than a human cell, invisible, shapeless, and mute. However, it boasted its potent presence through humans, claiming that they were the actual masters of the globe.

No one fled in panic but stayed orderly as required because they trusted the government and their compatriots elsewhere in the country. Their shouts and perseverance vividly illustrated the collective spirit and culture of the East. Though allegedly ostentatious as the Hubei people are known to the rest of the world, the Wuhan residents hemmed themselves in their apartment rooms. Everyone firmly believed that they were doing the right thing.

Zhong Nanshan lives and works in Guangdong, where the SARS epidemic had first broken out. Apart from Wuhan, the province was the hardest hit by the novel coronavirus. In Guangzhou, its capital, everyone was bracing themselves for a formidable enemy and far more anxious than in the SARS period. Not many Guangzhou residents had worn masks on the streets then, and even fewer people locked themselves down at home. Some even laughed at the mask-wearing people in Beijing, calling them chickens. When some Beijing residents landed in Guangzhou wearing their masks and saw most Guangzhou residents were bare-faced, they were so embarrassed that they took off theirs. But now, the people in Guangzhou behaved like the rest of the country, confining themselves to their residences. Lockdown management was prevalent among all the subdivisions, where food carryout service was also banned. Even package couriers weren't allowed into their territories. One or two daredevils might pop up on the streets, and they immediately became the focus of many others' attention. The outside world was so quiet that only wind or rain was audible.

At night, the lights decorating the landmarks of Guangzhou, ranging from the Canton Tower, the Liede Bridge, the Zhujiang New Town (Guangzhou's CBD), and the Guangzhou Bridge, were so dazzling that they made Guangzhou ever-bright. Though as gorgeous as an ever-exploding firework, the lighting also made the solitude more apparent. Occasionally a car stopped or drove away at a traffic light. Still open were a handful of convenience stores and fast-food restaurants, where only one or two salespersons were present while customers were nowhere to be found.

Though no one was riding in buses or waiting at bus stops, the drivers still stopped and went as usual. A sense of odd fantasy permeated the night that looked lonely, empty, and luxurious. It was a world of brilliant confusion and prosperous desolation.

Photos, videoclips, and textual messages circulated nationwide, showing the Chinese people dealing with the epidemic by all means. Carrying banners and beating gongs, some social workers or volunteers traveled through the alleys and streets and howled slogans to persuade residents not to come out,

"Resident friends, in your residences if you stay,
You'll keep yourselves from harm's way.
Resident friends, no drug works if you're sick;
Staying put at home is your best specific.
Resident friends, sleep and eat and eat and sleep;
Away from the virus yourselves you'll keep."

"Resident friends, don't crowd into a market as long as you've got a grain of rice/Don't venture into the streets as long as your edible oil will suffice/Don't charge into the wet market as long as you've got a stalk of scallion/As long as you want to survive, staying at home is your best advice."

"You're lucky if the weight you gain/Wandering around, you'll become a bane!" "I'm proud of staying at home/I'd waste the country's masks if I roam." "This is a war, not a child's play/If we win, we'll celebrate Spring Festival every day/if we lose, it'd be our last holiday!" The howler punctuated each line with the beating of the gong.

In some places, banner slogans were hung in the open air. Some read,

"Today's home visiting would be your tomorrow's tomb visiting." "Today, if you ran around, tomorrow, grass on your grave would be found." "Between a mask and a ventilator, you'll be a smart chooser."

A video went viral: a howler on duty was so sleepy that he dozed off without turning off his megaphone so that his snore permeated the night in the subdivision.

People who had to go out but had been unable to purchase their masks came up with various tricks: some covered their nose and mouth with half an orange peel. Others wondered where he had obtained such a giant orange. Some wrapped their whole body in a plastic film with the top tied with a rope or held open with a horizontal board, making them look like knight-errands. Some covered their heads and faces with a plastic bag, and others stuck their heads in buckets. Still, others wrapped their faces with towels, showing only their eyes....

The scene was as amusing as saddening. People calmly faced the disaster and quickly adapted themselves to the crisis. There were no riots, looting, or rushes to buy items of daily necessity.

Even war in its true sense couldn't have affected every fiber of the Chinese lives to such a degree. An epidemic transformed the behavior and lifestyle of everyone and every family in China. It was a war that's more like one.

– 7 –

As of 24:00 on January 27, the cumulative number of confirmed cases of patients infected with novel coronavirus in Hubei rose to 2,714. From that day on, the number increased by thousands every day.

After February 2, newly confirmed cases increased by over 2,000 per day, and the cumulative number of confirmed cases on that day exceeded 10,000.

After February 4, the number of newly confirmed cases climbed at a rate of more than 3,000 each day.

Hospitals were overcrowded, medical protective equipment was in short supply, and videos of doctors breaking down and crying became viral. On February 5, in principle, each designated hospital will only accept confirmed severe and critically ill cases and suspected critically ill patients.

On February 6, the cumulative number of confirmed cases exceeded 20,000.

On February 10, the accumulated number of confirmed cases surpassed 30,000. That day, all the subdivisions in Wuhan were placed under lockdown, with confirmed or suspected patients quarantined in the building units where they lived.

On February 12, Hubei Province issued the 5th edition of its "Plan for Diagnosis and Treatment, to which the item "clinic diagnosis" was added.

The revision bumped the confirmed cases up to 14,840 that day, making the accumulated number of confirmed cases total 48,206.

On February 18, the cumulative number of confirmed cases in Hubei exceeded 60,000.

Subsequently, the cumulative number of confirmed cases nationwide reached more than 80,000, and the death toll passed the 4,000 marks!

It's the largest epidemic that human beings have encountered since the 1918 influenza pandemic, also known as the misnomer Spanish flu. It is a virus that the world has never seen before. No other viruses are like the novel coronavirus, which combines the characteristics of contagion and lethality. The number of infected Wuhan residents exploded. In tens, hundreds, and thousands, people flocked to various hospitals with confirmed and suspected patients and their accompanying relatives crowding halls and hallways. Since the medical facilities couldn't accommodate so many patients, it was challenging to find a sickbed. Wuhan became a "barrier lake" of novel coronavirus patients. The "barrier lake" effect means too many infected patients crowded in a place would lead to a worse medical disaster.

A 90-year-old woman named Xu Meiwu had stayed in a hospital for five days and nights to wait for a bed for her 64-year-old son, diagnosed as a novel coronavirus patient. Grandma Xu asked the nurse for a pen and paper and left a message to her son on a piece of prescription paper, "Son, hang on there, be strong, and be alive!" She didn't bring enough money, asking the doctor to forward the only 500 yuan cash she had to her son. She said, "I still have two condos, and I'd sell them to redeem my son's life if need be."

The next evening, her son died in the ICU. The elderly woman had a mild fever and was admitted to the hospital. To avoid traumatizing her, the doctors held back the news of her son's death.

An infected middle-aged man could neither be admitted to a hospital nor stay in a hotel because the latter rejected him because of his abnormal body temperature. But he couldn't go home for fear that he might infect his family members. He went to a deserted warehouse and quarantined himself there. Some people quarantined at home couldn't be hospitalized even though their conditions worsened. They put their letter of request for help online....

"I cried for a time when I saw so many people unable to be admitted into hospitals and wail outside the hospital. Some even dropped to their knees and begged me to admit them. But I could do nothing because all the sickbeds had been occupied. I had to reject their pleas with pain and weep in secret. My tears have gone dry. It has been terrible. I've got nothing on my mind but to do more and save more lives."

That was what a doctor told a reporter. He was Peng Zhiyong, director of the Department of Critical Care Medicine at the Zhongnan Hospital of Wuhan University. He said with sadness that what he regretted the most was a pregnant woman from a rural area in Huanggang. She had been seriously ill and stayed in the ICU for over a week, which cost her RMB 2000,000 yuan. Her condition had improved while being rescued with an ECMO, and she could survive. Nevertheless, the pregnant woman's husband decided to give up the treatment. "I feel sorry for that woman.

"The deputy director of my department told me something that also made him cry. Wuhan No. 7 Hospital was a pairing unit that Zhongnan

Hospital was designated to help. He went to reinforce its ICU, where he found two-thirds of the doctors and nurses already infected. He told me about the working condition of that ICU, where the doctors were literally unprotected. They lacked protection gears and medical devices. It was only too natural for people there to be infected. But they must thrust forth into the storm of the epidemic. It's too hard on our public health workers...."

The pregnant Huanggang woman, Weng Qiuqiu, was only 31 years old when she died. On January 7, she went out to buy vegetables and had a hot pot meal with her husband and daughter. When she was sick, she first thought it was a cold. Three days later, she developed a fever in the middle of the night. After her husband took her to several local hospitals in a storage battery car, she was finally transferred to Zhongnan Hospital of Wuhan University. She was diagnosed with severe pneumonia and was immediately isolated.

The husband wanted to see her, talk to her, give her something to eat, or do something for her, but he wasn't allowed. Each time he called the doctor, he was told she was still in a coma and still in a terrible or even worse condition.

When his wife showed no sign of improvement, and he could no longer borrow any money, he was in despair and gave up the rescue effort. She passed away an hour later and was sent to the morgue. When he finally could see his wife, she had become the ashes in an urn. A dozen or so others were also there waiting for the ashes of their loved ones.

Soon afterward, China provided free medical treatment for novel coronavirus patients. Later, Weng Qiuqiu's family received state compensation.

– 8 –

The Wuhan residents under lockdown weren't left alone. They were closely related to the country's fate.

China's leaders expressed their thanks to the medical personnel and construction workers on the front line of epidemic prevention and control. They also visited the sites of prevention and control work and provided guidance.

On Chinese New Year's Eve, the Chinese People's Liberation Army issued an order to dispatch three medical teams of 450 members to aid Hubei. They flew from Shanghai, Chongqing, and Xi'an, respectively. They all arrived in Wuhan that night. Some of them didn't have time to say goodbye to their loved ones before their departure.

The medical teams from Guangdong and Shanghai also arrived in Wuhan that day. The first national team of traditional Chinese medicine (TCM) organized by the National Administration of Traditional Chinese Medicine got there simultaneously. Medical teams went to Wuhan from all parts of China every day from that point. On a record day, 6,000 health workers from over a dozen provinces arrived on 41 planes. Before celebrating the Chinese New Year with their loved ones, they had to part with them and embark on their journey with their luggage. They came by plane or train, wearing an expression of forgetting all else in pursuing their duties as if they were marching to a battlefield's front line like soldiers.

They said goodbye to their parents or spouses. Though their farewell might not mean they could never meet their loved ones again, who could guarantee they could all return safe and sound?

A doctor who was a medical team leader said that although his team member had been trained in protection against the virus many times, he still couldn't help shedding tears when he sent them into the doors of the front-line hospitals. No matter how they tried to protect themselves, it would be a challenge to dodge the "barrage of bullets."

Some of the female doctors and nurses had shaved their heads together, knowing that they would have no time to have their hair cut or do their hair anymore.

The academician team, including Zhong Nanshan, Li Lanjuan, and Wang Chen, also came to Wuhan.

With the speedy increase of infected people in the various cities of Hubei, the central government decided to pair 19 provinces with the cities outside Wuhan to reinforce their battles against the epidemic. Specifically, one of two provinces would support one city. PLA medical workers arrived in Wuhan in large numbers. It dispatched its Xi'an Y-20 military transport aircraft for the first time. The medical teams that came to Wuhan's help reached over 300, with more than 40,000 medical workers. The scale and speed of rescue mobilization greatly exceeded the 2008 Sichuan earthquake, with Wenchuan as the epicenter.

Having anticipated the severe shortage of hospital beds, the central government decided to have two hospitals constructed at the fastest speed possible so that the patients could be brought together and treated. The construction of the Huoshenshan (Mountain of Fire God) with 1,000 sick beds and Leishenshan (Mountain of Thunder God) with 1,500 sick beds immediately began on January 23.

Under the government's orders, 7,500 construction engineers and workers went to Wuhan. A hospital for infectious diseases usually takes two years to build, but they completed the Huoshenshan Hospital in ten days and the Leishanshan Hospital in 13. The progress of their construction was calculated by hours or even seconds. The feast only accomplishable by supernatural forces is known as "Infrastructural Wonders."

CCTV broadcast the construction site live 24 hours a day.

Some construction workers dropped on the earth slope and fell asleep in the severely cold season.

After completing the hospitals, some workers donated their wages to furnishing the hospitals. Donations came flooding in from various entities as well. The appliances, apparatuses, and the 5G communication software and hardware almost all came from the companies like Gree Electric, Midea Group, TCL, Galanz, Skyworth, and Huawei.

When the order of medical cabinets for the Huoshenshan Hospital was sent to a furniture factory in Luoyang City, Henan Province, the factory owner immediately replied that it would donate the cabinets. Due to the shortage of stock in the factory, the owner sent a message to the local furniture association's WeChat group, and 14 companies vied with one another to donate. They worked overtime and got the order together overnight. After the medical cabinets were loaded onto the trucks, the logistics company immediately delivered them to the hospital without charging a cent after learning that they were for the Huoshenshan Hospital.

On New Year's Eve, a CPC branch secretary of Shenqiu Village, Henan Province, delivered five tons of vegetables to the construction site. He got up at five in the morning and knocked on his fellow villagers' doors to wake them up. Two dozen of them worked hard picking 2,500 kilograms of green-leave vegetables and 2,025 kilograms of winter gourd.... He had been a serviceman stationed in Wuhan and participated in combating the 1998 China floods and the 2008 Chinese winter storms. He didn't want to be absent from being part of the fight against this epidemic. He was determined to do something about it.

When the 2008 Sichuan earthquake took place, over 100 injured people had been sent to Wuhan for treatment, including the villagers from Longzhu Village of Sanjiang Town in Wenchuan County, Sichuan Province. After the epidemic broke out, the villagers harvested 100 tons of vegetables and transported them in six trucks to Wuhan after traveling 36 hours. Over the front of the engine compartment of each truck, they hung a slogan banner reading, "Wenchuan is grateful to you! Wuhan, rise again!"

The Huoshenshan and Leishenshan hospitals were filled with inpatients as soon as they were completed. Subsequently, the Wuhan International Conference & Exhibition Center, Hongshan Stadium, and the Wuhan Keting were turned into makeshift hospitals to admit patients with mild symptoms. They were followed by the dormitories of the Party School of the Hubei CPC Committee. Still, they were unable to meet the demand. Then, more than a dozen makeshift hospitals were put into operation one after another. Many college dorms were also requisitioned, and dozens of hospitals and designated medical centers were expanded to add more wards, increasing the sickbeds to tens of thousands.

Like an intense race on the track, the number of sickbeds was racing against the number of infected patients. As if releasing a flood from a barrier lake, Wuhan spared no effort to admit and treat all the patients, trying to cut off the source of infection.

– 9 –

Zhong Nanshan once again became a public figure in the news. He kept appearing on Internet platforms, TV programs, and newspapers. People were concerned about what he said and did. People who cared about him could tell how he raced against time to fight against the epidemic from the news reports. For example, they found him doing the following between January 29 and 31.

On the morning of January 29, he video-conferenced with Prof. Jsm Peiris from the University of Hong Kong to discuss research design on the national cases. After the conference, he worked with Li Limin, Party secretary of the First Affiliated Hospital of Guangzhou Medical College, to study the treatment of critically ill patients. He collected the latest data on China's fight against the epidemic and mulled over how to effectively carry out clinical and scientific research to respond to the epidemic.

In the afternoon, he led a team of experts from the First Affiliated Hospital of Guangzhou Medical College in a remote video consultation with the ICU personnel from the medical team on the front line. Five critically ill patients appeared on the big screen. In the consultation room, he sat in the center, with nine other experts seated behind, watching the patient's condition from the video. They examined virus testing, whole-genome sequencing, medicating the patients, and treating methods....

While discussing them, Zhong Nanshan took off his mask, lest the ICU doctors couldn't hear him. The consultation lasted six hours and twenty-five minutes.

At a little past six on the morning of January 30, Zhong Nanshan received Prof. Water Ian Lipkin from Columbia University, U.S. Prof. Lipkin came to China for a visit on January 28. He flew to Guangzhou on the evening of the 29th as he wanted to see Zhong Nanshan. Their meeting was scheduled for ten o'clock the following morning. Dr. Water Ian Lipkin is the John Snow Professor of Epidemiology at the Mailman School of Public Health at Columbia University and director of the Center for Infection and Immunity.

This "master virus hunter" always rushes to the scene of a virus outbreak to investigate every time it occurs. He was invited to Beijing to help China fight SARS as early as 2003. That year, he flew to Beijing with oversized luggage. In addition to masks and shoe covers, it also contained 10,000 test kits donated to China. He and Zhong Nanshan became friends after their encounter during the fight against SARS. Zhong Nanshan's devotion, perception, and pragmatism left him with a deep impression. In the evening, Zhong Nanshan received a notice from the National Health Commission asking him to attend the National Symposium on Epidemic Prevention and Control Strategies the following day in Beijing. Therefore, he had to meet his old friend on his way and in the airport lounge.

As soon as he went downstairs at 6:30 a.m., Zhong Nanshan saw Prof. Lipkin waiting for him. After a brief small talk, they got into the car together and started exploring various methods that can be used to treat severe cases, such as drug and plasma therapies. Zhong Nanshan was looking for an accurate diagnosis method and a way to pinpoint the virus and find out how long it could survive on surfaces, such as doorknobs, subway balustrades, and railings. He wanted to determine how long a person could be contagious, what types of people were more virulent when they were contagious, and whether the virus would mutate. He hoped to maximize the protection of more people against the high risk of viral transmission.

They suspected that the novel coronavirus in the Huanan Seafood Wholesale Market in Wuhan might be a case of secondary transmission. They shared their feelings and explored how to bypass intellectual property rights, sovereignty, and greed and eliminate the factors hindering regular information dissemination from forming an effective global cooperation mechanism to face the worldwide challenge.

At this meeting, Zhong Nanshan expected Prof. Lipkin to lead his team in researching and developing a novel-coronavirus detection reagent and track how the virus would or would not evolve into something more likely to cause diseases or more quickly spread.

Someone took a snapshot of the two talking while wearing masks. They waved goodbye instead of shaking hands. Besides, Prof. Lipkin had to go through quarantine when he returned to the United States as required.... But, as infectious disease specialists, they had no alternative.

The conversation continued when they got into the car and the airport lounge. After they hurriedly said goodbye and asked each other to take care, Zhong Nanshan turned and left, leaving the vacant lounge behind him. The rising sun peeped into the glass walls and cast its rays upon this lonely old man. He trotted to the registration desk with his resonant footsteps trailing behind and echoing in the space. Hopefully, history will forever remember this scene on the way to the battlefield against the epidemic.

The airplane took off. Zhong Nanshan spread the plan for treating a few critically ill patients on the tray table. He would have to decide upon a remedy in flight.

The Beijing symposium was convened by the China Centers for Disease Control and Prevention and attended by state leaders to listen to experts' opinions on further strengthening the mechanism of scientific prevention and control of the epidemic.

As soon as the symposium concluded at 6:00 p.m., Zhong Nanshan rushed to the airport. On the way to the airport, a reporter from Beijing Satellite TV had an exclusive interview with him in the car, expecting him to answer many questions of social concern promptly.

Having hurried back to Guangzhou, he saw off another medical team from Guangzhou to rush to the rescue of Wuhan. Guangdong was the first province to dispatch Wuhan-aiding medical teams. It had sent over 20 successively. Some of the white-gowned angels were his students and some of his colleagues. He asked each of them to take care and addressed the team, "You're going to a tough place, the front line, where you'll find the greatest difficulties in your lives. It is also a battlefield where you're prone to infection. I salute you! I'm waiting for your safe return!" He walked them to the buses.

Afterward, he participated in a teleconference held by the National Health Commission, the Guangdong Health Commission, and experts. Based on the recent epidemic treatment work and virus research results, they discussed the epidemiological characteristics, clinical manifestations, diagnostic criteria, and plans for treating novel coronavirus. They also discussed, optimized, and revised the therapies, providing opinions to guide the clinical treatment of the novel coronavirus disease. The experts collectively formed three opinions, which were quickly conveyed to the medical workers participating in the fight against the epidemic across the country:

> 1. Digestive tract transmission cannot be ruled out, which is significant to epidemic prevention and control. The main route of virus transmission is the contact of droplets with the respiratory tract and mucous membranes, but the spread through the gastrointestinal tract cannot be ruled out. Meanwhile, experts are tentatively experimenting on patients' feces to determine whether live viruses can be isolated from them.
>
> 2. Patients with mild symptoms must also be hospitalized and treated in isolation to avoid community spread and clusters of cases. The treatment location should be determined according to the severity of the condition. Other places for treating patients with mild symptoms should be chosen because of the pressure on designated hospitals.
>
> 3. The treatment of critically and severely ill patients must be based on the therapy suiting the illness. We must actively prevent and treat complications, treat underlying diseases, and prevent secondary infections while providing organ-function support. We must adopt various life support methods for severe and critically ill patients. These adjuvant therapies: high-flow oxygen therapy, noninvasive

positive-pressure ventilation (NPPV), low tidal volume lung-protective ventilation strategy, and extracorporeal membrane oxygenation (ECMO), have proved satisfactory.

The teams led by the academicians Zhong Nanshan and Li Lanjuan respectively isolated novel coronavirus from the patients infected with novel coronavirus. Zhong Nanshan gave another interview to the media on whether the novel coronavirus was fecal-orally transmissible.

The novel coronavirus is shaped like a crown, invisible in the microorganic world and hidden in the human body and the air. It kills people without their knowing it.

A netizen deified Zhong Nanshan and Li Lanjuan by substituting their images for the gods believed to protect people by guarding their doors. There was even a rumor that Zhong Nanshan would appear in a special program to brief on the current epidemic situation on CCTV live on January 26. That night, many TV viewers found no such program.

Zhong Nanshan had to appear on TV frequently to respond to social concerns promptly to answer the public's questions. His appearance gave every Chinese confidence and calmed their nerves.

Zhong Nanshan demonstrated how to wear and take off masks on TV and answered one question after another in newspapers. For example, what symptoms required hospital examination or isolation at home, and what they could do themselves? If the patient had no fever, how could they identify people with asymptomatic infection or patients in the incubation period? When would novel coronavirus vaccines be available to them? How could they judge the trend of the epidemic, how long would it last, and when did Zhong Nanshan think the epidemic would reach its peak?

Now that the return trip of the Spring Festival travel rush had begun, what impact would it have on the prevention and control of the epidemic, and would there be another outbreak? What protective measures should those returning from their family reunions take? Zhong Nanshan's voice even affected the stock market, so many developers of stock-trading software paid close attention to Zhong Nanshan's every word.

What would the busy schedule mean to this 84-year-old man's health? He began joining the battle against the epidemic on January 18 and hadn't gone home, not even on the Chinese New Year's Eve, when the Chinese traditionally reunite. That morning, he called an emergency meeting at the First Affiliated Hospital of Guangzhou Medical College to set up a nucleic acid detection team, activated the first-level contingency plan, and declared a Class-A emergency response state in the hospital. Guangzhou Mayor Wen Guohui came to the hospital for investigation. He accompanied him and, while inspecting the epidemic prevention and control work with him, put forward suggestions for epidemic prevention and control. In the afternoon, as the deputy head of the Guangdong Provincial Leading Group for Prevention and Control, he attended the group's meeting and was then interviewed by reporters.

On the first day of the Chinese New Year season, the First Affiliated Hospital of Guangzhou Medical College held an epidemic-studying meeting to figure out countermeasures. Like what he had done during the combat against SARS, Zhong Nanshan suggested transferring all the critically and severely ill patients in other hospitals to his hospital's ICU. He required that they pull together the resources for treating infectious, respiratory, and critical illnesses to prepare for admitting and treating critically ill patients.

After making the arrangements at the meeting, he and the hospital's leadership extended New Year greetings to the doctors and nurses working on the front line. But his trip was interrupted by a phone call telling him about a severely ill patient. He received the request from the lab for an experiment on specimens at noon. He attended another meeting in the afternoon to discuss the plan for rescuing and treating the severely ill patient and demanded that the laboratory start solving a challenging problem. Subsequently, he came to the wards to ensure that the severely ill patients transferred from other hospitals were assigned to their respective zones in the hospital.

He rushed to the State Key Laboratory of Respiratory Diseases to discuss how to better treat severely ill patients with Prof. Song Yunlin he had invited from the Zhongshan Hospital, Fudan University. They decided to kick off a clinical medical research project on related injections in treating the novel coronavirus. The two studied it until 11:00 p.m.

Two critically ill patients were transferred to the First Affiliated Hospital's ICU from other hospitals the following morning. A tracheal intubation procedure was performed for the first patient. Zhong Nanshan waited and watched in the hospital starting in the early morning. The doctors and nurses threw themselves into the battle....

He was battling against the epidemic with his life, treating others' lives more important than his.

His wife, Li Shaofen, was the most worried about his health and safety. Seeing his red eyes due to lack of sleep, she was as angry as sympathetic, but she couldn't do anything. She knew she could by no means talk him into stopping what he was doing. To him, treating patients is more important than anything.

– 10 –

The death toll was rising day by day. Zhong Nanshan had trouble sleeping and eating and became prone to tears and melancholy. He always sees patients as living persons instead of statistical numbers. He pities and cares about them. He was always seen knitting his brows.

A poem about February, written by Boris Pasternak, a Russian poet, could best illustrate Zhong Nanshan's mood at the time,

"February, get out the ink and weep!
Sob in February, sob, and sing
While the wet snow rumbles in the street
And burns with the black spring...."

One day, one of his students rescuing and treating patients in Wuhan sent him a message telling him that the Wuhan residents sang the national anthem in the alleys and on the streets. Tears swelled in Zhong Nanshan's eyes. He knew how important to boost soldiers' morale in battles. Once spirited, people will unite as one and can solve many problems they can't otherwise do.

In an interview with a reporter from Xinhua News Agency, he mentioned that the people of Wuhan sang the national anthem. He believed that Wuhan could tide over the difficulties because it was a heroic city. While saying that, he suppressed the tears in his eyes and pressed his lips into a thin line. Zhong Nanshan knew how dangerous it was to let suspected and confirmed novel coronavirus-infected patients isolate themselves at home instead of admitting them to hospitals.

The ferocity of the virus and the intensity of its virulency were beyond his expectation. Releasing patients and letting their relatives risk infection, leaving patients at the mercy of fate, or allowing the deadly disease to torture them until they face death alone—all this was too much for a lifetime patient-caring doctor like him to bear. His sorrow was beyond words.

Zhong Nanshan had hated cell phones, but now he had to keep his on 24 hours a day to respond to the hospital's requests timely. He couldn't delay under any circumstance when a stress call came. He was distressed to see many of his colleagues fall ill or pass away. Many of his students fought on the front line in Wuhan, so he asked about them almost every day.

Zhong Nanshan's team was charged with doing the rounds to treat critically ill patients from the designated hospitals in Wuhan. It evaluated the patients' condition and treatment plans, identified patients who must be transferred for hospitalization, and ensured that critically ill patients were treated scientifically. Of his team, seven in leading positions were fighting hard in the ICU of the West Wing of the Wuhan Union Hospital. Their leader was Zhang Nuofu, associate head of the First Affiliated Hospital of Guangzhou Medical College. All who occupied the 20 sickbeds under the care of the seven-member team were the severest of the severely ill patients.

The uniqueness of this ICU lay in two large screens set side by side, connected online with Guangzhou 24 hours a day. Zhong Nanshan and his team of 50 doctors worked remotely to rescue and treat severely ill patients. They were all exhilarated every time they saved a patient from the jaws of death.

Zhang Nuofu led his working team to Wuhan on January 1. The team members were composed of the medical staff from the Department of Critical Care Medicine of the First Affiliated Hospital of Guangzhou Medical College. They were stationed in the West Wing of Union Hospital affiliated with Tongji Medical College of Huazhong University of Science and Technology. Union Hospital had already received over 200 inpatients, mostly with severe symptoms. The hospital treated Zhang and his team members as its saviors. The man in charge said, "The new ICU is waiting for you guys to put into operation."

Picking up the conversation thread, Zhang Nuofu cut to the chase, "Then, leave the most severely ill patients to us." He had the guts to take the task upon the team because he had participated in the combat against SARS, and all the SARS patients he had treated were critically ill. His team was worthy of Zhong Nanshan's, which had been good at fighting tough battles. Heading the team, Zhang Nuofu was an expert as well as an administrator. He had to appear at press conferences and meetings to discuss suspected and complex cases. To improve treatment efficiency and save more lives, he never shunned difficult questions and spoke frankly and boldly. He shared Zhong Nanshan's personality.

In the first few days, there was some confusion in the ICU because it wasn't up to the standards and needed rectification. After rationally dividing it into the buffer zone, the clean zone, and the contaminated zone, it welcomed the first batch of critically ill patients waiting outside. The twenty beds were all occupied in only five days.

On the evening of February 7, another medical team of 50 members came from Guangdong and joined Zhang Nuofu's people and, after helping reorganize the ICU, drastically increased its fighting capacity.

A patient with the family name Jin, who was first admitted to the ICU, experienced multiple dangerous situations: respiratory failure, pulmonary infection, myocardial injury, and septic shock. What's worse, she was resistant to various drugs. Zhang Nuofu managed to obtain antibiotics from other hospitals and found her responding to only one. He consulted Zhong Nanshan twice via teleconference. After more than 20 days of hard work, they finally successfully removed the tracheal intubation from Ms. Jin and transferred her out of the ICU.

A patient with Wang as her family name was admitted to the hospital. They put the high-flow oxygen ventilation mask on her, but her face was still flushed. For many days, her condition fluctuated: her asthmatic suffocation worsened; she coughed and had blood in her piss, stool, and phlegm; and her oxygen saturation continued to drop. Her life was hanging in the balance.

The medical team communicated via videoconference with Guangzhou and concluded that she suffered from gastrointestinal bleeding due to ischemia (inadequate blood supply). They must immediately stop the bleeding.

In the early morning of February 5, Ms. Wang's fingertip blood oxygen saturation was as low as 61%, and after masked pure-oxygen ventilation, it was only 84%. Her heart rate was 130 beats per minute. The medical staff immediately communicated with her family members by telephone. Ms. Wang suffered from acute respiratory distress syndrome and must be instantly transferred to the ICU.

Led by Xu Yuanda, the head of the ICU and director of the Department of Intensive Care, the medical team, comprising Xi Yin, Lü Zheng, and Meng Lei, worked hard to rescue and treat her. They carefully considered the dosage of the anti-virus, anti-infection, and acid-suppressing, stomach-protecting medication for symptomatic and supportive treatment. They also adjusted her ventilator parameters and medication timely according to the progress of her condition. But the novel coronavirus in her system was too "cunning" to be eradicated after repeated setbacks, and her condition couldn't be stabilized.

Zhang Nuofu video-conferenced with academician Zhong Nanshan and his team in Guangzhou three times. They discussed her condition and treatment plan. They racked their brains, China's best in the field, to figure out the cause of her recurrence.

On February 18, the medical staff found that Ms. Wang had too many oral secretions. Continuing orotracheal intubation would choke the patient. After the expert team discussed the situation, they substituted the nasotracheal intubation therapy. Though cumbersome to the medical staff, it kept the patient's mouth clean. The nurses also stepped up her oral care.

Ms. Wang's nucleic acid test indicated negative on February 21. However, after finally overcoming the challenging novel coronavirus, the medical team found many multi-drug-resistant bacteria in the sputum culture that day. After repeated deliberations and discussions with Xu Yuanda and experts from other hospitals and consultation with Zhong Nanshan, Zhang Nuofu kept adjusting the anti-infection therapy according to specific situations.

When the medical staff handed over their duty to the next shift every morning, Zhang Nuofu would emphasize, "We must also care for our patients' mental health besides their physical health." He asked them to pay attention to their psychological care, saying that solace was also crucial to their recovery.

Ms. Wang always looked sad whenever she was conscious because she was worried about her family members. Wen Deliang, an attending doctor, phoned her husband every afternoon and relayed what was going on in her family. He also played the video and voice messages her husband sent over and over on the duty cell phone to alleviate her anxiety.

The doctors and nurses were extremely busy. So to prevent Ms. Wang from suffering from her wild imaginations while they weren't around, the nurses pasted a note on the wall visible to Mr. Wang, and it read, "Cheer up! Trust us! Your family will be reunited soon!"

On the afternoon of February 25th, after a comprehensive evaluation, experts agreed that Ms. Wang's vital signs were relatively stable, and she no longer needed the support of an invasive ventilator. The doctor removed the nasotracheal intubation for Ms. Wang to free her from the "shackles" at long last.

Per the Anti-Epidemic Headquarters' request that as many patients are admitted and treated as possible, the Union Hospital's sickbeds increased to over 800. Still, the ICU beds were far from enough to meet the needs. Zhang Nuofu realized that it would be impossible to reduce the mortality rate simply by increasing the number of beds without proper treatment. He suggested to the working group of the National Health Commission that invasive ventilation treatment be carried out in the other 16 general isolation wards of the hospital, which should be equipped with many non-invasive ventilators. The working group approved the decision right away, and the move was tantamount to adding dozens of ICU beds, thereby alleviating the pressure on the ICU from critically ill patients waiting for its beds.

The ICU admitted 62 critically ill patients in a month, removed tracheal tubes from 13 patients, and transferred 15 patients to the hospital's general wards. This "report card" gave Zhang Noufu some relief: he "seemed to see the light in the tunnel."

On the afternoon of February 22, Zhong Nanshan video-conferenced with front-line medical staff in Hubei. They studied the issue of dispatching epidemic prevention and control personnel and treating patients. Simultaneously, Zhong Nanshan expressed his concern that the number of the infected medical staff exceeded 3,000, and doctors and nurses were dying one after another. He asked in detail about their physical condition, whether they had put isolation measures in place, and whether their families had any difficulties. He assured them, "If your family members have any problems, we'll do our utmost to solve them for you whether they're difficult, urgent, or psychological."

The Federation of Trade Unions, the Youth League, and the Women's Federation of Guangzhou immediately learned about the problems that the medical staff's families had. They formed a team to provide one-on-one services to relieve their stress, communicate with them, offer them moral support, and provide psychological counseling. They also took it upon themselves to care for the medical staff's aged parents, pregnant wives, or babies and infants. They also helped their family members do their chores and delivered free fresh food, wet wipes, and other maternal and childcare supplies. They granted relief funds to their directly related family members whose infection with the novel coronavirus was confirmed. In addition, they also purchased life insurance for the medical staff on the front line to fight against the epidemic.

Besides leading the fight against the epidemic on the main battlefield in Wuhan, Zhong Nanshan was also an expert in charge of the anti-epidemic work in Guangzhou. The number of confirmed cases of the novel coronavirus in Guangdong had reached more than 1,000, making it the province with the most infected people next to Hubei Province. The pressure was also immense and could not be taken lightly. Zhong Nanshan even rushed to the ICU in Shenzhen to treat patients.

The most potent weapon for humanity to fight against diseases is science and technology. The victory of humankind against catastrophes and epidemics is inseparable from scientific development and technological innovation. Zhong Nanshan hoped to find out the regularities of the incidence and infection of the novel coronavirus through scientific research, provide scientific and reliable guidance for improving the plans for its diagnosis and treatment, and give helpful references for preventing and controlling the epidemic nationwide and even globally.

During the fight against novel coronavirus, Zhong Nanshan's team published a paper online in the top international medical journal, *The New England Journal of Medicine*. It studied the clinical data of 1,099 cases of confirmed 2019-nCoV infection collected from 552 hospitals in China and discovered that nearly half of the patients infected with novel coronavirus did not have a fever when admitted to hospitals. The discovery was significant for conducting vaccine and drug research and formulating prevention and control policies. The team also developed a hydrogen generator with a nebulizer or healthgen that helped alleviate patients with the novel coronavirus symptoms. Nearly 3,000 units were produced in Shanghai and donated to the front-line medical staff for clinical use.

The device also followed the Chinese medical expert team to Iraq to support its rescue and treatment work. Simultaneously, Chinese medical experts brought some effective therapies it had mastered to treat the novel coronavirus to countries like Iran, Iraq, and Italy to reinforce the global fight against the epidemic.

The epidemic prevention and control products such as isolation beds, isolation reception counters, and isolation infusion chairs developed by Zhong Nanshan's team were produced by the Nanhai Biomedicine Industrialization Base in Guangdong and used by many hospitals in China. The team and the Shenyang Institute of Automation of the Chinese Academy of Sciences jointly put forward the plan for pharyngeal-swab sampling with intelligent robots, which could reduce the medical staff's risk of infection.

His team and Harvard University jointly established an expert research task force to work on tracing the novel coronavirus to its source, research and develop antibodies, and step up researching and developing vaccines. Simultaneously, it strengthened the exchanges of anti-epidemic experience with the medical teams and related medical societies in Japan, Singapore, Italy, and other countries to jointly promote global epidemic prevention and control.

On January 21, the Ministry of Science and Technology of China and relevant departments jointly carried out emergency scientific research on the novel coronavirus epidemic. It established a scientific research expert group with the novel coronavirus epidemic's joint prevention and control mechanism, with Zhong Nanshan as the team leader.

China quickly launched emergency scientific and technological research projects on the national level, focusing on ten aspects: virus traceability, transmission routes, animal model establishment, infection and pathogenic mechanisms, rapid immunological detection methods, genome mutation and evolution, optimized treatment plans for critically ill patients, development of emergency protective antibodies, rapid vaccine development, and therapies of traditional Chinese medicine prevention and treatment.

On January 22, the first batch of eight emergency key projects of the "Technical Response to the Novel Coronavirus Epidemic" was launched. The funds were allocated to where they were needed.

With Zhong Nanshan in the lead, his team devoted itself to medical and pharmaceutical research.

He brought in traditional Chinese medicine from the beginning and conducted basic experiments and clinical trials with traditional Chinese medicine to discover new treatment methods through observation. His team conducted its research based on Lingnan's climate, natural environment, diet, and human ecology, using the data of diagnosing the novel coronavirus with the TCM's methods: observation, auscultation, and olfaction, inquiry, and pulse feeling and palpation. They quickly formulated a herbal tea recipe for epidemic prevention and made it available to medical staff and citizens according to their preferences.

The Nanshan-Yiling Lung Collaterals Joint Research Center joined the "battle against the epidemic" only half a year after its founding. Jointly formed by the teams led respectively by academicians Zhong Nanshan and Wuyiling, it was a platform for preventing and treating respiratory diseases with integrated traditional Chinese and Western medicine. It explored integrated Chinese and Western medical treatment plans and carried out clinical experimental research on Lianhua Qingwen granules in treating the novel coronavirus. The study results confirmed that the Lianhua Qingwen Granules was an effective drug to improve the clinical cure rate of the novel coronavirus disease, proving a potent weapon for fighting it.

Chapter

Two

The Pain of SARS in 2003

A SARS epidemic required that someone tell the truth, but lying would prove too costly to China and its people. The whistleblower might be God-sent or chosen by moral principles and historical responsibility. This person who has iron-like shoulders is none other than Zhong Nanshan.

SARS made Zhong Nanshan famous not for his medical skills but for his moral courage to shoulder the responsibilities. He stepped forward out of more than a billion people and marched on alone. History placed such a mission and test in front of him.

– 1 –

The SARS outbreak 17 years ago seemed to have passed in a blink of an eye. We thought that the infectious disease caused by the coronavirus was gone, and everything with it was history. But the novel coronavirus pandemic suddenly appeared. It raged and shocked the world with more ferocity and contagiousness.

It brings back our memory of those days. As we peer deeper into the time tunnel, we'll find striking similarities between the past and the present. We may put it in other words: the present time hasn't stepped out of history. We thought we had gone far, but while busying ourselves in our daily routines and suddenly looking back, we see nothing but the years blurred in the distant past. Comparing the two coronavirus epidemics can help us understand a man who comes as a profound revelation.

The year 2003 was like a mirror, into which let's take a hard look.

Heyuan City, Guangdong Province, boasts a crystal clear river known as Xinfeng. It forms a vast body of blue water when blocked by Wanlü Lake (Xinfengjiang Reservoir). The beautiful landscape with the appearance as naïve as a wonderland teems with various exuberant lives.

However, an ominous moment broke the millennial peace. In Baipu Town, Zijin County, Huang Xingchu's illness worsened. He worked in a restaurant in Shenzhen as a chef, good at fixing Hakka-cuisine dishes. He hadn't felt well ten days before with the symptoms of a cold: fever, aversion to cold, and lethargy. He went to a hospital for intravenous treatment without recovery. Therefore, he went back to his hometown per his family's persuasion.

Huang Xingchu's fever still lingered after resting at home for a week. His mother tried to nurse him back with folk medication, but his condition worsened.

Ye Junqiang was the attending physician on duty in Heyuan People's Hospital on December 15, 2002. A stout man was helped into his clinic that afternoon, coughing with headache, continual fever, and shortage of breath. Ye Junqiang diagnosed him with pneumonia and applied antibiotics to him.

The patient was none other than Huang Xingchu, later known as the "King of Virus" because he was the first-named SARS patient.

(Subsequently, a nationwide campaign to trace the source of the virus began, involving doctors, epidemiologists, media, and citizens. Huang Xingchu felt guilty and desperate at once. He was more scared and disappeared after donating his blood serum. He had to donate it a second time a few months later under the pressure of public opinion. The search for the source found someone who had been sick with the SARS virus a month earlier than Huang Xingchu. The earliest eleven cases mostly had a history of close contact with civet cats. Some of them were engaged in transporting or trading wild animals, and others cooked and served them in restaurants. But they had no connections with one another.)

The following day, another middle-aged man with Guo as his family name came to the hospital with symptoms similar to Huang Xingchu's. He had spots on his lungs without increased white blood cell count. Like

Huang Xingchu, he was unresponsive to antibiotics.

Huang Xingchu had been hospitalized for two days, and his condition kept worsening. His fever ran as high as 40°C and wouldn't go down even with ice bags placed on his limbs and groin. Ye Junqiang decided to transfer him to a hospital in Guangzhou and escorted him there.

The ambulance blared its siren all the way. To bring his temperature down, Ye Junqiang purchased ice water on the way to feed him. They arrived at the Guangzhou Army General Hospital of Guangzhou Military Region at sunset.

Huang Wenjie, director of the Respiratory Medicine Department of the Guangzhou Army General Hospital, was preparing to get off work. The patient was carried to his presence by ambulance. He immediately started rescuing and treating the patient. He gauged his body temperature, which read 39.8°C, and found him suffering dyspnea and obnubilation and having purple skin. He was such a maniac that four to five doctors were barely enough to press him down.

Huang Wenjie treated him after immobilizing and sedating him.

The patient's condition continued to worsen, and Huang Wenjie decided to put him on a ventilator and under intubation.

The patient Guo's condition also deteriorated in Heyuan People's Hospital. He had chills and a high fever and coughed so much that he couldn't speak. On December 22, Ye Junqiang escorted him to the GIRH of the First Affiliated Hospital of Guangzhou Medical College.

Guo was Zhong Nanshan's first SARS patient. He was the director of GIRH of the First Affiliated Hospital of Guangzhou Medical College. The doctors worked on him for five days running but still couldn't find the cause of his illness. His condition deteriorated, which was reported to

Zhong Nanshan when he made the rounds.

Zhong Nanshan checked and analyzed the patient and found both his lungs have diffuse and exudative legions and respiratory distress. The X-ray showed "white lungs." After his deterioration, the doctors intubated him, but they found his lungs as hard as plastics without elasticity: the doctors could neither expand nor shrink them. Conventional ventilation caused pneumothorax and punctured the lungs.

Zhong Nanshan realized that the patient didn't suffer from common pneumonia, suspecting it to be a particular type of acute lung legions or an acute respiratory distress syndrome. He tried intravenous therapy with high-dose corticosteroids as appropriate.

To his surprise, Zhong Nanshan found the patient's condition significantly improved on the third day, with his symptoms of dyspnea alleviated.

Zhong Nanshan determined that the virulency of this pneumonia was rare. It came as a fierce onslaught, but it was tough to treat. He intuitively felt that something horrendous was looming large.

Sure enough, shocking news came from Heyuan: the eight doctors and nurses from Heyuan People's Hospital involved in rescuing and treating the patient Guo had all been infected with the same disease!

On December 23, You Li, a nurse in Zone No. 1 of Heyuan People's Hospital, became the first medical staff infected with SARS. She was four months into pregnancy.

That night, Ye Junqiang dreamed that he was in a wilderness, surrounded by darkness, and the cold wind blowing toward him made him shiver.... After waking up from the cold, he found that he had had a dream. He hurriedly got out some padded bed covers and wrapped himself in two of them. But he still felt chilly. Then, he felt his body heating up. He was also infected.

Soon afterward, another nine people showed the same symptoms, and six of them were the medical staff. A total of 11 people had been infected.

On January 2, other cases with the same symptoms were found in Zhongshan City.

Zhong Nanshan sensed danger. He called the medical staff together and told them to get prepared. He asked the hospital to report the patient Guo's case to the Epidemic Prevention Station in Yuexiu District, Guangzhou.

The Guangdong Provincial Department of Health received the warning on the morning of January 2, 2003, and in the afternoon, quickly organized several experts to go to Heyuan People's Hospital for consultation.

A patient also came to Zhongshan Traditional Chinese Medicine Hospital on the same day. He was a restaurant chef suffering from the same disease. On January 5, another chef in Zhongshan fell ill. On January 20, the number of patients in Zhongshan City reached 28. Cases also appeared in Shunde, Foshan, Jiangmen, and other cities in the Pearl River Delta. Some medical staff in Zhongshan and Jiangmen were also infected.

On the evening of January 21, Zhong Nanshan rushed to Zhongshan to conduct on-site investigations on the three hospitals that had admitted patients with the same symptoms for treatment in Zhongshan City. Together with the expert group sent by the Guangdong Provincial Department of Health, they consulted and rescued the patients.

The next day, he wrote "Provincial Expert Group Investigation Report on Unexplained Pneumonia in Zhongshan City," a formal report with the experts of the investigation team based on their investigation. It explained this atypical pneumonia's clinical symptoms, treatment principles, and prevention measures and named the infectious disease "atypical pneumonia" ("Atypical" for short in Chinese) for the first time.

On January 23, the Guangdong Provincial Department of Health distributed the report as its official document to various local governments. It thus became a significant basis for guiding the diagnosis and treatment of atypical pneumonia.

In March 2003, the World Health Organization (WHO) named it Severe Acute Respiratory Syndrome (SARS) according to its clinical manifestations and epidemiological characteristics.

Everyone felt a storm was about to burst and sweep over.

– 2 –

Spring Festival was a few days away. New Year's Eve fell on the 29th day of the last lunar month as the month didn't have the 30th. The migrant workers in South China had packed the train and long-distant bus stations. Those returning to their hometowns were anxious and restless. Though tickets were hard to come by, and the uncertainty on their journey home was scary, their determination to reunite with their families was unshaken.

It seems that only the Spring Festival celebrated in the hometown counts as the actual Chinese New Year. The land south of the Nanling Mountains may have a flower market preparing people for the advent of the New Year, and the locals of Guangdong enjoy every bit of their New Year celebration. But to those from the north, the colorful flowers and lush trees can't match their freezing winter because they won't give them a sense of a Chinese New Year and deprive them of their childhood memories. Unable to go back, they feel a deep sense of loss. Sometimes, they find themselves distracted as their souls wander back to the land where they came.

Except for the medical staff, everyone had nothing but the New Year celebration on their minds. The doctors and nurses, however, became increasingly anxious. The epidemic loomed larger as the New Year drew closer, and it developed rapidly, with more people falling ill. Over 20 had been transferred to the GIRH.

Rumors began to spread: "A hundred or so doctors have died in a certain hospital." "A certain hospital is closed." According to even more terrifying hearsay, "A strange disease has spread over to Guangzhou from Shunde and Zhongshan. Anyone infected suffers respiratory failure the following day. No medicine can cure the disease, and many people have died." Some rumors were wide of the mark: "The disease is so contagious that people can get infected in a bus shared by a sick person." "The doctors and nurses infected in the morning showed white spots on their lungs on X-rays in the afternoon, and they weren't rescuable in the evening." Some even claimed that avian influenza (bird flu), plague, and anthrax came simultaneously....

Rumors even traveled the Northeast, which was the farthest from Guangdong. People there also said, "Deadly pneumonia broke out in Guangzhou."

People rushed to buy things like the indigowoad root medicine, antiviral oral liquid, and distilled white vinegar until they were sold out. Some people hoarded the commodities and profiteered, selling white vinegar for 100 yuan per bottle.

To escape the epidemic, those Hong Kongese who had set up factories and settled in the Pearl River Delta returned to Hong Kong early to celebrate the Chinese New Year.

The news media's coverage of the incident was extremely subtle and obscure, saying that special attention should be paid to a "flu" this year's Spring Festival. Ordinary people paid no heed to such reports. Only a few well-informed people understood the implications. Such statements were counter-productive: they slackened people's vigilance. The 2003 Spring Festival was as lively and joyous as usual. The topics of people's conversations were nothing but the current events that excited, angered, and saddened them: mobile phone service had entered the digital age from the analog mobile communication network, the Chinese soccer team made its World Cup debut, actress Liu Xiaoqing was arrested on suspicion of tax evasion, Chen Shui-bian put forward the "one country on each side" theory, and two planes crashed one after another....

For these people, the jubilant Spring Festival was bound to be tragic. After the Chinese New Year, the epidemic outbroke in clusters at home and hospitals. Patients flocked to the Second and Third Hospitals of Sun Yat-sen University, the Eighth People's Hospital, and Guangzhou Chest Hospital. The medical staff at the Second and Third Hospitals of Sun Yat-sen University weren't prepared, unaware that the disease was infectious. They panicked after some of them were infected.

The Guangdong Provincial Department of Health held a press conference on February 11. To calm the panicky people's nerves, it invited

Zhong Nanshan to appear before the media. He put his academician's reputation on the line by assuring the people that SARS wasn't so scary because it was preventable, curable, and controllable. He told people not to panic and asked them to cooperate with government health agencies to combat this demon of the virus.

At this juncture, Zhong Nanshan stepped forward and volunteered to have the patients with severe symptoms transferred to his respiratory institute. It took a lot of courage to make such a decision: he would be accountable if the patients could not be cured. If that happened, his institute's reputation would be damaged. What's worse, the infectious disease was lethal. But Zhong Nanshan was very calm and showed no fear. It's not that he wasn't worried or scared. What was on his mind was, "If those engaged in the research and treatment of this disease feared and flinched, who else would dare to take the risk of rescuing and treating the patients?"

– 3 –

Heroes are ordinary people. But people who have become heroes because they didn't back down in times of crisis. They always think of others first, have the big picture in mind, and cherish universal love. Then, dangers can arouse their courage, and fighting against threats can reveal their determination, thus manifesting the best and most beautiful qualities of human nature.

Zhong Nanshan was entrusted with a mission at a critical moment, as he would 17 years later, leading the Guangdong Provincial SARS Medical Rescue Expert Steering Group.

Facing this menacing epidemic, Zhong Nanshan showed not only a doctor's compassion but also a soldier's bravery. Many critically ill patients were sent to the GIRH. He and his colleagues lost no time joining the battle to save the patients' lives. None of them shrank from the life-threatening epidemic. They repeatedly charged at the demon of the SARS disease like vanguards of an army. Like blowing up enemy bunkers or taking over enemy citadels, they saved the lives of one critically ill patient after another.

The GIRH formed four echelons. The second echelon dashed forward when the first was infected and fell during the battle. The third echelon replaced the second when the latter had to disengage from the campaign due to infection, and the fourth took over when the third succumbed to the disease. Those who had been sick returned to the front line as soon as they recovered.

The hospital was still the one by the Pearl River, and the buildings remained the same. So did the wards in them. Everything changed overnight: stepping into the premises, the medical staff couldn't believe how close death was approaching them and lurked in every nook and cranny. It would bring you down without knowing it if you occasionally let your guard down. Twenty-six of the GIRH's doctors and nurses were infected and fell ill, but they never left their familiar buildings.

What if the disease struck you? Would you be absent from work with the patients hospitalized? Those colleagues not yet infected still went into the buildings. They might feel death brush by them with cold terror, but none of them flinched in the wards.

The infected medical staff went back to work after their recuperation. Unyielding to the disease, they buckled on their armor and went into action again. People jested that they had acquired antibodies that made them immune to any virus. When someone from WHO asked Zhong Nanshan if anyone had ever left the hospital, Zhong Nanshan proudly told him, "None!"

It was a heroic collective with the spirit of heroism led by a courageous leader. And that leader was Zhong Nanshan. He was always the first to enter the ICU, checking on the patients and formulating treatment plans. He always dashed forward whenever dangers arose. His example encouraged his fellow medical staff to fight bravely.

He would have merely put on a show if he had been a talker than a doer fighting such a tough battle.

Unfortunately, Ye Xin, the head nurse of the Guangdong Province Traditional Chinese Medicine Hospital, died in the line of duty. Deng Lianxian, the chief physician from the Department of Infectious Diseases of the Third Affiliated Hospital of Sun Yat-sen University, also succumbed to SARS. He was infected by the phlegm coughed out by the patient known as the "King of Virus" while performing the intubation procedure on him on the first day of the Chinese New Year season. Chen Hongguang, director of the intensive care unit of Guangzhou Chest Hospital, was also cut down by the disease.... Three medical professionals would be affected by rescuing and treating each SARS patient because the contact between them wasn't completely cut off. These infected medical staff all converged in the GIRH. Zhong Nanshan's heart ached as he watched the colleagues he worked with suffering from the disease for many years. He felt the weight of the colossal responsibility on his shoulders. Medical personnel's infection caused greater panic in society, and he must ensure that they could stand up again.

Zhong Nanshan realized that he had the weighty responsibility of keeping the medical staff safe besides plucking up their courage in the face of danger. Every day, he carefully checked whether the medical staff's protective measures were in place and asked about their physical condition. He asked the doctors to turn on a fan blowing in a patient's face when checking his mouth. The nurses in the ICU commented, "No one is more considerate than Academician Zhong. He'll correct us when he sees us wearing our masks wrongly."

He extended his regards to the doctors hospitalized with the infection every day. He would call to inquire about their conditions even if he was away on business. He couldn't feel at ease. Zheng Zeguang, a doctor from the ICU, had emotional disturbances after his infection. Zong Nanshan learned about it when he was at a meeting away from the hospital. He sent him messages to cheer him up.

Zhong Nanshan often forgot he was in danger when concentrating on rescuing and treating SARS patients. Once, an emergency occurred when the ventilator used to save a patient with respiratory failure needed adjustment. Zhong Nanshan pushed the Gatch bed with the patient on it to an ICU bed himself and gave him artificial respiration with an Ambu bag. It was a risky procedure because many doctors who had done so were infected by the blood or phlegm squirted from a patient's windpipe. The squirts would splash on their faces and clothing. But Zhong Nanshan had only the patient's rescue on his mind.

The act of Zhong Nanshan deeply moved the patient's family members after they learned about him performing such heavy physical work at 67.

There was a family of five, four of whom were infected with SARS. After their admission to the GIRH, the eldest son was so emotional and impetuous that he stormed out of the isolated wards attempting to see his wife. He missed her and was grieved at this life-and-death juncture. Seeing that no one else could calm him down, he volunteered himself. Chilling a patient out is a prerequisite for saving a patient's life. Empathetic with his patients, he knew how they felt and what they thought. This particular patient read consolation and confidence from his assuring and intelligent look.

During that crisis, hospitals of various sizes in Guangzhou that had admitted SARAS patients often asked him for help. He would visit each upon request as long as he had time. It was common for him to take off upon a phone call.

To overcome the difficulty in treating SARS, Zhong Nanshan set up a team of veteran and young respiratory disease experts with Xiao Zhenglun, Chen Rongchang, and Li Yimin as the backbone members. SARS flares up suddenly and acutely, and its condition changes rapidly and unpredictably. To understand its regularity of occurrence, Zhong Nanshan wouldn't let a single patient slip off his scrutiny.

After countless sleepless nights, Zhong Nanshan finally figured out an effective therapy. He summed it up as the following:

First, the treatment integrating Chinese and Western medicine is advisable when the disease acutely attacks a patient, especially when he has a high fever and muscle ache. Antipyretic-detoxicate herbal medication is particularly good at alleviating the symptoms.

Second, when a patient's condition develops to a certain degree, timely use of steroids or corticosteroids can prevent the development of lung fibrosis and more severe respiratory failure.

Third, artificial ventilation should be used when a patient suffers apparent hypoxia. But no intubation or tracheotomy should be used for ventilation at first, and a non-invasive nasal or face mask should be used simultaneously. This therapy proves to be working because it has saved many patients' lives.

Fourth, an infected patient, whose natural resistance to the virus is deficient, is prone to superinfection. Therefore, such infection must be prevented as early as possible, which is critical in reducing the death rate.

These specific guidelines were issued to the medical units under the direct and subordinate jurisdiction of the province and its municipalities as a document titled "Guidelines for the Hospitals in Guangdong to Admit and Treat SARS Patients."

These guidelines gradually became well-known to the medical professionals as "Three Early's and Three Appropriates": "early diagnosis," "early quarantine," "early treatment," "appropriate use of corticosteroids," "appropriate use of ventilators," and "appropriate treatment of complications."

The timely introduction of these therapies was a turning point in Guangdong's battle against SARS: its rage in Guangzhou was gradually suppressed.

Seven experts from WHO visited Guangzhou on April 3, 2003. They asked to meet Zhong Nanshan as soon as they arrived. Zhong Nanshan made a 40-minute report on behalf of the Guangdong Provincial SARS Medical Rescue Expert Steering Group. The WHO experts praised his report, stating that they found the experience of treating SARS in

Guangdong. By then, the epidemic had spread to over 20 countries and regions. Still, they saw the best result in Guangdong, where the number of cured SARS patients accounted for 86.3% of the reported cases, and the mortality rate was only 3.7%.

– 4 –

Patients flooded into the hospital. Zhong Nanshan knew that the more important task than rescuing and treating individual patients was to cut off the source of infection. To do this, he must find the pathogen and its transmission route as quickly as possible. Otherwise, the situation would be out of control!

The logic is easily understandable: it's like when water gushes from a faucet, it's more effective to stop the continual flow of liquid by finding and turning off the tap than scooping the water. Who would have taken the responsibility if he, an academician of the Chinese Academy of Engineering, a lead researcher, and a respiratory diseases expert, had refused to do it? Zhong Nanshan felt it his duty to locate the faucet and turn it off.

But finding the source was no easy job. Zhong Nanshan was anxious but, at the same time, more tenacious, a quality acquired as a pioneering scientist. This intricate path of exploration made him inexplicably excited. A scientific inquiry without encountering any difficulty would be meaningless for a scientist. Therefore, discovering the cause of the disease as soon as possible and figuring out an effective way to treat SARS became Zhong Nanshan's greatest concern.

The lamp in Zhong Nanshan's study often stayed on all night. His colleagues warned him that burning night oil was harmful to his health, but he paid no heed. He wouldn't feel at ease before finding a way to save the patients from the epidemic. He hadn't cared about risking his life for an experiment when studying in the UK, let alone trying to save thousands of lives now. Nothing but curing his patients and seeking truth and scientific results matter to Zhong Nanshan in his life. They all came together as his goal today, and he was willing to exchange his life for its achievement.

Zhong Nanshan spent most of his time at the sites rescuing and treating the patients he observed. Finally, he and his assistants found more detailed emergency treatment methods. When lung shadows continue to increase, and the level of blood oxygen decreases, it is advisable to apply non-invasive ventilation in time to increase oxygen supply and prevent alveolar collapse. When there is a very obvious high fever and aggravation of pulmonary inflammation, apply large doses of corticosteroids to reduce the non-specific inflammation of the alveoli. Although there are no effective antibiotics, targeted antibiotics should be used when patients are found to have secondary infections. Those were the experience distilled from his cases. Clinical practice proved them effective: most critically ill patients' conditions were improved or stabilized, and those infected earlier had already recovered and been released from the hospital.

Despite working hard, they still hadn't achieved a breakthrough in searching for the pathogen. Zhong Nanshan gathered and researched data and established contact with other experts as he groped in the dark. A colleague reminded him that the provincial government had set up a technical steering committee for pathogen detection and suggested that he stop doing it. Otherwise, he would have been accused of stepping on their toes, which meant he would have done a hard but thankless job.

Zhong Nanshan ignored the warning. Finding the pathogens is undoubtedly a scientific breakthrough and a significant accomplishment, But curing patients is more important for him because it is the duty of a medical worker.

On February 18, a Beijing authoritative expert officially released his definitive conclusion through CCTV and Xinhua News Agency, "The pathogen causing SARS in some areas of Guangdong can be identified as chlamydia." They claimed that they observed typical and clear images of chlamydia particles under the electron microscope from the specimen sections of the lung tissue of two dead cases that Guangdong had delivered to the lab. They added that they didn't find other microorganisms like mycoplasma and rickettsia.

On February 19, CCTV broadcast an interview with the authoritative expert. He said that the treatment of chlamydia had become very simple, and it would suffice to use antibiotics effective against chlamydia.

The authority's conclusion shocked the experts in Guangdong. It would greatly simplify the treatment if the recommended tetracycline and erythromycin antibiotics could effectively cure the disease. But if the judgment were wrong, it would cost many lives!

At 4:00 p.m. on February 18, the Guangdong Provincial Department of Health immediately held an expert meeting to analyze and discuss the test result of China's highest authoritative professional department. Zhong Nanshan didn't think it was chlamydia, believing that it was only one of the causes that ultimately caused death to patients, and the leading cause might be a new type of virus. The conclusion from the electron microscopic observation of two lung tissue specimens wasn't scientific enough.

The Guangdong experts agreed with Zhong Nanshan, didn't support the chlamydia conclusion, and believed that the possibility of viral infection was high based on the analysis of the clinical manifestations and treatment. The discovery of chlamydia particles could only indicate that these two patients had chlamydia infection or coinfection, but it didn't mean that other patients were also infected with chlamydia. Guangdong Provincial Department of Health braced itself as it decided to overturn the authoritative test report. It mobilized the experts to test the serum obtained from various hospitals for Chlamydia pneumoniae antibodies overnight. They tried 90 cases, of which 17 were positive, accounting for 18.9%. The tests proved that the conclusion that the SARS-causing pathogen was identified as chlamydia was incorrect.

Zhong Nanshan negated the authoritative department's conclusion on the media. His confrontation with the authority was seen as publicly challenging it, which worried everyone who knew him. He would face a "disaster" if his judgment were proved slightly incorrect. It took great courage, which he obtained from the patients waiting for him to save them. They would die if he didn't waver from his opinion. His rationale was as simple as defending science and truth and saving people's lives. Zhong Nanshan was fully aware of the consequences. It might be a personal "disaster" for him to stand up, but if he didn't correct the authoritative expert's mistakes in time, it would be a calamity for all patients!

He fell ill that day, struck with a fever, perhaps because of stress or fatigue. His colleagues sent him home against his will.

The Guangdong Provincial Department of Health adopted Zhong

Nanshan's view, which became a significant watershed in the fight against SARS. This tough guy stepped forward as an academician of the Chinese Academy of Engineering and saved countless lives!

– 5 –

Scientists are usually unsophisticated and care less about playing politics and cultivating personal relations. But an epidemic involves all aspects of society, going far beyond clinics and operating rooms. When Zhong Nanshan searched for the source by himself like a lone hero, something unexpected happened to him. Because of this incident, he didn't sleep for 38 hours and finally collapsed beside his patient.

The fall of Zhong Nanshan would mean that the raging epidemic might be entirely out of control!

To say that it was a misunderstanding is an understatement after what has happened. This incident was a psychic trauma, and the victim didn't want it to be mentioned again. Zhong Nanshan isn't afraid of hardships and has never flinched from the most challenging problems. Compared with rescuing patients at the risk of being infected, this kind of mental damage is more unbearable.

Zhong Nanshan is physically strong enough not to collapse after rescuing patients for 38 hours running. But the sudden occurrence of this incident knocked him down. He fell ill after the intense hours. His illness seemed to be destined.

The incident had to do with searching for the pathogen. Zhong Nanshan needed close collaboration in the etiology and clinical aspects of the disease, which he believed to be humankind's, not a country's. It couldn't be tackled by a country's medical personnel alone. A country's strength was limited, so it was necessary to pull the wisdom of all people in the world and rely on humanity's collective knowledge to overcome the fulminant disease and the disaster it might bring.

The search for pathogens depends on the detection of viruses, but China didn't have such detection equipment at the time. Hard-pressed for time, he thought of his two students: Guan Yi and Zheng Bojian. He trusted them and recognized their academic accomplishments. Both were microbiology professors at the University of Hong Kong, specializing in animal viruses. Hong Kong had an advantage over the mainland in terms of etiology research. It had laboratories of the same standard as developed countries and a high level of detection technology. To find the pathogens, Zhong Nanshan went to the University of Hong Kong and immediately started cooperating with it after an on-site inspection.

One day in late February 2003, Zhong Nanshan attended a conference on anti-infection in Shanghai. The meeting, related to SARS, was crucial to the fight against the epidemic. But someone from the Guangdong Provincial Health Department called him in the middle of the meeting, telling him to rush back to Guangzhou on the same day because the matter was urgent!

Although he hesitated, he had to leave the meeting and flew back to Guangzhou overnight.

The plane landed at Baiyun Airport at about 10:00 p.m. Walking down the gangway, Zhong Nanshan saw a car parked next to the aircraft illuminated by something like spotlights. As soon as he appeared, someone walked up and asked him to get into the car. Without delay, it drove from the parking area to a hotel.

Some people were waiting at the door. As soon as he got out of the car, they took him to a conference room. Walking into it, Zhong Nanshan saw everyone sitting upright and expressionless. He felt the atmosphere exceptionally tense.

He quickly scanned the people and spotted an acquainted leader among several others he didn't know. His seat had been arranged, and someone led him to it.

As soon as he was seated, one of the leaders cut to the chase, staring into his eyes, "According to what we know, Hong Kong will announce the discovery of pathogens tomorrow. We've learned that you cooperated with someone there in secret. We want you to tell us about it."

Silence reigned in the venue, and it was so quiet that a pin falling to the floor could have been heard.

Zhong Nanshan was dazed a little.

The acquainted leader also spoke, questioning him gravely, "How did you do it?"

Zhong Nanshan found out later that he had been called back from Shanghai because the leaders from above thought he had considered the SARS outbreak as chicken flu. What made it worse was that Hong Kong's release of the evidence of bird flu would lead Hong Kong and the international community to criticize the mainland. They would question the reason for concealing the outbreak and why it wouldn't publicize it timely. If so, China would find itself in an unfavorable situation. The leaders were worried that Zhang Nanshan might have sold information to someone in Hong Kong for personal gains. In their eyes, he might have disregarded national interest or even betrayed the country if his action were elevated to the level of principle.

Zhong Nanshan maintained that he did nothing wrong but only what a doctor was supposed to do. The search for pathogens relies on advanced detection equipment. Only Hong Kong was conveniently close while other countries were far apart. Zhong Nanshan asked them to use their research equipment to test serum and sputum specimens to detect viruses, which was necessary for research cooperation. To this end, Zhong Nanshan signed a cooperation agreement with his two students to jointly study pathogens. Per the agreement, he provided the patient's serum and sputum samples. Considering that only the Ministry of Health of China had the right to issue announcements about pathogens, he specially wrote a clause in the agreement. It read, "If either party finds a pathogen, both parties must verify it and won't release it to the outside world until they get the Ministry of Health's approval.

Zhong Nanshan felt more at ease when realizing that his recall from Shanghai had to do with Hong Kong. He gave the leaders detailed explanations and asked someone to get the agreement over to show to the leaders.

Their stern questioning gave Zhong Nanshan a feeling of hostility, making him look like a criminal. He felt that he was more dangerous than the epidemic in their eyes.

It seemed that the atmosphere lightened. But they wondered what to do tomorrow when Hong Kong released the result.

After deliberating for a while, they failed to develop a good solution.

It was 1:30 a.m. Zhong Nanshan proposed that he rush to Hong Kong overnight.

He decided to leave immediately without returning home. He called Li Yimin, his fellow expert at the GIRH, over and left for Hong Kong in a car with Guangdong and Hong Kong plates.

– 6 –

The two crossed the border via Shenzhen's Luohu Bridge, and the car drove in the direction of Kowloon on the empty road illuminated by the orange light of the street lamps. The sea's salty smell permeated the air, the number of tall buildings kept increasing, the few vehicles on the street ran at high speed, and this bustling internationalized metropolis was fast asleep. Zhong Nanshan was exhausted by traveling from Shanghai to Hong Kong via Guangzhou and Shenzhen, covering four municipalities overnight.

They arrived at the University of Hong Kong at daybreak. Prof. Li Yimin asked Zhong Nanshan to call his students on his mobile phone, but the latter said they were still asleep and suggested they wait for a while. He feared that they would have scared his students if they had called them so early. His students would have thought the matter must have been so grave that it had brought them to Hong Kong late at night and would have been too scared to see them. That would have bungled their visit.

Zhong Nanshan didn't call Guan Yi until it was almost time for work.

Guan was happily surprised by his mentor's phone call and asked after him. He wanted him to take care, knowing he had been so busy.

After chatting for a while, Zhong Nanshan told him that he had come to Hong Kong. Guan Yi was very excited and asked him where to pick him up.

Zhong Nanshan responded that he was right in front of his building.

Guang Yi was stunned, asking him when he had arrived. Hesitating a little, Zhong Nanshan told him the whole story.

Guan Yi felt guilty after hearing his teacher had waited in the car for two hours. He said he was about to come down and apologized for having his teacher wait for so long. Zhong Nanshan told Guan Yi that he was by his dormitory and asked that he bring Zheng Bojian with him. He said he had something to talk about with them together.

When the three met, Zhong Nanshan's students asked their teacher to have breakfast with them. Zhong Nanshan said, "We'd better put off our breakfast. Let me ask you a question: Are you going to release information on the pathogen today?

Guan Yi was puzzled and asked, "Where did you hear the news, teacher? We haven't found the pathogen yet, let alone confirmed it. Even if it were confirmed, don't we have an agreement? The timing of the release is explicitly written."

Zhong Nanshan stared into Guan Yi's eyes without blinking once. In Guan Yi's memory, his teacher had never been so severe.

Guan Yi repeated emphatically, "How can I lie to my teacher? If I wanted to release the result, I would have to get your consent, and we have to get the Ministry of Health's verification and approval. I know this basic principle."

Zhong Nanshan breathed a deep sigh of relief, finally feeling relaxed. He said, "Let's go to dinner together with a smile on his face."

They had walked a few steps when he came to a halt, saying to Guan Yi, "Can you two go to Guangzhou with me? Let's go now."

Guan Yi and Zheng Bojian guessed something might have happened. They'd better go with the teacher as he had requested. They immediately asked the university for a day's leave. They followed Zhong Nanshan to Guangzhou without bothering to eat breakfast.

– 7 –

Guan Yi was born in Meijiang Town of Ningde County, Jiangxi Province. The year following the resumption of the college entrance examination, he was admitted to Jiangxi Medical College. He entered the University of Hong Kong to study for a Ph.D. at 30. After graduation, he worked in WHO's Animal Influenza Research Center, jointly established by the University of Hong Kong and the United States.

Guan Yi first studied pediatrics, but his interest led him to give up his medical career for basic science, devoting himself to studying bird flue. Besides his curiosity, he believed that physicians could only save a limited number of patients. But he could save tens of thousands of people's lives if he worked as a microbiologist to find the culprit of a viral epidemic and stop its spread.

The first case of human-to-human bird flu broke out in Hong Kong in 1997. At that time, he was a postdoctoral fellow at St. Jude Children's Research Hospital in Memphis, Tennessee, with world-renowned influenza researcher Robert Webster. The breakout prompted him to focus on the research on bird flu. After returning home, he entered the University of Hong Kong to engage in animal influenza research.

Guan Yi isolated the SARS virus a little over a month after this 2003 trip to Guangzhou with his teacher and his quick return to Hong Kong. In October, he found the SARS virus in civet cats. At the end of the year, he announced to the world in Hong Kong and Guangzhou at the same time that the SARS virus had been found in civet cats.

Four SARS cases appeared in Guangzhou again in the spring of 2004, a year after its outbreak. The timing was similar. Guan Yi isolated coronaviruses from civet cats and humans, and all four cases were highly homologous. After Zhong Nanshan notified the governor, Guangdong immediately slaughtered all the civet cats in the wild animal markets, effectively curbing the spread of the disease.

During the SARS outbreak, Zhong Nanshan, Zheng Bojian, and Wen Yumei conducted vital research on the "Inactivated SARS Virus Immunization Prevention Nasal Drip" at Guangzhou First Military Medical University. Twenty days later, they successfully developed the nasal drip for use by front-line medical staff, effectively blocking the virus from invading the human body.

Guan Yi and his team successfully collected samples from more than 100,000 birds and extracted the gene sequences of more than 250 H5N1 avian influenza viruses from the samples. They figured out the regularities of avian influenza's origin, occurrence, and changes in China. Theirs has become one of the eight WHO reference laboratories worldwide and has identified all the world's 20 or more variants of H5N1 avian influenza. It has also isolated a human-infected bird flu virus in Indonesia. The U.S. *Time* magazine featured them in January 2004, September 2005, and November 2005. Guan Yi was selected as one of the 18 medical heroes globally by the U.S. *Time* magazine in 2005.

The unexplained pneumonia breakout in Wuhan also attracted Guan Yi's attention in 2020. Reports said that human-to-human transmission couldn't be proved. But when he heard Zhong Nanshan announce on CCTV that the new crown pneumonia was passed from person to person on the evening of January 20, Guan Yi could no longer sit still. He rushed from Hong Kong to Wuhan before dawn the next day and appeared on the streets of Wuhan in the morning. He hoped to find the culprit of the disease and help Wuhan curb its ravages, as he had investigated the SARS pathogen in Guangdong.

However, his enthusiasm was met with a cold welcome and even suspicion. He even found himself on the wrong side of the door in many research institutions. Few of them would cooperate with him. Some people even defined his trip to Wuhan as coming for his academic achievements and wanting to steal scientific research data. After he left, they said he went back in disgrace due to failing to achieve his goal. Many ordinary Chinese also criticized him. Guan Yi felt that epidemic prevention experts in particular and scientists at large weren't welcome here. He was deeply disappointed.

He had a taste of what his teacher had suffered when he was misunderstood 17 years before.

He went to the Huanan Seafood Wholesale Market but found it

sealed. It had been cleaned, no animal samples were kept, and no CCTV cameras could be found. The "scene" wasn't there anymore. He couldn't find the specimens for his laboratory studies.

He didn't know if it was the result of the idea of trusting luck or not. How could he develop an antidote without finding the source of the disease? He found that the characteristics of the novel coronavirus were similar to SARS and even more dangerous: people who didn't have the symptoms of cold and fever could still spread it to others! The first wave of transmission had begun. It was a war! He came to Wuhan at the risk of being infected. He returned to Hong Kong without success because he couldn't collect animal samples.

While staying in Wuhan for two nights, he found its residents undisturbed by Zhong Nanshan's announcement that the novel coronavirus was transmissible from person to person. They still lived their lives as they used to, traveling here and there without wearing masks and crowding wet markets and supermarkets like sardines doing Spring Festival shopping. Many of them even prepared themselves for tours outside Wuhan. Spring Festival mass greeting gatherings were going on like in previous years. The citizens seemed not to have woken up. Not until January 22 did the municipal government issue a public notice of its decision to implement control measures for wearing masks in public places across the urban area. But some people still advocated that young people and children weren't vulnerable to viral infection.

When he went through a security check in the Wuhan Airport on January 22, he saw a young female transportation security officer wearing a disposable mask. When asked, she told him she put it on voluntarily against the will of the airport administrators, who wouldn't let her lest she would tarnish the airport's image.

It was already an epidemic-stricken area! The scene reminded him of such a scenario: people were still partying without being mobilized and prepared for an atomic bomb attack while it was imminent. He wanted to cry out. He wished to take extensive isolation measures and immediately lock the city down. But he had no authority to do so, which made him feel utterly helpless as an expert.

He decided to evacuate from Wuhan at once, and his self-deprecating remarks immediately drew sarcasm and attacks from some netizens.

On January 23, 2020, the central government locked Wuhan down with lightning speed the next day after Guan Yi's departure. In the early morning of that day, he reminded everyone to pay attention to aerosol transmission and eye protection, prevent fecal-oral transmission, and understand that children and young people are equally susceptible to infection.

– 8 –

Zhong Nanshan and his students Guan Yi and Zheng Bojian traveled fast and reached Guangzhou Hotel at noon. Zhong Nanshan asked them to explain the rumored bird flu announcement to the leaders.

After getting over the incident, Zhong Nanshan attended an epidemic prevention and control conference. He gave a presentation on how to implement prevention and control.

Zhong Nanshan, who had known no fatigue, felt lethargic for the first time. As if his legs didn't belong to him anymore, he walked with great difficulties, like carrying a thousand-kilogram burden on his shoulders. He was as different from another person compared with himself, who had used to walk briskly. The once tireless Zhong Nanshan finally realized that his ability fell short of his wishes. He felt more than wronged as the word "country" repeatedly rang in his ears and thumped his nerves. He wondered why the country didn't trust him at all and turned him into someone like an infidel overnight.

He had spent 38 hours without sleep and rest: he got up at 7:00 a.m. in Shanghai and arrived in Guangzhou at 10:00 a.m. He then rushed to Hong Kong overnight and returned to Guangzhou the following day. Besides a conference, he also participated in rescuing patients and didn't finish until 9:00 p.m. He was hit by a high fever and started coughing. A timely x-ray showed inflammation on the left lobe of his lungs.

He wanted to go home, which he missed sorely. He had never been so homesick before. He was in Guangzhou now, but his family members weren't aware of his whereabouts yet. He missed his wife Li Shaofen, her eyes filled with loving care, and her smile.... She had retired very early and been taking care of him. He also missed his young grandson, who had recently returned from New Zealand. He hadn't seen him for two years, and he was six. He hadn't returned home to spend some time with him, even on New Year's Eve. How much he wanted to hold him in his arms....

Zhong Nanshan fell ill. It would become a bombshell if leaked out and undermine the morale of the anti-epidemic battle.

Is he infected with SARS? If he can't treat himself, who can trust doctors anymore?

Bouts of dizziness didn't deprive Zhong Nanshan of his soberness. He didn't allow getting the word of his illness out and asked those around him to keep it a secret for him.

But how could the secret be kept if he were hospitalized? Where medical treatment was concerned, his GIRH would be the best option. Apart from the specialized medical skills and equipment, it had his comrades-in-arms who had gone through thick or thin with him. Each would go all out to treat him. Therefore, all of them asked him to get his treatment there.

Zhong Nanshan was reticent. Placing a hand on the desk to support himself, he closed his eyes and pinched his glabella with the forefinger and thumb of the other hand. The bulging veins on his hands were particularly conspicuous. He bent his upper body a little and straightened it up again. He was contemplating. He usually rested his hands on his hips and never placed them on the desk when he did so. He was severely ill. Someone went up to steady him, but he waved his hand to say no. He was too proud to allow others to regard him as a sick man.

He couldn't get himself confined to the GIRH's sickbed. If people learned of his condition, how could SARS patients have any confidence in doctors? Who could lie in their sickbeds waiting for the medical staff to treat them? If it took a long time to get him to recover, it would be more damaging to public confidence. He wanted to get treatment in a place unknown to the public. Pinching his glabella, he racked his brain, thinking: *Whom shall I go? And what's the right place?*

Now that he had figured out whom and where, Zhong Nanshan straightened his bent back and asked all his colleagues to leave the room except one. Zhong Nanshan discussed with the colleague, asking him to find him a comrade-in-arms and admit him to a hospital unit designated for cadres. He asked him to keep his hospitalization a secret. Before long, his colleague sent him a message to inform him of the result of contacting the hospital. Someone from the hospital said that a patient would have a kidney transplant operation in the cadre's unit, and some reporters from Hong Kong would come to interview him. Therefore, the unit would be messy.... That meant the hospital turned down his request politely. Zhong Nanshan sympathized with the hospital's worries that he might be infected with the contagious SARS. He could understand their fear of being infected.

Zhong Nanshan was so dizzy that he almost hallucinated and didn't have any strength to keep himself on his feet. He could only rely on his family members at a time like this. He found his son's phone number and called him, "Weide, dad's fallen ill. Take me back home, where I'll get treated."

– 9 –

The father and son went back home. Zhong Nanshan's wife walked over as usual and looked at him tenderly as if nothing had happened. In her brief gaze, Zhong Nanshan felt her boundless love and care. Her signature gentleness jolted and lit up his lifetime memory like a thunderbolt.

Living their lives of vicissitudes through thick or thin, they kept each other company till they reached their sixties. But still, they cherished the love they had had when they first met, and Zhong Nanshan felt the tenderness mellowed by the depth of time.

The housemaid had cleaned the room and made the bed. She was somewhat anxious, not knowing what to do.

Zhong Nanshan's wife took off his clothes and asked him to take a bath. She changed all the clothes taken off and placed the medicine Zhong Nanshan had brought back with him where it was conveniently accessible. Then, she went to the kitchen.

A nurse came to give Zhong Nanshan an intravenous drip but couldn't find where to hang the bottle. Zhong Nanshan asked his on Weide to hammer a nail into the upper-left corner of the wooden door, and it was perfect for hanging the bottle. Making his home a makeshift hospital, Zhong Nanshan would treat himself.

As soon as his back touched the bed, he saw stars and felt like he was falling into an abyss. He sank into a heavy slumber.

He had no idea how long he had slept. He hadn't had such a sound sleep for years. He had worked like a spinning top that stopped and rolled on its side only when the illness hit him. He wore a straight face though asleep: he still had something weighing heavy in his mind.

Sitting by his side and staring at his haggard face, Li Shaofen felt deeply sorry for him and couldn't help shedding tears. He had fallen ill twice since SARS broke out, but he had never been sick before. About a month ago, he had a fever and felt listless due to overwork. His colleagues sent him home against his will. He rested less than two days before returning to the hospital, not wholly recuperated.

He was always busy and seldom at home, even in his sixties. His pet phrase when he returned home was "I'm tired." Li Shaofen was unhappy, and they had had many rows over his constant absence. She entertained no high hopes of going on a sightseeing tour together. She would have been satisfied if he could have kept her company briefly. But after their rows, he remained busy outside the home.

Li Shaofen has a bold disposition, having the courage to shoulder responsibility while being restrained and gentle at the same time. She hates to be ostentatious and show herself in public. She enjoys peaceful and uneventful family life. After her husband became famous, many reporters tried to interview her, but she rejected their requests each time. She doesn't like dealing with journalists, still less with their interviews because of her husband.

Zhong Nanshan was full of apologies to his wife. He knew she needed his company and missed her when away from home. He was worried about her health and would scrutinize her health examination report each time she had her physical. But he felt uneasy staying at home when his patients' lives were in danger.

Li Shaofen understands Zhong Nanshan, and no one knows him better than she does. Initially, she had rows with him because she couldn't suppress her impulsiveness. Later, she gradually got used to her husband's work pattern. Eventually, she feels satisfied if he can return home safe and sound.

Their husband-wife relationship seemed to be predestined. Zhong Nanshan's maternal aunt and Li Shaofen's paternal aunt had remained single all their lives and lived together from their youth till their later years. One was a physician and the other a pianist. After being recruited into the national basketball team, Li Shaofen often visited her aunt. After being admitted into Beijing Medical College, Zhong Nanshan frequently came to see his aunt. Li Shaofen was from Huadu, Guangdong. Both the young people from the same province shared the same obsession with sports. The happy match of the two with the same interest meeting away from their shared hometown was godsent.

They came close soon, found each other agreeable, and fell in love. Other lovers typically dated in romantic environments featuring colorful flowers or gentle moonlight. But their rendezvous mainly was on a soccer field, where Zhong Nanshan practiced running while she accompanied him. When she was tired, she would stop to clock his time.

In his junior year, Zhong Nanshan participated in the Beijing University Games and won the 400-meter hurdles championship. He caught Beijing Sports Commission's attention, and it transferred him to the Beijing Team of Athletes for training, preparing him for the coming 1st National Games of China. The selective trials started, but he wasn't selected. It was like cold water poured on Zhong Nanshan, who had been full of confidence. A young man of indomitability by disposition, how could he swallow this defeat? It was the first setback in his life.

Li Shaofen solaced and encouraged him, saying that she had faith in his ability to win. Zhong Nanshan decided to challenge himself. The couple tried to figure out the reason for the defeat and especially a way to win: giving Zhong Nanshan's explosive force full play.

As a result, he won the final tryout. In September 1959, Zhong Nanshan broke the national record for the 400-meter hurdles with a time of 54.4 seconds at the first National Games! He also won the Beijing decathlon runner-up in 1961.

Li Shaofen was a national basketball team player, and Zhong Nanshan was also a basketball lover. She was fond of talking about the basketball team and what she thought of each match, and he liked everything she told him. The couple always had a lot to say to each other. Playing basketball together perfected their physical coordination so that verbal communication seemed unnecessary.

They supervised and encouraged each other to strengthen their training. They didn't know how much sweat they had shed, and their perspiration brewed and mellowed their passionate love.

Zhong Nanshan could be as romantic as playing his clarinet on a quiet night or in a secluded corner of a park. Both loved Russian songs like *Katyusha, On Night in Moscow's Suburb*, and *Troika*. When discussing literature, they talked about the works of Soviet writers most of the time. As a Russian major, Zhong Nanshan knew a lot about the history and culture of the Soviet Union. Li Shaofen had been to the country to receive training from Soviet basketball experts. She often consulted him about the Soviet Union, and the two always had endless topics for their conversation. Zhong Nanshan was wittily humorous. He often took Li Shaofen to college dancing parties, where he would sing when excited. His youthful vigor and tenaciousness appealed to her.

Her adoptive mother brought up Li Shaofen as her biological mother lived in Shanghai. Li Shaofen is the youngest of her siblings and was adopted soon after birth. Her adoptive mother, a lifetime single, lived with another woman as her companion for the rest of their lives. Li Shaofen loved playing piano and basketball when young. She was selected by the Central Institute of Physical Education and recruited by the national basketball team. Her adoptive mother had been unwilling to let her go but gave her consent after persuading herself that her adoptive daughter might not have a future otherwise.

They both attached great importance to their careers. Li Shaofen was worried that marriage might affect her career, and Zhong Nanshan had a strong desire to advance in his career path. As a result, they dated eight years before tying the knot. Their bridal chamber was a 10-square-meter, plainly furnished room the National Sports Commission provided. But they thought that it was their world big enough for them to live a happy life.

They were separated more often than being together from the beginning. Training and participating in matches abroad took most of Li Shaofen's time. To help China get rid of the insulting name of a "Sick Man in East Asia," everyone must work hard. Soon after their marriage, Zhong Nanshan was sent to Rushan County (present-day Rushan City), Shandong Province, during the "Down to the Countryside Movement." When he returned to Beijing, Li Shaofen had been transferred to Guangdong Province, so the couple lived apart for six years subsequently, meeting once a year at most. They could appreciate the joy and sorrow of the Cowherd and the Weaver Girl.[1]

---

1. *The Cowherd and the Weaver Girl* is one of the four classic Chinese folktales of love. It tells the romance between a mortal cowherd and an immortal maiden. The heavenly mother intervened in their love and called the maiden back. With the help of his cow, the cowherd chased her to the sky with their two children. Before he caught up with the Weaver Girl, the celestial mother drew a line between them with her hairpin, and the line became the Milky Way. Each year, magpies, touched by their love story, flocked to form a bridge so that the couple could meet once. That day, the 7th day of the 7th lunar month, became the Chinese version of Valentine's Day. The Cowherd and the Weaver Girl are symbolized by the Vega and Altair stars. For details of the folktale, see Yuan, Haiwang. *The Magic Lotus Lantern and Other Tales from the Han Chinese*. Westport, Conn: Libraries Unlimited, 2006.

Zhong Nanshan went to the UK to study in his early forties. During those two years, the couple only communicated by correspondence. When he occasionally ran into a pharmaceutical factory agent, he would ask him to make a phone call to his wife in China.

However, Zhong Nanshan is far busier than in those years. He even doesn't have the time to talk with his wife today. But he has persisted in exercising. He runs for a while if he has ten-minute spare time before going to bed. Then, the couple will have time to chat—Zhong Nanshan talks while running.

– 10 –

When Zhong Nanshan was ill at home, Li Shaofen became his gatekeeper. She wouldn't allow him to go out no matter what. Neither did she permit visits from anyone except Zhong Nanshan's leaders. Only nurses came to give him injections. She didn't want him to answer anyone's phone calls. When some of his leaders called, she would tell them that he was on his business trip. She prepared congee, soup, and other easily digestible dishes and served them to her husband.

His son Weide returned to attend to Zhong Nanshan. Like father, like son: he was also a doctor, a famed urological specialist, and a winner of the "New-century, Hundred, Thousand, and Ten-thousand Talent Project." He is a professor and a doctoral advisor at the Guangzhou First People's

Hospital. He is also a lover of sports, especially keen on basketball. Like Zhong Nanshan, who admires his father, Zhong Weide also reveres his father, Zhong Nanshan.

Under the utmost care of his wife, Zhong Nanshan began to recover: his fever subsided two days later, and the chest X-ray retaken revealed no spot anymore. He broke into a smile. His judgment had been correct: he was less likely to be infected with SARS. SARS patients have difficulty breathing, but he didn't have the typical symptoms. He had chosen antibiotics administered orally and intravenously. At the time, SARS patients weren't sensitive to large doses of antibiotics. His experience of treating himself proved that SARS was no ordinary pneumonia, and traditional therapies must be abandoned.

Overwork and psychological trauma had stricken Zhong Nanshan ill. He was robust enough to fight one of the causes back, but a mental blow was more terrible because it could eventually destroy its victim's health.

Zhong Nanshan felt the urge to go to the hospital three days later. Many people's lives were hanging in the balance because the epidemic was spreading. With the situation worsening, he thought there was no time to delay.

Though still feeble, he arrived at his office and felt it difficult to unlock the door. He came to the wards pretending nothing had happened to him and greeted everyone with a beam on his face. A few of his colleagues who knew of his illness couldn't believe their eyes. They whispered, "Our director has come to work."

Some colleagues didn't know that he had been struck by pneumonia. They only knew that he was under the weather due to overwork and needed to rest a few days. They hadn't expected that he should have lost a lot of weight and suddenly gained many gray hairs. They were sorry to see him so haggard.

Zhong Nanshan, however, wasn't aware of his weight loss and worn looks. He appeared stoic and curved the corners of his lips up unnaturally like an upward convex. Everyone could see that he wasn't fully recuperated. A few subtle observers caught sight of the medical certificate and laboratory test report almost slipping off his hand, trembling without him knowing it. Tears welled up in some of the beholders' eyes, and they turned away their faces to void Zhong Nanshan catching sight of them crying. Those who knew nothing about Zhong Nanshan's condition asked, "What happened to his health?" "How come he's become so weak?" "How can he work in such a poor condition?" "Doesn't he insist on going to the ICU isolation room?"

Zhong Nanshan may be easy-going and gentle, but no one dared to question his unequivocal remarks. When he said he would go to ICU, no one could stop him by persuasion.

While putting the mask, cap, protective clothing, protective goggle, and gloves on him, they secretly felt worried that he might collapse at any time.

Even though he mingled with other doctors in his protective gear, the patients could still recognize him as their patron saint. They sensed his arrival by his every move. It must be out of their human instinct for survival.

A patient with the last name Liang said, "I know it's him. Although he was in his white gown and covered his face up, and I was half-conscious, I could still tell he was Academician Zhong. It must have been telepathy. I felt at ease with him in my presence."

Mr. Liang was critically ill and in a coma for five days. While under emergency treatment, he went maniac and hallucinated. He was even paranoid, pulling off all the tubes from his body and crying hysterically. So much so that no one could control him.

Zhong Nanshan came over and subdued him without much effort. The latter calmed down immediately. Finding him still in his right mind, Zhong Nanshan asked, "Do you know who I am?" The patient responded, "I know. You're Academician Zhong."

Zhong Nanshan said, "Great. Since you know who I am, you must lie down still."

Mr. Liang simmered down and began to allow the nurse to give him an injection.

– 11 –

While fighting the SARS disease and saving patients' lives, Zhong Nanshan found himself in a crisis of confidence that grieved him exceedingly. He sensed something quietly brewing behind him but didn't understand why he should have stood opposite some people. Many distanced themselves from him. SMS messages like "Academician Zhong, we're on your side" appeared on his mobile phone.

Zhong Nanshan no longer appeared in public, and those who wanted to hear him answering questions wondered what happened to him. Medium coverage of the epidemic also dwindled. Some reports said that the epidemic wasn't supposed to be exaggerated because it wasn't that terrible.

It was hard for Zhong Nanshan to state his loneliness. He felt an invisible pressure looming larger than the SARS epidemic. He could face it with his team and comrades-in-arms, but he had to meet the challenge of this formless pressure all by himself and couldn't tell anyone about it. SARS was a complex problem to tackle, but this permeating psychological strain made him apprehensive. But Zhong Nanshan had his patients, who became his most significant source of strength in the fight against the SARS epidemic, thereby mitigating his stress.

During that delicate period, the coverage of SARS became exceedingly cautious. Reporters weren't allowed to interview Zhong Nanshan. When a major southern newspaper communicated its reporting on Zhong Nanshan at a weekly meeting, it almost characterized him as an enemy, claiming that he had a personal purpose and wanted to use this opportunity to gain fame and fortune. No reports about him were allowed to be published in the newspapers. An influential newspaper that had reported on Zhong Nanshan's deeds was demanded to make an in-depth self-criticism. His exchanges with Hong Kong were seen as leaking state secrets. Even relevant departments were dispatched to investigate him....

In early April 2003, Dr. Evans, an official of the World Health Organization, and his party came to Guangdong. They asked to see Zhong Nanshan. Evans had two doubts: whether Guangdong had concealed the number of patients and underreported it and whether many people had died in Guangdong. The Guangdong Provincial Department of Health called Zhong Nanshan over.

Zhong Nanshan had recently given a presentation on SARS to the Hong Kong medical community, and Dr. Evans had been present. Hearing the report, Dr. Evans hadn't expected that there should have been such good doctors in Guangdong, China. Based on his in-depth research on SARS, Zhong Nanshan dwelt on how to prevent, diagnose, and treat the disease with a clear understanding. Dr. Evans thus had a deep impression on Zhong Nanshan and wondered why his experiences hadn't been released to the world sooner?

After arriving in Beijing, Dr. Evans mentioned his trip to Guangdong and complimented it for its excellent job. He particularly praised the contributions made by Zhong Nanshan. As a result, Beijing notified Zhong Nanshan to participate in a WHO meeting in Beijing.

Zhong Nanshan knew that his trip to Beijing would be another grave test, and he felt deeply disturbed. It would be unbearably tormenting if he couldn't speak the truth but would have to say the high-sounding words already drafted for him.

– 12 –

At the Qingming (also known as Tomb-sweeping) Festival in 2003, Zhong Nanshan decided to fly to Xiamen with his family to visit his parents' graves despite being busy. Zhong Nanshan had scattered his father's ashes in the sea around Gulang Island per his father's will. Regarding his father as his pride, Zhong Nanshan was full of respect and filial piety toward him. An annual visit to his parents' tombs has been the Zhong family's routine. But this year, he wanted to talk to his father: he found himself at a dead end and felt the pressure almost strangle him.

His father was his most respected person, telling the truth and doing practical things all his life. He had been full of justice and conscience. A family with the family name Zhong on Gulang Island in Xiamen adopted Zhong Nanshan's orphaned father and named him Zhong Shifan. He had been aspiring when young and was admitted to Peking Union Medical College from Tongwen Institute in Xiamen. After eight years of study, Zhong Shifan graduated with a doctorate and stayed at the college as a teaching assistant. He met Liao Yueqin, a classmate from Gulang Island, Xiamen, at Peking Union Medical College, where Liao Yueqin studied nursing. Coming from the same place and running into each other away from home, they soon liked each other and fell in love.

Zhong Shifan went to the University of Cincinnati College of Medicine to study virology and obtained a doctorate in medicine two years later. He resolutely chose to return to China and became the director of the Pediatrics Department of Nanjing Central Hospital. Liao Yueqin was also sent to Boston to study advanced nursing. She co-founded Guangdong Cancer Hospital later. After the two got married, they gave birth to Zhong Nanshan, their first child.

Zhong Shifan devoted himself to his patients. People often asked him to see patients while he was reading at home after work. Most of those who came were in a hurry, and Zhong Shifan would set aside anything he was doing and left in a hurry, rain or shine. The visitors were from various financial backgrounds, but he would treat everyone, poor or rich, equally. The patients he was invited to see mostly suffered from acute diseases, and treating them was beyond his duty. But he still treated them without delay. He insisted on making rounds of the wards and always created each medical record truthfully and clearly, so much so that it was legible to people without medical training. He would administer as less and inexpensive medicine as possible.

In the 1950s, Zhong Shifan founded the Pediatric Virus Laboratory of Sun Yat-sen University of Medical Sciences in Guangzhou, one of China's earliest clinical virus laboratories. He used the laboratory to engage in virus research and train postgraduate students. He thus became one of the well-known "Eight Great Doctors" in the Chinese medical community at that time.

Zhong Shifan's love for medicine and concern for patients came from the heart, so he was conscientious and devoted all his life. He decided to write a book in his 70s to share his decades of valuable clinical experience with future generations. However, his vision dropped so that he could only read and write with the help of a magnifying glass. When the glass wasn't helpful enough due to cataracts, he had to ask others to read to him.

He went to the library every day, consulting data and writing. Few people except Zhong Shifan often visited the reading room at that time. He wrote his Differential Diagnosis of Pediatric Diseases with great difficulty as he had to cover one of his eyes with one hand. He completed the 400,000-word book in four years, and it became a hit when published. He donated half of the remuneration to those who helped him refer to the data and purchased copies of the book to give to others with the other half. He treated others well because he wanted them to live happily.

Like father, like son, Zhong Nanshan inherited not only his father's profession but also his character and medical ethics. Seeing his father able to save lives and garner respect from others, Zhong Nanshan set his mind on being a doctor himself when he was young.

During the "Cultural Revolution" (1966-1976), Zhong Nanshan and his father were in the countryside. A child suffered kidney disease and urinated blood. A local doctor diagnosed him with kidney tuberculosis. Zhong Nanshan knew a lot about nephrosis and wanted to flaunt his knowledge to his father by explaining how to treat kidney tuberculosis in detail. His father asked him how he was confident of the disease as there were various causes of hematuria, and kidney tuberculosis was merely one of them. "How can you be sure that blood in the urine must mean kidney tuberculosis?" added his father, "You must base your conclusion on facts."

The warning "You must base your conclusion on facts" sounded like a wake-up call, which Zhong Nanshan remembers for the rest of his life. His way of thinking and handling things has since changed. He ensures that each viewpoint must be well-founded instead of being far-fetched at will. Science is not taking things for granted. His understanding of his father's words and their significance deepened with the advance of his age.

When national authority experts claimed that the source of SARS was Chlamydia, he questioned them about the base of their conclusion. If they based it on autopsy, he asked if they had seen and treated the patients? Antibiotics were required if patients were treated based on Chlamydia, but SARS patients weren't responsive to antibiotics. Therefore, the claim that the pathogen of SARS is Chlamydia is baseless and must be incorrect.

His father had been reticent, and if he spoke, he must have based his statement on solid ground. He was more intolerant of telling lies.

As a 3rd-grade elementary pupil, Zhong Nanshan was naughty and excessively fond of play. He even played truant for the sake of having fun. Instead of submitting to his school the money on meals that his parents had given him, he spent it on snacks. When his mother asked him about the money one day, he lied that he had handed it in. But sensing something was wrong, his mother checked with his teachers.

After learning about the incident, the always stringent father didn't scold Zhong Nanshan. Instead, he only said, "Nanshan, go and think about what to do with your lying." Zhong Nanshan, who had long revered his father, had anticipated receiving his dressing-down but hadn't expected that his father would have said only that. But that simple question tormented Zhong Nanshan with shame the whole night, making him sleepless. He vowed never to lie again and to tell the truth forever.

– 13 –

Kneeling before his father's tomb, to whom he had secretly vowed to tell the truth forever, Zhong Nanshan was thrown into panic and depression by the forthcoming situation where he had to lie. He knew his father could admonish him no more, but he still cried out, "Father...." in front of his grave mound. Then, he poured out his heart to him. Father always lives there. Zhong Nanshan calls "Father" to the sky whenever he wants to talk with him, feeling that his soul always accompanies him between heaven and earth.

Zhong Shifan had been a medical advisor to WHO. Now, would Zhong Nanshan conceal the facts from the officials of WHO and even lie to them? He could end his troubles by doing so. But could he have peace of mind anymore? No. Once he told a lie, he had to keep telling more and could never tell the truth. Then, he would be haunted by a heightened sense of guilt instead of enjoying any mental peace. He would be unfair to the patients struggling for their lives, especially his colleagues who had died of SARS infection. But the consequence of telling the truth was unpredictable. He wished that his father could give him some hint from the other world, telling him what to do.

Zhong Nanshan recalled the most challenging period of his father's life. During the "Cultural Revolution, he was denounced and humiliated in public, expelled from the CPC, and sent to a pediatric department to wash milk bottles. Meanwhile, Zhong Nanshan's mother committed suicide to avoid further humiliation. Under such circumstances, his father still taught Zhong Nanshan to be honest in conducting himself, clarify his views, and express his most genuine feelings. When his father's book Differential Diagnosis of Pediatric Diseases was published, the publisher requested that Mao Zedong's quotation be added to the preface. But his father insisted that it was a mere medical monograph that had nothing to do with politics.

Zhong Nanshan treated his father as a mirror. He wouldn't be muddle-headed when looking into it.

Li Shaofen was sympathetic with his torment and wept silently, standing behind her husband.

A spring rain started drizzling densely, fuzzing the mountains on Gulang Island in the distance and hazing the sea waters surrounding it. The chilling rainwater fell on his face, hands, and clothes, soaking his garments so that they clung to his body.

It's already unfortunate to encounter an epidemic in his life. But Zhong

Nanshan was subjected to such a mental ordeal on top of it. Who could be empathetic with his frustration and pain?

The malpractice of lying and indulging in cliches, big words, and empty talk was too common to surprise anyone. Under its influence, people tended to share the good news while concealing the bad ones. Very few people could tell the truth. It was challenging for naked truth to be revealed in such a social atmosphere. But faced with the SARS epidemic, someone must tell the truth. Lying would be too costly to the country and its people.

This truth-teller might be God-sent or chosen by moral principles and historical responsibility. This person who has iron-like shoulders is none other than Zhong Nanshan. His life of faith, professional ethics, personality, sense of decency, genetic heritage, and father's earnest teachings did not allow him to betray his conscience.

SARS made Zhong Nanshan famous not for his medical skills but for his moral courage to shoulder the responsibilities. He stepped forward out of more than a billion people and marched on alone. History placed such a mission and test in front of him.

Zhong Nanshan knew the benefit of lying, but he knew better the value of telling the truth. The significance of telling the truth doesn't lie in its right or wrong but in the fact that truth comes from the heart. Harmony reigns wherever the truth can be told, be it a group of people, a working unit, or a family. He is aware that it's essential to maintain social stability. But he is also conscious that concealing facts would destabilize society, whereas making the truth public is good for stability, which is the end result, not a measure to maintain the status quo.

He saw a crisis in the Hong Kong people's ignorance of the SARS epidemic. It was oblivious of the grave SARS situation in Guangdong, albeit its geographical adjacency. It was not until the epidemic broke out in Hong Kong in March did its residents understand the situation in Guangzhou, where the fight against SARS was already in full swing.

In late March, Zhong Nanshan met with Margaret Chan Fung Fu-chun, the health officer of the Hong Kong Special Administration Region (SAR). Hong Kongese blamed her for the outbreak and the Department of Health for delaying the release of news about it. They were dissatisfied with its responses when they telephoned to consult it, trying to get information on preventing and treating the disease and its explanations of the epidemic's severity due to its lack of understanding.

Margaret Chan Fung Fu-chun had long been worried about the spread of SARS into communities in Guangdong. She tried every means to collect data about the epidemic but found it hard to learn about the province's situation. At that time, the relevant people in Guangdong didn't know the higher authority's official version of the epidemic yet. Therefore, they dared not "make irresponsible remarks" and even considered the information about the epidemic national secret. Margaret Chan Fung Fu-chun told Zhong Nanshan that she had done all she could and had a clear conscience.

It was the severe consequence of not telling the truth.

– 14 –

Before the Qingming Festival, Zhong Nanshan heard the news released by the authority in Beijing. On March 26, the Beijing Municipal Health Bureau spokesperson announced that the imported atypical pneumonia in Beijing had been effectively controlled. He also proclaimed that the source of the disease hadn't spread, and no primary case had been found locally.

On the April 2 "Focus Report" program of CCTV, Zhang Wenkang, the then Minister of Health, claimed that there were only 12 SARS patients in Beijing and three deaths. The following day, he attended a press conference. He repeatedly reiterated, "The SARS epidemic in some parts of China has been under effective control" and "It's safe to work, live, and travel in China."

On the contrary, on March 6, someone posted a SARS case in Beijing online, which was dismissed as a rumor.

The epidemic was getting worse! Zhang's statement was a big lie!

Zhong Nanshan couldn't accept the statement so contrary to the truth, let alone understand the logic of these liars.

Zhong Nanshan knew that the consequences of doing so would get the epidemic out of control. Infectious disease is a national fight that requires everyone to participate. Without the truth, there will be no participation. It was different from anything that had happened in the past; it was a matter of life and death, and the Chinese would have to pay an unimaginable price in their lives.

Tensions in Beijing had been at their peak. Citizens were increasingly panicked because they had no idea how serious the epidemic was. Government officials were increasingly worried that the epidemic would affect social stability, and the more worried they felt, the more afraid they were to disclose the truth of the epidemic. The situation had become a vicious cycle.

Zhong Nanshan felt the same way when giving an exclusive interview with a foreign media. He could hardly suppress his emotions when he mentioned the young doctor Li Wenliang, who gave up his life. Each of his words sounded teary.

Zhong Nanshan said, "Most people think he's a Chinese hero. I also think so, and I am very proud of him. He told the truth to the Chinese people at the end of December, then he passed.

"On the following day, people in Wuhan and some other cities performed a brief mourning ceremony in honor of Li Wenliang, holding up their phones with lights turned on for a few minutes. Then they went back to work. People admired him and considered Dr. Li to be a hero. So do I. He's a Chinese doctor, and, to my mind, most Chinese doctors are like him.

"Most doctors want to tell the truth. So many of them will join Dr. Li in doing the same."

Li Wenliang had been a doctor in the ophthalmology department of Wuhan Central Hospital. The first case of COVI-19 was admitted to the hospital where he worked on December 16, 2019, followed by the second case on December 27. A total of seven people from the Huanan Seafood Wholesale Market went to the Wuhan Central Hospital for treatment and were subsequently isolated. He saw a patient's test report showing a high-confidence positive indicator of SARS-CoV. That meant the patients were infected with SARS-CoV.

On the afternoon of December 30, 2019, Li Wenliang posted several messages from 17:43 to 18:42 on the WeChat group of his college classmates: the WeChat Group of the 04 Clinical Class of Wuhan University School of Medicine. He wrote, "Seven cases of SARS are confirmed from the Huanan Seafood Wholesale Market." "They were isolated in the Emergency Department of the Houhu Zone in our hospital." "The latest news is that the coronavirus infection is confirmed, and virus typing is underway." "Please don't spread the word, but just let your family members take precautions." He concluded his posting with the origin of the coronavirus and a picture of "Clinical Pathogen Screening Results," with the words "SARS-CoV" circled with red ink.

Besides the 04 Clinical Class of Wuhan University School of Medicine, someone in three other medical institutions, including the Department of Neurology of Wuhan Red Cross Hospital and the Oncology Center, also posted related information on their WeChat groups.

At around 1 a.m. on December 31, Li Wenliang went to the Wuhan Municipal Health Commission to attend a meeting to deal with the epidemic. After going to work, Li Wenliang was repeatedly asked by the hospital administrators if he admitted the "mistake of spreading rumors." They demanded that he write a reflection and self-criticism to denounce his mistake of "spreading disinformation."

On January 1, 2020, the Wuhan police issued a public notice, "Some netizens published and forwarded false information on the Internet without verification, causing adverse social impacts. After investigation and verification, the public security bureau summoned eight law-breakers and dealt with them according to law. Li Wenliang is among them.

On January 3, 2020, Li Wenliang, accompanied by his colleagues, came to the Zhongnan Road Police Station of the Wuchang Branch of the Wuhan Public Security Bureau in the Zhongnan Road Subdistrict. At the police station, he was questioned by Hu Guifang, a police office associate and an auxiliary police officer. The Zhongnan Road Police Station told Li Wenliang to write a warning letter for "publishing untrue remarks about the seven cases of SARS diagnosed in the Huanan Seafood Wholesale Market."

He signed his name and put his fingerprint on where it was marked "The Admonished."

On January 6, 2020, Li Wenliang admitted an 82-year-old female eye patient who had a fever on January 7 and was later confirmed to have been infected with the novel coronavirus. Li Wenliang also had a fever on January 10 and saw a doctor in the Fever Clinic of Wuhan Central Hospital. He began to cough and was hospitalized on January 12 and transferred to the hospital's Respiratory and Intensive Care Unit to receive isolated treatment on January 14.

He had trouble breathing and was intubated with oxygen. He was neither able to get up nor speak. He occasionally used his mobile phone and had to type to communicate with others.

He slept 5 to 6 hours every night and dozed for a while during the day. The hospital cafeteria came to deliver meals every day, including rice, vegetables, and meat. He urinated on the bed. Every day, he videoconferenced with his family members and chatted through text. His parents also contracted Covid-19 and were treated in a Wuhan hospital.

A screenshot of Li Wenliang's dialog with someone has survived him:

Li Wenliang: "The epidemic won't go away soon."

Friend: "So, what will you do after your release from the hospital?"

Li Wenliang, "I'll go to work after my recovery" "I've registered for going to the front line."

Friend, "Aren't you afraid?"

Li Wenliang, "It's my duty."

He said, "The epidemic is still spreading. But I don't want to be a deserter." "What shall we do if no one dares to go and fight the disease?"

On January 23, 2020, the number of COVID-19 cases increased sharply, and the epidemic erupted like a volcano. Wuhan was urgently placed under lockdown.

At 3:30 a.m. on January 23, 2020, Li Wenliang was transferred to the ICU.

On January 28, 2020, the Supreme People's Court's WeChat public account published a text message saying, "Although the novel coronavirus is not SARS, the content posted by the information publisher is not entirely fabricated. Suppose the public listened to this 'rumor' and took the measure of wearing masks, disinfecting themselves, and shunning wildlife markets based on the fear of SARS. In that case, it might be a blessing for us to do a better job preventing and controlling the novel coronavirus today."

The Supreme People's Court News and Media Headquarters stated, "Attempting to crack down on all ungrounded information is neither legally necessary nor institutionally possible. It will even push the crackdown on rumors to the opposite side of our value of legal justice."

On January 30, 2020, Li Wenliang said in an interview with a reporter from the *Beijing News* that he didn't think he had spread rumors. Instead, he just tried to remind everyone to take precautions. "If everyone paid attention to this matter at the time, there might not be an outbreak of today's epidemic."

On February 7, 2020, the official Weibo of Wuhan Central Hospital issued a message that read, "Li Wenliang, an ophthalmologist in our hospital, had unfortunately been infected with the novel coronavirus while fighting it. After all rescue efforts were ineffective, he passed away at 2:58 a.m. on February 7, 2020. We deeply regret the loss and mourn his death."

Li Wenliang died at 34, survived by his wife, a five-year-old son, and a baby in his wife's womb.

WHO issued a message of condolences soon after Li Wenliang passed.

On February 7, 2020, the website of the National Supervisory Commission announced that, with the approval of the central government, the National Supervisory Commission decided to send an investigation team to Wuhan, Hubei Province, to conduct a comprehensive investigation on the relevant issues reported by the public involving Dr. Li Wenliang.

On March 19, the investigation team of the National Supervisory Commission announced the investigation result. It maintained that the admonition letter issued by the Zhongnan Road Police Station was inappropriate, and the law enforcement procedures weren't up to the standard. The investigation team suggested that the supervisory organ of Wuhan City, Hubei Province, supervise the rectification of the case and urge the public security agency to revoke the admonition letter and hold relevant personnel accountable.

That night, the Wuhan Public Security Bureau decided to revoke the admonition and sincerely apologized to Li Wenliang's and other people's family members for its mistake. A demerit disciplinary action was imposed on Yang Li, deputy director of the Zhongnan Road Police Station, for neglecting his duty: getting Li Wenliang admonished by police officers, incorrectly citing the law, wrongfully enforcing it, and being ineffective in supervision and management of the police station's law enforcement work. A warning disciplinary action was imposed on Gu Guifang for substandard enforcement of legal procedures and breaking the rules to issue the admonishing letter.

The situation among the medical staff in Li Wenliang's Wuhan Central Hospital was grim: 68 of them were infected, and the death toll was high. Besides Li Wenliang, the virus also took the lives of two deputy directors of the Ophthalmology Department: Mei Zhongming and Zhu Heping, and Jiang Xueqing, director of thyroid and breast surgery; Liu Li, member of the ethics committee; and Hu Weifeng, deputy director of the Department of Urology. Wang Ping, associate head of the hospital, and Yi Fan, deputy chief physician of the Thoracic Surgery Department, were under rescue in the ICU. They were in critical condition with multiple organ failures.

– 15 –

In April 2003, WHO's official Dr. Evans and his party stopped by Beijing after inspecting Guangzhou, with Chinese and foreign reporters following them. Evans publicly talked about how he had discovered Zhong Nanshan. The reporters had long targeted this unfamiliar Chinese scholar-a doctor fighting the SARS epidemic on the front line.

The global press conference was about to start. To be cautious, Beijing convened a meeting first, and all officials from the WHO participated. At the meeting, the Chinese person in charge released the positive information that the epidemic had been brought under control, medical staff protection had been put in place, and the pathogen had been found.... Evans was very relieved to hear this.

The positive news had spread rapidly in China before the WHO officials arrived in Beijing. The Beijing authorities had sent Zhong Nanshan a notice, asking him to attend the press conference for the WHO officials and Chinese and foreign journalists. For this reason, Zhong Nanshan visited his parents' tombs at the Qingming Festival.

At 10:30 am on April 10, 2003, the press conference was held under the auspices of the State Council Information Office.

The meeting started, and the venue was so quiet that the sound of flipping notebook pages could be heard very clearly. The world's cameras were aimed at the podium. Zhong Nanshan's voice sounded in the venue, "As a doctor, I think this cooperation and communication with WHO is very pleasant." He was calm but a little excited and continued with a slight guttural tone, "We actually communicated three issues together: first, the diagnosis and treatment of patients; second, some laws related to epidemiology; and third, the study of etiology. So far, more than 50% of the SARS patients have appeared in Guangdong. WHO is very interested in how the patients are diagnosed and treated, especially in early treatment and reducing mortality."

Zhong Nanshan also mentioned that he had good communication with Dr. Evans and his party. They established a friendly relationship in just five days. He said he hoped that China would develop closer ties with the WHO. Everyone's goal was the same: to face human diseases together.

At the meeting, an expert from the WHO immediately commented, "The treatment experience gained by the Guangdong expert group headed by Zhong Nanshan has guiding significance for the world's fight against SARS."

As soon as Zhong Nanshan's voice fell, an overseas reporter asked him about the number of sick people. According to what he had been instructed to say before the press conference, Zhong Nanshan replied, "Why haven't we discovered some patients? The truth is, some doctors at that time were not in this line of work and could not identify them."

The reporter was not satisfied with his answer and continued to ask questions. Zhong Nanshan always responded along the same line adopted beforehand, "As a doctor, I think this disease can be controlled if the isolation is in place. You have also heard that it's spreading quickly in many places, but the number of people publicly reported is still low. Why? I'm afraid you must understand that some patients have been transferred to other medical departments not specialized in respiratory diseases. Therefore, it will take some time for these patients receiving treatment there to be diagnosed."

How familiar this rhetoric was to what he would hear during his investigation in Wuhan when the novel coronavirus hit it!

The press conference would last for two days, and the first day was finally over. Obviously, the leaders of the relevant departments were relieved to hear the result.

On April 1, the mayor of Beijing, Meng Xuenong, when receiving Masaaki Okamura, president of Corporate Japan, Japan Inc., said, "For

Beijing, a city with a population of more than 13 million, twenty-two cases is a small proportion. Besides, we have put it under control. So, there's no need to worry."

The fact is that as early as April 3, the 309th Hospital of the Chinese People's Liberation Army admitted 60 "SARS" patients in one day. The figures released by the media on the same day were 12 patients and three deaths.

The press conference on the second day was smaller in scale, with about 70 participants and fewer leaders attending. The reporters were mainly from Japan and the regions of Hong Kong and Taiwan. Despite the smaller number of reporters, their questions were much more aggressive than the previous day.

In the beginning, several reporters repeated the questions raised in the first press conference session, and they were not satisfied with the previous answers. A reporter asked Zhong Nanshan bluntly, "So, in your opinion, the epidemic has been brought under control, hasn't it?" This question directly hit Zhong Nanshan's sore spot. The reporters were unrelenting, like cross-examination, their questions getting increasingly sharper. Zhong Nanshan couldn't bear it anymore. He responded, "What is under control now? There is no control at all!"

No one could believe their ears. Silence reigned briefly and soon gave way to a hubbub of exclamations and comments. Zhong Nanshan was so emotional that he couldn't close the "sluice gate" he had opened. The man sitting next to him began to wipe his cold sweat. Zhong Nanshan continued to speak, and the venue quickly quieted down. He said, "The most important thing is, what is control? We still don't know where the disease came from or how to prevent it. Neither do we have an effective way to treat it. Without knowing the source of the disease while it is still spreading, how can we say it is under control?"

He paused for a second and went on emphatically, "We've contained it at best, not controlled it."

The reporters' mood suddenly changed, and they scrambled for the microphone, eager to ask questions. A foreign reporter questioned, "You mean the protection of the Chinese medical staff isn't in place yet?"

Without any hesitation, Zhong Nanshan responded immediately, "No!"

He also talked about the need to conduct more research on the virus, strengthen the protection of medical staff, and conduct more international exchanges.

The next day, the media at home and abroad reported the press conference, causing a sensation.

On April 12, the WHO announced that Beijing was an epidemic area.

Zhong Nanshan's answers to the reporters at the press conference spread throughout China and shocked the Chinese. The information about the seriousness of the SARS epidemic reached the central government. The CPC Central Committee and the State Council clearly stated that governments must be highly responsive to the people to detect, report, and announce the epidemic promptly. They demanded that no delay in reporting, underreporting, or concealing reports be allowed.

The State Council immediately decided to list SARS as a notifiable epidemic disease in China for legal management. The central government severely criticized the malpractices in some places, such as "imperfect working mechanisms of information statistics, monitoring reports, follow-up investigations, significant omissions in epidemic statistics, and inaccurate reports of the epidemic figures to the higher authorities."

On April 20, the central government dismissed Beijing Mayor Meng Xuenong and Health Minister Zhang Wenkang. The fight against SARS in China finally opened up new dimensions.

On the afternoon of April 20, the State Council Information Office held a press conference. Executive Vice Minister of Health Gao Qiang briefed the country on the prevention and control of SARS and answered questions from Chinese and foreign journalists. He admitted that the work of the Ministry of Health was flawed, and the epidemic reporting system needed urgent improvement. He said: "The Ministry of Health has been insufficiently prepared to deal with public health emergencies, the epidemic prevention system was relatively weak, the requirement for local reporting wasn't clear, and the guidance for epidemic prevention and control was ineffective.... Relevant departments had imperfect working mechanisms for information statistics, testing reports, and follow-up investigations. There were significant omissions in epidemic statistics, and the number of cases was accurately reported."

The press conference attracted nationwide attention, and the TV viewers listened to every word of Executive Vice Minister Gao Qiang's answer.

The State Council decided: Starting from April 21, the epidemic situation would be announced once a day instead of once every five days, in line with the WHO's requirements.

On April 23, Premier Wen Jiabao presided over an executive meeting of the State Council and decided to establish the State Council's SARS Prevention and Control Headquarters, with Vice Premier Wu Yi as the commander-in-chief, and decided to set up a 2 billion SARS prevention and control fund from the central finance.

To prevent SARS, Wu Yi met with Zhong Nanshan twice. The first time was to learn about the SARS epidemic and its prevention and control, and the second time was to understand what Beijing should do to prevent and control SARS and listen to Zhong Nanshan's opinions.

Zhong Nanshan was always straightforward and never beat about the bush. He told Vice Premier Wu Yi that Beijing's medical level was better than Guangdong's, but it has done a poorer job in preventing and treating SARS. The main reason was that many senior doctors had not played their role. They were indispensable to treating critically ill patients. But Beijing didn't mobilize them on a large scale and did not put good doctors on the post of treating critically ill patients. Zhong Nanshan suggested concentrating critically ill patients in one or two places and then gathering doctors with high medical levels to rescue and treat them.

On April 29, 2003, Premier Wen Jiabao went to Thailand to attend the special meeting of China-ASEAN leaders on SARS. Zhong Nanshan accompanied him.

Zhong Nanshan's fate has reversed. He was no longer shrouded with a haze but basked in the bright sun. His fate was China's chance to conquer SARS and the future of countless patients.

– 16 –

Zhong Nanshan was in the full flush of his fame because of the conversation on CCTV.

On April 15, CCTV news anchor Wang Zhi and the team of the special program "Face to Face" of *Oriental Horizon* interviewed Zhong Nanshan. The program team went into the ICU to interview and videotape the scene of rescuing patients. The actual fight against SARS shook and moved the whole country and the world.

At the end of April, a telephone poll conducted by the China Social Survey showed that 89% of the 1,200 respondents in Beijing, Shanghai, Guangzhou, and other places believed that Zhong Nanshan was a hero.

Zhong Nanshan ranked second in CCTV's *2003 Touching China's* "People of the Year," next only to Yang Liwei, "The First Person to Go to Space in China."

The title of the award statement to Zhong Nanshan was "Touching China with Fearlessness." His deeds were, "Faced with the sudden outbreak of the SARS epidemic, Zhong Nanshan stabilized the country with a single sentence, 'SARS is preventable and treatable!' When the epidemic was at its worst, he volunteered himself based on a doctor's medical ethics, 'Transfer the most critically ill patients to the GIRH.' The casual remark is tantamount to a hero's call during the Battle of Triangle Hill to bring in artillery fire on himself to kill the enemy around him. After the call, he worked 38 consecutive hours at 67 to rescue and treat the patients. He said, 'In our post, it's the political task of prime importance to do a good job in preventing and treating the disease.' Zhong Nanshan has superb medical skills and is known for his moble medical ethics. But his moral character and intellectual courage of respecting science, seeking truth from facts, and daring to speak up earn him more respect and admiration. The most precious spirit of Chinese intellectuals is vividly reflected in him: not at higher authority's bidding, not scared by evil forces, and dare to shoulder responsibilities. At a critical juncture, he bravely rejected the relevant authorities' view that 'typical chlamydia is the cause of SARS,' thus providing grounds for argument for the Guangdong health administrative agencies to formulate treatment plans promptly. As a result, Guangdong Province has become one of the regions with the highest cure rate and lowest mortality rate for SARS patients globally."

The award statement read, "In the face of the sudden SARS epidemic outbreak, he was calm and fearless. He saved lives with his skillful hands and the kind heart of a doctor and responded to the disaster with the scientific attitude of a scientist seeking truth from facts. He said, 'In our post, it's the political task of prime importance to do a good job in preventing and treating the disease.' These powerful words show his life principles and professional ethics. With his admirable academic courage, noble medical ethics, and spirit of in-depth scientific exploration, he has given people the strength to overcome the epidemic."

On April 26, the "Face to Face" TV program was broadcast, attracting countless viewers. They saw the scenes of Zhong Nanshan and other medical staff doing a life-and-death battle against SARS, and they knew that there were so many twists and turns in the fight. They were exposed to the topics such as pathogens, international cooperation, control or containment, diagnosis, treatment, and disease prevention.... The topics even included "system," "democratic politics," "scientific outlook on development," "medical system," and many others.

Afterward, even Zhong Nanshan found it hard to believe that he had such courage. That was tantamount to Don Quixote fighting the Windmill: one person had to say "no" to a roomful of people. He thought the circumstances had made him fearless. If he hadn't stood up, the consequences would have been disastrous. Working with patients every day, he saw them carried to the morgue one by one. What else could have given him more pressure than death?

He wasn't afraid of telling the truth because he had evidence as a doctor fighting on the front line of rescuing the patients. The only pressure came from a doctor's duty. There's no greater thing in the world than saving lives, and nothing is more significant in the face of life and death.

The media focused on him because he was outspoken. He always has a strong sense of right and wrong and speaks boldly in defense of justice. His outspokenness has earned him high prestige. However, no matter how grave the problem, he adopts a business-is-business attitude, never concerned with the particular person involved. He never wants others to suffer because of his words. He intends to help society break itself of the habit of lying and build it with healthier social conduct, promoting social civilization.

Zhong Nanshan has his principles. He may be easy-going, but he's never compromising on matters of significance. Take credibility, for example. He once told a major newspaper, "When I said good faith and honesty were always the best policy, I referred to the leaders." But the newspaper didn't publish the report. Zhong Nanshan has since lost faith in this particular media and his interest in granting it any interview. He asked the reporter who came to interview him again, "Since you can't publish that type of article, why did you waste so much of my time?"

On April 12, the Guangzhou GIRH held a press conference, announcing for the first time that the pathogen found in SARS patients in Guangdong was "coronavirus."

On April 16, the WHO announced in Geneva that, through the concerted efforts of scientific researchers worldwide, it officially confirmed that a coronavirus variant was the pathogen that causes SARS. It had been the most valuable phased achievement since the global SARS outbreak.

Unfortunately, the GIRH had submitted its report of having isolated the coronavirus through a complex bureaucratic hierarchy, but in the end, some domestic research institutions preemptively released the research result. The scientific research achievements that should have belonged to Guangzhou fell by the wayside, but Zhong Nanshan didn't complain. In his view, the most important thing was that Guangzhou won the victory in the battle against SARS.

Zhong Nanshan earned a worldwide reputation for his scientific spirit and achievements in effectively rescuing and treating SARS patients. He was invited to share his experience and give lectures globally. He wanted to tell the world the actual situation of China's fight against SARS and overcome their prejudice. He also recommended Chinese medicine, especially TCM, to foreign counterparts. Like an iron man, Zhong Nanshan is always energetic with inexhaustible strength....

The fight against SARS may not have been the same without Zhong Nanshan.

– 17 –

In May 2003, the fight against the SARS epidemic began to end. On May 12, International Nurses' Day arrived on schedule. This red-letter date was destined to be exceptional for the medical staff who had achieved results in the fight against SARS and a day when victory in the battle was in sight.

On the eve of International Nurses Day, Guangdong held a nine-hour "Hand in Hand as One to Fight the SARS Epidemic" TV gala with 100 hotlines opened to the public, involving 150 volunteers. The TV program featured nurses recounting their days and nights of the fight to treat the ill and rescue the dying and sharing their sorrows and joys. On the stage, there were songs and dances to celebrate love and sacrifices, clips of documentaries, experts' question-and-answer sessions, and one after another family being reunited via visual telephones.

The TV gala received over 51,000 hotline calls. Each brief conversation was recorded to document the actual social psyche and emotions during the SARS epidemic. If compiled into a book, the phone conversations could be titled *Tonight, Love Shines*. But it was hard to put the 51,000 callers' names on it as the author. Regardless of age or region, they voluntarily participated in its creation and completed it overnight. A portrayal of the spirit of the period, its weight cannot be measured by paper and ink.

The "book" has a distinct theme. No other books contain such profound feelings and simple words because they come straight from people's hearts.

That night, love from the bottom of people's hearts drove the shadow of fear away and boosted confidence like the sun. Love surged, settled down, converged, and presented itself like drops of water coming together to form a river rushing torrentially forward. Love spread like sparks of fire to scorch a wilderness.

That scene reappeared 17 years later when the Hubei people said goodbye to the medical teams from various provinces in the drizzling season of the spring equinox. They flanked the five-kilometer street crying, some elderly people kneeling on the ground in gratitude, some bowling low, some calling out their rescuers' names, some holding slogans high, and some holding flowers in their hands.... In various cities, police motorcades led the way for the processions of busses carrying the leaving medical professionals. The Hubei people sang the song *Listen to Me Saying a Thank-you*! Such demonstration of universal love, thicker than the atmosphere of spring, brought tears from anyone who saw it.

Among the people seeing the medical teams off were heroes who had participated in the War to Resist US Aggression and Aid Korea, the Battle of Laoshan, the 1976 Tangshan Earthquake, and the 1998 China Floods. They shared the same inner voice: these angels in white gowns fighting on the front line of the fight against SARS are the most beloved people.[2]

---

2. It refers to *Who Are the Most Beloved People,* a famous essay extolling the People's Volunteer Army during the War to Resist US Aggression and Aid Korea written by Chinese journalist Wei Wei.

These young women, facetiously labeled as "the weaker sex," had to face death in its face and shoulder the nation's heavy responsibility of fighting back a fulminant disastrous epidemic without flinching.

These girl nurses dressed in white gowns bravely and calmly walked into isolation wards in such a spring. Before leaving home, some had kissed their sleeping babies goodbye, some had kept their departure from their aged parents, and some had said farewell to their newlywed husbands. Duty-bound, they left their loved ones to come close to SARS patients, fighting the demonic disease together with them. Some nurses gave up their lives, never able to return to their families.

Yesterday, they might still be facetious girls, quibbling about a dress or worrying about the skin bruised in an accident. They might still be faint-hearted students in the eyes of their professors as they could be too scared to enter the classroom with a zoological specimen. They might still be a pampered child in their mothers' eyes, never having done any family chores. They might still be endearing wives in the eyes of their husbands. But today, they were brave soldiers in front of hospital heads; in the face of the disaster, they looked straight into the eyes of death without backing down; and they became guarding angels of their patients. "It doesn't matter. It's our duty, and it's what we should do." A faint smile would warm the hearts of the people around them.

That spring, the Chinese premier cited a line from a poem to express the aspiration of the Chinese medical staff when meeting with journalists in the People's Great Hall, "I'll dedicate my life for the country's interest/ And never shirk my duty for personal weal or woe." Each word was powerful and rousing. Lin Zexu wrote this oath at the juncture of China's life and death. It has inspired many aspiring Chinese to devote themselves to the liberation and prosperity of China. When the Chinese nation was in crisis again, most medical staff also practiced the oath with their actions! A Miss Zhou from Yueyang, Hunan Province, wrote such a poem:

Where you came from, I've no idea
But you stand by my bed with no fear.
Your dazzling white gives me hope to live.
Although I can't see your face clearly,
You must be as beautiful as a fairy.
Your gaze is clear from your eyes watery;
Your hands are gentle, and your voice silvery;
Your footsteps are light though you're hasty.

Do you remember Jingwei, the drowned fairy bird,
Avenging its death, it filled the sea with a spirit undeterred?
You are the fearless white fairies under the blue sky,
Having saved many lives with your hands untired.
With your love, you've built a lengthy levee
Against SARS, because you believe firmly:
The disease is about to collapse,
While standing up will always be human dignity!

The poem represented the shared inner voice of the people.

Some school children called in, their voices tender and innocent. One of them, named Li Shi, said their classmate was infected with SARS, and he had been scared. But his fear had gone because a nurse attended to him every day. An eight-year-old boy from Chaozhou read an entry in his diary, "I watched the news about SARS on TV and saw doctors and nurses wearing thick protection clothing and masks. They risked their lives to rescue the patients, tired and sweating. They provided safety to others while keeping danger to themselves. I must emulate their example and learn to become a man." Ye Liuhang, an elementary pupil from Guangxi, exclaimed heartily, "The nurses are great! I'll follow their footsteps and become an angel in a white gown to save people's lives when I grow up."

A 14-year-old elementary pupil missed Ye Xin very much. She asked someone to relate her words, "How are you, Sister Ye Xin? Although you can't hear our greetings, we can't help thinking of you because you've left us your selfless devotion and unlimited giving. Why didn't Heavens turn me into a magic doctor so that I could wake you up from your eternal slumber? Please come back, Sister Ye Xin. I miss you!"

Senior citizens were also moved. Huang Shuying from Zhuhai Center for Maternal and Child Health Care called, "I watched the entire TV gala with teary eyes. As a medical professional myself, I'm deeply touched by the medical staff fighting on the front line to save lives at the risk of theirs. I've got five granddaughters and five grandsons, and I wish they could become angels in white gowns when they grow up to carry on the proud profession."

Deeply touched were also overseas Chinese. Cambodian Chinese Zheng Huafu and Singaporean Chinese Li Yuanxiang saw medical staff in their country of origin devoting their lives to their work and the Chinese uniting as one. They said with tearful voices that they were proud of being Chinese. The Overseas Chinese Association in Tijuana, Mexico, sent an email message reading, "The selfless dedication of the angel in white has baptized and sublimated our hearts and souls!" Mr. Jia, studying in the UK, stated, "I'm touched to see in the UK how my motherland's angles in white battling the demonish disease. Next month, I'll return to my motherland, and I'll fight against the disease with the medical staff nationwide."

Here is a true story: an electrician surnamed Dong in Wuhan whose daughter Xiaoqian worked as a nurse in Guangzhou. A few days ago, Xiaoqian was very nervous and called him, saying that she had just taken a patient's temperature, and the patient's seemed to have SARS symptoms, which frightened her. Upon hearing her complaint, her father was anxious and told her, "If you don't come back tomorrow, don't blame Dad for ignoring you! If you aren't obedient, don't come back anymore." However, Xiaoqian didn't listen to him in the end. Although she was terrified, she still chose to stay. Her father regretted his threat. He called the operator on the hotline and insisted on apologizing to his daughter Xiaoqian, a nurse in Guangzhou. He said emotionally, "Now that I think about it, I shouldn't have said those words to Xiaoqian. I hope she can hear my apology. I'm sorry, Xiaoqian. Your mother and I respect your choice. SARS and hope you will concentrate on the anti-SARS work."

A mother came to downtown Guangzhou from Huadu District to see her daughter, Pan Lili, a nurse in the First Department of Orthopedics, Guangdong Provincial Hospital of Traditional Chinese Medicine. On March 8, she entered the ICU, with the SARS disease following her like a shadow. Three of her colleagues were infested the same day: one in the morning, another in the afternoon. Even the head nurse wasn't spared. When a critically ill patient was put on a ventilator, Pan Lili grabbed her hand, saying, "Auntie, it's alright! You'll get well." The patient was in a coma, but tears overflowed from the corners of her eyes. But she succumbed eventually, which struck fear in Pan Lili, and her mother stayed with her. However, Pan Lili told her mother the truth and begged her to go home, worrying that she would pass the viruses on to her mother if she contracted them. Her mother said, "If something happens to you, what's the point of my living in this world? I won't leave; I'll take care of you. Her daughter dropped to her knees and sobbed, "But you'll interfere with my work like this!" Her mother left her daughter crying. At home, she sent a text message to her daughter every day, prompting Pan Lili to feel like she wanted to cry. A message she had kept all the time read, "The US and Iraq are at war, so is my daughter. She can win her fight without planes and cannons because she's my daughter!" Her mother's caring love gave her moral support. She left the ICU on April 9 and entered the isolation ward on April 28. This time, she didn't tell her mother. It was a news segment broadcast at the TV gala.

(Seventeen years later, Pan Lili received a phone call from her hospital asking her if she could go to Hubei. Pan Lili immediately responded, "No problem," even though something did happen at home. But she packed up immediately and rushed to Huadu overnight to say goodbye to her mother. Unlike 17 years before, Pan Lili was now a head nurse and a mother of two. Before seeing her mother, she had to part with her two daughters. Pan Lili's mother saw her daughter late at night, but when told her daughter was going to Jingzhou, Hubei Province, the mother cried sorrowfully again.)

The hotline received calls from many medical staff's family members, who were more concerned and had more mixed feelings. But they were all more determined than before....

Two elderly parents from Shanghai called their daughter, a nursing department director. They said, "You are our daughter. Since you've chosen the nursing profession, you must be courageous. A nurse must attend to critically ill patients, so you must be cautious while being brave." However, the elderly parents themselves needed their daughter's caregiving as they were 76.

A man who didn't give his name called from Gansu, saying that it was the first anniversary of his wedding with his wife, who was on the anti-SARS front line in Langzhou University No. 1 Hospital. He wanted to bless her in secret.

A man with the family name Gao said his girlfriend had been fighting on the front line against SARS in the Emergency Department of Nanfang Hospital. He said he and his wife hadn't seen each other for months, and he wanted to bless her on this particular festival. He said with tears, "I love her forever!" His statement was full of gnawing worries and prolonged concern.

Mr. Zhang from Jiangsu Province was worried about his wife, a head nurse on the front line of the fight against SARS. It had been 15 days since she left home.

The wife of Mr. Zhang, a civil servant in Nanshan District, Shenzhen, was a nurse fighting on the front line against SARS in Dongpu District. They had married less than a year before and separated for over 20 days due to the SARS epidemic. He was worried that she was young and hoped she would take good care of herself.

A man surnamed Zheng said, "My girlfriend worked on the front line of the fight against SARS. I respect her decision and promise not to tell her parents about it. He hoped she would return early and safe and sound.... Please tell her I love her... and take care!"

Zhang Yunsheng from the Sanitation and Epidemic Prevention Station of Nanyang City, Henan Province, was an epidemic prevention worker. His wife and her companions fought SARS in the wards. But unfortunately, they were infected and were fighting for their lives. He and his colleagues were also fighting day and night, rushing wherever there was a situation. He said, "We are willing to exchange our lives and blood for the people's health nationwide! A mother said, "My daughter is studying in a health school, and I hope she can make progress in her studies and become your qualified successor."

Miss He from Guangzhou Chest Hospital called, "I thank my parents for bringing my sister and me up, enabling us to become glorious angels in white."

Wang Yuanhang from Guangzhou said on the phone with emotion that he used to think that heroes were far away from real life. But only when the epidemic loomed close to us did I realize real heroes and heroines were by our side!

On the phone, a village teacher said that a senior in her high school had a phobia of white color, but she chose nursing as her option for her college entrance examination. She did so because she was moved by the sanctity and sublimity of this profession. Mr. Feng, a private business owner in Shantou, had always wanted to do something in the fight against SARS. So, he thought of donating blood. He said, "I'm well aware of the medical staff's current physical and mental pressure. I set an example for my employees by encouraging them to donate blood as a token of our support for the medical workers.

In a remote rural area of Guizhou Province, a township official didn't grudge showing his love because he was far away from the epidemic area and his family was poor. He said emotionally, "We in the remote villages also support and care about the angels in white fighting against SARS.

A farmer shed tears while watching the TV gala. He felt that his respect for the medical staff fighting SARS on the front line was beyond words. He said that they were the pride of the Chinese nation!

Wu Feng was from the hometown of Head Nurse Ye Xin. He called and said, "Head Nurse Ye Xin is the pride of the people in my hometown. I'm proud that the people in my hometown have brought forth such a heroic daughter who gave her precious life in the fight against SARS! The people of her hometown will always miss her!"

Mr. Zhang was a nutritionist at Shenzhen Central Hospital. He was a friend of Fan Xinde, an ambulance driver who had died in the fight against SARS. He said, "Fan Xinde has left us, but I want you to convey my condolence to his wife, Sister Yu, a nutritionist from the 2nd Sun Yat-sen Memorial Hospital, Sun Yat-sen University. I hope she would take good care of herself."

Mr. Liu, a part-time worker in Guangzhou, had a lot to say, but he didn't know where to start. He said he had been thinking a lot after learning about Head Nurse Ye Xin's deeds. "Please tell Ye Xin's mother that although Ye Xin is gone, there are still thousands of young people who'll be her good sons and daughters."

Liu Hui from Shenzhen couldn't help shedding tears when she saw the medical staff taking good care of the patient. She said she was all the more determined to become a doctor.

Mr. Gu from Dongguan worked as a security guard with a low income. But he said he would do his bit by donating to the medical staff. Mr. Wang from Shenzhen left his phone number because he was concerned with the nine-year-old boy in the program A Head Nurse's Diary, eager to know his state of illness. He said he'd like to make some in-kind donations if need be. "I want to do my part to help with the fight against SARS," he added.

A TV viewer wrote a poem to give his blessings to the angels in white. It read, "If a drop of water can represent a blessing, I'd rather send you the Eastern Sea / If a star can represent a sense of happiness, I'd rather give you the Milky Way / If a tree can represent my longing, I'd rather gift you with a forest."

Greatness is often conceived in the ordinary, and heroism lies in the conquest of cowardice. As people wade through this disastrous time minute by minute, everyone has gained a new perspective on everything around them. The catastrophe has changed everyone.

In this war without gunfire, the medical workers aren't alone. Leaders at all levels, from the central to local governments, news media, military, public security, and traffic police—all walks of life gave them their support. As devotion inspired people's desire to give, many people stepped forward to volunteer on the front lines. A company's general manager in Beijing left his company and worked as a janitor in an isolation ward. In the hotline, people who expressed the same inner voice one after another....

Sun Xiangdong from Shenzhen left her phone number and said, "I am only a migrant young woman doing the most ordinary job. I think I'm in pretty good health. So, if need be, I hope to chip in for the fight against SARS. I'm willing to work as a janitor or a food delivery woman in any hospital. I'm eager to have a chance.

Mr. Wang called to say, "My wife is a nurse. She may not be on the front line, but I'll encourage her to go to the front line to fight against SARS if she is needed.

Mr. Tan from Guangzhou left his mobile phone number and said that he wanted to take some family photos or videos for the medical staff who could not go home and send them to the medical staff in the hospital on the same day.

A young lady surnamed Xiong left her mobile phone number, saying, "I am a hairstylist. I want to cut the hair of SARS patients and medical staff and design beautiful hairstyles for them so that they can live as they did before. I'm not scared of being infected because I'm willing to do something for them!

Yang Long from the Yimeng Mountains, Shandong Province, said, "I hope you can convey my sincerity that I'd love to be a volunteer taking care of SARS patients. I want a reply as soon as possible."

Wei Handong from No. 62 Workers New Village, Changjiang Road, Wuhan, called the hotline, saying, "I'm a 60-year-old veteran. I wish Academician Zhong Nanshan would take care of himself and the 1.3 billion Chinese. I'm very concerned about his health. I have a request to attend to patients at the front line voluntarily. I prefer the wards in Guangdong to any other places to protect the southern gate of our motherland. Please grant my request!"

In his call, Lin Hanxiong from Chaozhou, Guangdong, said, "I'm a driver. If you need me, I'd love to work for any hospital as an ambulance driver without pay as a token of my support for the fight against SARS.

An unemployed worker said that he was compassionate though knowing nothing about medicine. So, if need be, he'd do odd jobs like sweeping the floor or cleaning rubbish anywhere in the country regardless of pay.

How quiet the deep night is!
How cool the evening breeze is!
Who's she, with her warm hand,

Gently stroking his forehead frowned,
To relieve him of his wound's pain.
Ah, it's you, our dear nurse
With love profound,
In the ward, she's on duty!
She has ideals lofty,
Longing for the soldier gusty
To rise and fly without bound....

The song Girls in White rang on the stage again to commemorate Nightingale on International Nurses Day.

Listen to the phone calls from the infected and cured patients, and you'll understand why nurses are referred to as "angels in white" and "Nightingales of the New Era."

Miss. Huang: "I couldn't see my loved ones while sick. They cared for me like my sisters, making me a member of a large family in the ward. I'm so grateful to them."

Miss. Chen from Guangdong: "I'm a SARS survivor, and I sincerely thank Director Liao of the Department of Psychology of the Chest Hospital. He was always beaming, and his smile meant a lot to us. Director Liao, please take care of yourself!"

A rejuvenated man who was too excited to leave his name said emotionally, "I was lying in bed and witnessed the medical staff infected with the disease while rescuing the patients. One fell, and another would come to work in her place. Their devotion has contributed to the success of the fight against SARS. I want to salute the doctors and nurses who have saved my life. Thank you all!

A SARS patient admitted to Dongfu Hospital in Shenzhen said, "Though a SARS patient, I'm confident that I can surely recover because the whole country cares about me, and the angels in white are taking care of me."

Zhang Wenzhong from Beijing: "I'm an ambulance driver. I was infected with the SARS disease while fighting against the epidemic. I'm now being treated in an isolation ward. I sincerely wish that the medical staff on the front line take good care of themselves while rescuing and treating others. I hope that epidemic will be defeated as early as possible so that they can reunite with their families."

The sudden surge of love and warmth moved the medical staff fighting SARS on the front line!

A head nurse at Guangzhou Second People's Hospital said, "I used to think my job was insignificant. But now, I realize that it's so important that I may even face death. I hope that all medical staff will pay more attention to their safety so that they can do a better job."

A nurse from the GIRH of the First Affiliated Hospital of Guangzhou Medical College called. She said, "I've received care and support from many fellow nurses during my hospitalization. Thank you! I want to express my heartfelt thanks to all walks of life for the gifts and health products sent during the fight against SARS. It was the support of these friends that brought me back to life so that I could work again.

All the nurses from the 157 Hospital called and said, "While in quarantine, we watched the gala, knowing that people outside the hospital are loving and caring about us. Since it's Mother's Day today, we want to give our greetings to all mothers and wish all the patients recover soon!"

In her call, a nurse surnamed Chen in the isolation ward of the

Emergency Room of Guangzhou Hospital of Traditional Chinese Medicine said, "I'm greatly encouraged to see my colleagues around me actively fighting SARS. I believe we can eventually overcome the disease."

A nurse named Lin from Guangzhou No. 8 People's Hospital: "In the past days of fighting against SARS, I was moved by the spirit of our hospital and all the front-line medical staff who gave up their lives and feared no danger. I wish all medical staff good health and an early victory over SARS."

A chest doctor with the family name Zhang called, "I'm under the weather and resting for now. My wife is working on the front line to fight against SARS. I'll join the battle without hesitancy when I get a little better."

Miss. Ye from Longgang, Shenzhen: "My two sisters and I are all nurses. Unfortunately, we didn't get to go to the front line. I can't help crying as I watch the TV gala."

Miss Xi: "As a doctor, I've never felt the profession is so lofty. I'm glad we're better understood by society. With the joint efforts of the medical staff and everyone in the country, SARS will undoubtedly end as soon as possible.

Luo Qiling, a nurse in the Department of Infectious Diseases of Guangdong Provincial People's Hospital, called: "I've worked on the front line for over three months. I want to take this opportunity to express my gratitude to my family. Without their support, I couldn't survive until now.

All we second-line nurses from the First Affiliated Hospital of Sun Yat-sen University: "We, on behalf of all the nurses from the second-line, extend our wishes on this festive occasion. We hope that all the First Affiliated Hospital of Sun Yat-sen University's medical staff will do well!

We hope you'll take care of yourselves while working hard. We'll do our part of the job as second-line medical workers and go all out to support you!"

Dr. Peng of Guangzhou Chest Hospital, who fought on the front line, called, "Both my mother-in-law and elder sister are nurses. Whenever I go around the wards, I see the nurses taking care of the patients day and night. Their hard work touches me. I'd like to wish all the nurses a happy holiday! I hope they can take care of themselves. SARS isn't scary, but what is frightening is panic. We have the confidence to defeat SARS.

A head nurse surnamed Zhao retired from Guangzhou People's Hospital: "Seeing the nurses working hard to fight SARS, I remembered all the past events in my line of work. If necessary, I hope to come out again and contribute to the fight against SARS."

Yan, a nurse from Guangzhou Military Hospital: "I'm a nurse under quarantine. I'm willing to dedicate everything to the fight against SARS! I hope my fellow nurses will enjoy this festival to do a better job fighting the SARS disease."

Miss Rao from Meizhou, Guangdong: "Greetings to my fellow nurses fighting on the front line! We nurses in the mountainous areas always pay close attention to you. Your work has deeply moved us. As long as there is a need, we can always go to the anti-SARS front line to enforce you."

A medical officer: "I'm a military doctor dispatched from Guangzhou Military Region to Beijing to support the fight against SARS. We soldiers are always indispensable in times of crisis. We'll work hard to live up to the expectations of the Guangdong people."

……

The messages left on the hotline from the 51,000 callers were like spring drizzles falling on the land of China. Here, everyone learned to take responsibility and gained courage, thus sublimating the dignity and sanctity of life.

Florence Nightingale bravely went to the battlefield to rescue the wounded over a century ago. She made the rounds, holding an oil lamp when all was quiet. She saw the wounded soldiers lying on sickbeds kissing her shadow in the lamplight. She said, "Amid horrific sickness and death, I see human nature's divine and heroic sublimation." In the face of disasters, the national emotions are being purified and sublimated, the national spirit awakened, and the national strength consolidated.

That night, the silent melody echoing in China beautified its mountains and rivers. As we wade through this disastrous time minute by minute, we gained a new perspective on everything around us.

Chapter Three

The Best Doctors Are Those Who Care about Ordinary People

Zhong Nanshan has a famous saying: When you see a patient, you only examine his condition, not his background. He sticks to the principle of "Three Same's": he'll show the same dedication, the same meticulous care, and the same responsibility concerning patients regardless of their social position, financial status, and regional importance. "I may be an academician and a hospital head, but I am first and foremost a doctor." A doctor without his patients is like a farmer with land and a fisherman without water.

– 1 –

May 6, 2008, is World Asthma Day. SARS was five years behind, and everything that had happened during the epidemic had become a collective memory.

The bustling metropolis goes on like a machine day after day nonstop. No one knows where it gets its energy and vitality.

One day, Zhong Nanshan had a lecture to give to the public. Academician Zhong appeared in front of the audience with the same serenity, composure, and scholarly temperament. He also looked self-confident and sociable. His look was profound and full of various feelings, and his face was angular, revealing an unswerving determination. His hair, grayed during the SARS outbreak, had miraculously black again.

Due to air pollution and other reasons, human asthma is rising worldwide. Chinese asthma patients are also on the rise. China Asthma Alliance held various forms of publicity activities across the country on this day. As the Chinese Medical Association president, Zhong Nanshan insists on doing his duty by giving lectures on asthma to the public.

It was a small auditorium located on the eighth floor of the Medical Technology Building of the First Affiliated Hospital of Guangzhou Medical College on West Yanjiang Road, Guangzhou. It was also where Zhong Nanshan's GIRH is located. Close to the Pearl River, the venue faces the historic Aiqun Hotel across the street. There are buildings with verandas all around, and these old architectural structures are reminders of old Guangzhou. The steel Haizhu Bridge in the east and the Shamian island with a European-style landscape in the west integrate the actual life with the modern historical sites.

Before 8:00 a.m., the auditorium, with a capacity of several hundred people, was packed. Most of the people who came to listen to Zhong Nanshan's lecture on asthma prevention and treatment were patients.

Zhong Nanshan arrived at the venue on time and walked up to the podium. Like the countless presentations he had given, he talked eloquently in front of the images, charts, data, and text projected on the wall with a laser pointer in his hand. He directed the red dot on the screen to highlight the blocked shapes of the trachea when it was normal or attacked by asthma.

He said that it wasn't enough to treat asthma alone, which tackled only the symptoms but not the root cause. Therefore, it was also necessary to simultaneously treat inflammation, which was nonspecific, not bacterial or viral, and could only be effectively controlled by inhaled corticosteroids. Asthma can be cured clinically through standard treatment.

People kept streaming into the auditorium and took all the adjustable folding chairs distributed additionally. Those who couldn't get the chairs had to stand at the back.

A little boy tried to strike up a conversation with his mother, causing many people to look back, expecting the mother to quiet him down. The mother's tactic of ignoring the boy backfired, and he burst into tears, asking his mother aloud why she abandoned him. The mother was reluctant to leave though her son wouldn't listen to her. The mother was in a predicament. However, undisturbed, Zhong Nanshan continued explaining earnestly and methodically. He said it was better to prevent than treat asthma when it attacked. The disease must be treated early.

The boy gradually calmed down, and the audience listened to Zhong Nanshan attentively.

No one noticed Zhong Nanshan was ten pounds thinner than before. He had just been released from the hospital and had recovered from his thyroiditis.

This illness enabled him to understand his physical condition better. He had thought that he was always in good health. He had worked day and night during the fight against SARS. He might have felt exhausted, but he didn't care too much due to his "good condition."

Once, when he came back from a business trip in Beijing, he didn't rest until 2 o'clock in the middle of the night. He was already fatigued. But the next day, several students came to ask him to play badminton, and he played two games in a row. In the early morning, he suddenly felt heart discomfort, chest tightness, and slight difficulty breathing in his sleep. The family rushed him to the hospital.

He suffered a minor myocardial infarction in his heart. Fortunately, his condition was detected early, and he was sent to the hospital in time. He underwent a heart stent operation and recovered quickly. Later, atrial fibrillation developed. To live and work normally, he chose to take the significant risk of a defibrillation procedure. When he was taken to the operating room, he felt like parting from this world. Only then did he realize the importance of his physical fitness.

The heart surgery made him bid farewell to the basketball court, and he dared not do confrontational sports rashly. But he persisted in exercising. After getting off work in the afternoon, he would jog or run for 20 to 25 minutes before doing sit-ups and parallel and horizontal bars. The whole routine would take about an hour, and he did it three to four times a week.

– 2 –

But facing his audience each time, he still looked high-spirited and pronounced every word correctly and in a sweet, mellow voice.

He was surrounded by TV reporters and patients when the lecture ended an hour later. His sallow face could hardly conceal his tiredness. But, instead of being perfunctory, he answered each of the audience's questions earnestly.

The question-and-answer session had timed out before he knew it, and he had other appointments after that. The anxious staff wanted to tear him away from the podium.

As Zhong Nanshan was leaving, a girl who couldn't squeeze to the front asked loudly from a distance, "If the airway is narrowed, what will happen to the heart…?"

Zhong Nanshan paused and asked about the condition. She told him it was her father, and Zhong Nanshan said he couldn't tell without seeing the patient. The girl's father then responded in a raised voice, "I'm here…." He elbowed to the front, wheezing.

Zhong Nanshan waited patiently and turned around to ask about his condition.... Half an hour later, he was still answering his questions thoroughly with exceptional patience.

Zhong Nanshan finally walked off the podium, but TV reporters crowded around him, shooting a barrage of questions at him. He was stopped after moving every few steps forward. Simultaneously, someone was already awaiting him in his office. A few dozen reporters and photojournalists from various newspapers had been waiting for him in a small meeting room next door for a long time. He had to see outpatients in the afternoon.

"By the time Academician Zhong sat down for my exclusive interview, not much time had been left in the morning. I had to take up his lunch break.

"Our chat ranged from his physical condition to his way of maintaining good health. He believed the self was the best physician. What affects health is generally divided into internal and external factors. Genetics is the internal factor and plays a 15% role. The social and natural environments, medical conditions, and lifestyle all belong to external factors, among which the influence of lifestyle accounts for the lion's share of 65%. The most significant difference between lifestyle and other influencing factors is that it is the only factor we can choose. We can control it and change it to live a healthier life. Therefore, the first step on the road to fitness and delay of senility should be choosing a healthy lifestyle."

He talked with ease, fluency, and clarity of thought. He went on without feeling tired.

He maintained that the essential "cornerstone of health" is psychological balance, the most significant and challenging for many successful people to achieve. A famed doctor once said, "Among all the factors detrimental to health, a bad mood and poor state of mind are the worst as they can shorten people's lives. These moods and states of mind include worry, fear, desire, cowardness, anger...."

Another crucial factor in striking a psychological balance is knowing how to deal with setbacks, which is indispensable in life. He believes in the saying, "Good fortune lies within bad, and bad fortune lurks within good." It's actually to let us learn to view life's setbacks dialectically.

It's a little surprising for someone so successful to speak of setbacks. Zhong Nanshan seemed to have a deep understanding of his setbacks. Before learning about his life experience, I had thought he talked in generalities. Therefore, I hadn't been convinced. As I understood him more, I realized that setbacks almost accompanied every stage of his life. Setbacks had been his stepping stone to success. On second thought, I found that successful people all had close contact with setbacks. Did that have to do with the factor of society, human nature, or destiny?

So, he was talking about learning to live happily. He said people must learn to enjoy the "happiness" in life. "We have to master the three methods of being happy. The first is 'enough is as good as a feast.' We must have a goal in life and persistently pursue this goal. But it doesn't mean that we have to be harsh on ourselves. Therefore, we should set our goals within our achievable limits, appreciate our achievements, and learn to pat ourselves on our backs.

The second is finding contentment in something. Confucius said, "They who know the truth are not equal to those who love it, and they who love it are not equal to those who delight in it." Zhong Nanshan's understanding of this hypothesis is that for the same job, people with proficiency in their career aren't as good as those liking what they do, and those who love their work aren't as good as those who can indulge in it. "Therefore, if we can immerse ourselves in our lives and jobs, we can forget a lot of the troubles around us and revel in our own happy world."

The third is to help others, making them happy. People who like to help others can always enjoy friendships, which enable us to get along well with the people around us, giving us much more happiness than lonely people.

– 3 –

There are two desks in Zhong Nanshan's office, with windowpane storage cabinets full of books and reading materials. With a traditional sofa placed in it, the 20-square-meter study appears crowded. The office supplies look old and cheap.

Several photos are on the windowsill, all of his own, the most prominent being photos of him exercising. Though extremely athletically talented, he can only choose between sports and medicine. After studying medicine, he bid farewell to the sporting world, no longer able to bring his sporting talent into play. These photos may reflect his mixed feelings of regret, memory, and compensation. There are also group photos of him with others, one of which is with General Secretary Hu Jintao. There is a photo of Zhong Nanshan during the SARS period.

He likes to use gestures to express his feelings when he speaks, waving his hands in front of his chest. Sometimes, he combed his hair, falling behind the head, with the spread fingers of his hand. People kept coming to consult him, and he always received them each time.

Sitting face-to-face with him, we chatted away. I asked him, "What kind of person do you think you are?"

He responded, "I'm a person who always pursues goals. I am emotionally fragile, sentimental, and sometimes depressed. I'm not particularly eager to participate in social activities. I'm asked to relay the coming Olympic Games' torch to Yunnan. Although I was born an athlete and loved playing basketball all my life, I don't want to spend so much time."

He's a celebrity now, but he takes fame and fortune lightly. He is typical of the character of a Cantonese: honest and practical.

I asked again, "Are you satisfied with your life?"

He responded, "What I'm most dissatisfied with is that I pay attention to my health too late. I have had high cholesterol for a long time. My mother had a family history of coronary heart disease and myocardial infarction. What makes me most satisfied is that I have finally made some contribution to society. I've fulfilled my vow, so I'm not living my life in vain."

He even thought that he wasn't in good health.

Perhaps, it was because he talked about his health and what he had experienced during the SARS epidemic. He might not be able to forget it five years later and felt a little sad. For the first time, I saw the fragile and sensitive side of a hero in the small office of his GIRH. I understand that everyone is an individual, after all. When facing the complex society and the mundane world, any individual will have moments of loneliness and helplessness. Fortunately, he can constantly surpass himself and come out strong from each challenging situation.

It's the real Zhong Nanshan, coming out strong from weakness. And it's all because he respects humanity and life.

His speech on health care reform during the Two Sessions (the annual sessions of the People's Congress and the Chinese People's Political Consultative Conference) concerned me the most. He was the first to speak as a representative of the National People's Congress when he came to the Guangdong delegation for discussion. He was performing his duty as a deputy to the National People's Congress and speaking for the benefit of the masses.

Medical reform is an issue of significance that concerns all the Chinese. It worries Zhong Nanshan all the more because he's a doctor.

Zhong Nanshan had reflected for a long time on the ongoing medical reform meant to solve the problem of being difficult and expensive to see doctors. He believed that the situation couldn't be improved by one department, some monetary investment, and a newly established system. Nor was it a matter of treating and curing patients. The medical reform wasn't a "shock-absorber," either. It must be treated from the perspective of creating a healthy nation.

He said that we must first make people conscious of 1) treating and curing diseases, 2) keeping fit, and 3) preventing diseases.

We have worked out more than a dozen plans for medical reforms, all of which are talking about reform methods and community medical care. However, none mentions who will carry out the reform. It involves multiple departments, and it is not something that any department can do. There must be a concept of general health. All the departments need to join forces and consider medical insurance simultaneously.

Third, the focus is on the community, but we haven't solved the problem of human resources. We need to train medical professionals willing to go and remain in the community or rural medical clinics. To this end, we must ensure and improve their income and working conditions. Our current medical university's guidelines and professional education are geared toward training medical personnel for big hospitals but pay too little attention to public health and disease prevention. Is it possible to consider exempting tuition fees for medical students like those in teachers' colleges and work as interns in big hospitals for two years before going to the grassroots clinics, with the government and big hospitals responsible for their training?

Training such medical professionals is the key to medical reform....

– 4 –

Zhong Nanshan has a famous saying: When you see a patient, you only examine his condition, not his background. He sticks to the principle of "Three Same's": he'll show the same dedication, the same meticulous care, and the same responsibility concerning patients regardless of their social position, financial status, and regional importance.

In his opinion, when a doctor faces a patient, he should have nothing but the patient on his mind regardless of his financial status or political influence. He even believes that a doctor must save patients from their sufferings in a time frame unlimited by eight hours. A doctor who prefers to work within the eight-hour time frame isn't qualified, let alone good.

Zhong Nanshan does what he says, which is his nature and hasn't changed for decades.

Zhong Nanshan goes to the ward for rounds every Wednesday morning and has never stopped doing so since 1992. He mainly checks on patients with diseases challenging to diagnose and treat, trying to solve some unsolved problems. He is always followed by the chief physician, the attending doctor, the head nurse, the nurses, and interns during the rounds.

He sees outpatients in his capacity as an expert doctor every Thursday afternoon. Except for exceptional circumstances, he appears at two o'clock in No. 1 Clinic on the third floor of the Outpatient Department of the First Affiliated Hospital of Guangzhou Medical University. The outpatients come from all over the country due to their admiration for his reputation. Patients make appointments through the expert hotline and submit their medical records to be screened by Zhong Nanshan's assistants. Emergency patients may get priority reservations and receive Zhong Nanshan's one-on-one diagnosis and treatment for at least half an hour. Because of their large numbers, patients have to wait three to six months on average before they can see him.

During his rounds, Zhong Nanshan likes to sit next to the patient, listen carefully to him, and ask about his condition, holding his hands. Some patients had terrible body odor, while others were severely ill, but he never minds.

When seeing outpatients as an expert, he and his graduate students always prepare beforehand, the former half an hour in advance and the latter an hour. He habitually rubs his hands to warm them in winter, lest his cold hands may make his patients feel uncomfortable.

Zhong Nanshan became excited as soon as he entered the outpatient clinic. The more patients he had, the harder he worked. He has come up with a way to prevent the patients from being tired as they await him. He has set up several consultation desks in the clinic. He allows the patients to sit at their desks while his doctoral students record their medical history and conditions and measure their blood pressure. Zhong Nanshan then sees the patients one desk after another. The patients sit as he walks around, which not only takes care of the patients but also improves efficiency.

The outpatient clinic hours start from 2:30 p.m. Zhong Nanshan begins at 2:00 and works till 8:00 p.m. Zhong Nanshan's schedule has made his wife and his graduate students form a habit. Every time at 9:00 p.m., Li Shaofen will carry a thermos bottle containing her cooked food and deliver it to Zhong Nanshan. Simultaneously, his graduate students, assistants, and nurses have also adapted to eating their supper late.

He tells his students, "All the patients who have registered with him have waited for several weeks before getting their chance to come to see him due to his reputation. They must have suffered a lot from their illnesses for a long time. They may be incoherent when speaking. That's because some are nervous, and some are panicky. We must be considerate to them." When prescribing medication to his patients, he always tries to learn about their affordability before racking his brain to find the cheapest drugs with the best efficacy.

Zhong Nanshan has become an academician and the dean of Guangzhou Medical College (now University). But he has insisted on working on the medical care front line despite his busy schedule. He said,

"I may be an academician and a hospital head, but I am first and foremost a doctor." "Only when working on the front line can I experience the joys and sorrows of a doctor, know what the ordinary people think and what problems they have that need to be solved so that we can make our decisions accordingly. At the same time, only when I work on the front line can I find the clinical problems that need to be solved urgently. That means that our research inspiration must come from practice. "A doctor without his patients is like a farmer with land and a fisherman without water."

Considering himself a "clinical medical scientist," he always works hard in his laboratory, trying to find a cure for a complicated case he has seen in the outpatient clinic. He treats cases of that nature as his research topic. "Practical medicine means researching while treating disease in practice. It can be research only because solving the problems the patients have is essential." Soon after becoming the GIRH's director, Zhong Nanshan proved the hypothesis of "hidden asthma (later known as "cough variant asthma" or CVA for short). He was the first to put forward a correction formula for basic energy consumption in Chinese patients with COPD (chronic obstructive pulmonary disease) in China.

The concept of "hidden asthma" has come from the patient. Zhong Nanshan found from a large number of cases that many patients from South China coughed repeatedly but were unresponsive to various antibiotics. He wondered if there were any therapy to deal with this unexplained intractable cough. He started his exploration with airway hyperreactivity (AHR), trying to figure out how it functioned or what role it played as an indicator of bronchitis asthma and if it was closely related to asthma.

He conducted the AHR surveys in two middle schools and found that the more severe AHR was, the greater the possibility of new asthma attacks. On the contrary, AHR weakened when asthma symptoms disappeared. He also found from the survey observation indicators that when the AHR reached a specific value, up to 45% of the subjects without asthma suffered from it two years later. The "sub-patients" can be discovered through testing to improve the cure rate of asthma with treatment before its onset.

Because the overseas medical community hadn't recognized the "hidden asthma" concept, Zhong Nanshan immediately wrote the paper "Does Asymptomatic Airway Hyperreactivity Indicate Hidden Asthma?" The thesis has perfected the "hidden asthma" notion and has been recognized by the medical community after publication in Chest, a famous American thoracic journal. The American Thoracic Association also awarded him the "Special Commissioner" title.

Zhong Nanshan started treating chronic obstructive pulmonary disease by exploring the causes of pulmonary heart disease and acute respiratory failure in patients. He experimented with pigs. By dissecting live pigs, he found out the relationship between hypoxia and pulmonary arteries, the cause of pulmonary hypertension, and the pathogenesis and principles. He also studied nutritional therapy to treat patients with pulmonary heart disease and acute respiratory failure, formulated the primary energy consumption correction formula for Chinese people, and developed a high-density nutrient with the commercial name Nutrient. He has also verified that biofuels can cause COPD based on epidemiology and has discovered that two old drugs can effectively treat it.

Throughout his life of practicing medicine, Zhong Nanshan understands people better. The deeper he explores the miraculous human body, the more he marvels at the greatness of life and appreciates life's preciousness. The human body is a magical world with endless mysteries. To explore diseases, we can use both the microscopic aspects of Western medicine—cells and microorganisms—or the macroscopic aspects of traditional Chinese medicine—the holistic concept and *bianzheng-lunzhi* (determination of treatment based on pathogenesis obtained through differentiation of symptoms and signs). In his eyes, diseases are just sets of challenging questions for him to answer. He feels exceedingly happy whenever he's gotten the correct answer.

Zhong Nanshan pays equal attention to both Chinese and Western medicine. He carries out pathological analysis and makes diagnoses based on the understanding he has gained from traditional Chinese medicine. When he diagnoses patients suffering bronchiectasis with hemoptysis, he can quickly associate the symptom with pelvic congestion, lochia, multiple abscesses, or endometriosis. Or perhaps there are various reasons in the uterus that cause bronchiectasis with hemoptysis. If so, the patient won't respond to anti-inflammatory drugs. The cause of such a disease is diagnosed based on the pathological understanding gained from TCM—the discovery of the mystery of man and nature united as one—instead of Western medicine. Asking a female patient with hemoptysis if she has a period seems, as it were, to head in the direction opposite to the intended destination.

One day, an old lady in her 80s came to see Zhong Nanshan. He found the shadows on both sides of the lower parts of her lung lobes resembling a pair of open wings. Such an exceptional case plunged Zhong Nanshan into contemplation. He thought of TCM and finally traced the cause of the disease to esophageal reflux: the patient suffered from organizing pneumonia. Ordinary pneumonia medicines were useless in her case.

A female Guangzhou Post Office employee named Aqiong had had asthma for over a year. Coughing often and responding to no medication, she found her condition worsening. She came to Zhong Nanshan, who gave her an asthma test and found its result positive. He could have prescribed some medicines for her now that her diagnosis was unquestionable. However, Zhong Nanshan was still concerned because his intuition told him that Aqiong's symptoms seemed slightly different from asthma. His gut feelings told him there might be some hidden symptoms though he wasn't sure if it was true or, if so, what disease it was. He suggested admitting Aqiong to the hospital for a period of observation.

Zhong Nanshan carefully observed her symptoms, looking for problems from the slightest irregularities. After all, no disease can escape -trained eyes. Zhong Nanshan believed there was a tumor in her trachea. He performed fiberoptic bronchoscopy on Aqiong to confirm the diagnosis. Sure enough, the cancer was there. The operation started, and the surgeon who operated on Aqiong with Zhong Nanshan was stunned by the tumor hidden so well in Aqiong. It took up four-fifths of her trachea. It was such a close call!

A patient suffering from an intractable cough saw many doctors and took a lot of medicines with no effect. After coming to the GIRH, he was initially suspected of lung cancer. Zhong Nanshan examined the patient with a fiberoptic bronchoscope. After careful observation, he took out a few chicken bones from the patient's right bronchus, thus ridding the patient of years of persistent ailment. Zhong Nanshan was the first to remove a foreign object from the trachea with fiberoptic bronchoscopy. He started research and wrote a high-quality paper based on the case.

A patient drove all the way from Zhanjiang to see Zhong Nanshan. He hurriedly invited Zhong Nanshan to a lavish dinner and tried to bribe him with a red envelope filled with cash because he was worried that Zhong Nanshan might not see him. Zhong Nanshan understood his anxiety and found time to treat him without either going to the dinner or taking the money.

A student from the South China University of Technology felt unwell before studying abroad. He went to the hospital for examination, and the result did not rule out that he had a tumor. He came to see Zhong Nanshan. Zhong Nanshan, empathetic with the patient's eagerness to study abroad with a bill of health, carefully examined his CT scan and concluded that he didn't have a tumor.

Some patients have their diseases treated with little or no effect for a long time. Zhong Nanshan almost became their only hope and moral support for survival. A patient from the rural area of Chaozhou got himself admitted to the GIRH so that Zhong Nanshan could treat him. He was in a severe condition, repeatedly coughing with blood. He was pretty pessimistic, thinking he was doomed. Such a mental state was unfavorable for his treatment. The GIRH had to contact Zhong Nanshan to prevent his illness from deteriorating.

After learning the situation, Zhong Nanshan decided to return from his business trip ahead of time. He went straight to the ward after landing at the airport without returning home. The old man from Chaozhou had been ill for a long time, and his psychosomatic problem could add to the difficulty of his diagnosis. To find the pathogenesis, Zhong Nanshan presided over seven consultation sessions.

After finding out the seed of the disease, Zhong Nanshan prepared to go to Beijing for another meeting. But worried about the patient, he saw him before his departure. The patient's face had turned a lot rosier. Zhong Nanshan asked about the treatment again, holding his hands in his. He said apologetically, "I have already made a surgical plan for you, but I'm urged to attend a meeting in Beijing…" Before Zhong Nanshan could finish speaking, the patient, who had regained confidence, waved his hand and said, "Don't worry, go ahead. I trust that your student can do the surgery." They shook hands like old friends and said goodbye.

In Beijing, Zhong Nanshan was still worried about the patient's operation and called the GIRH every two days to inquire about it until the surgery was successful. When Zhong Nanshan returned to Guangzhou, he went directly to the ward to see the patient like an old friend. His hands held in Zhong Nanshan's tightly, the old man from Chaozhou burst into tears.

Zhong Nanshan could be impatient at times. A patient surnamed Liao had seen Zhong Nanshan many times. Every time he came to Zhong Nanshan, he would tell him that he hadn't recovered. He saw Zhong Nanshan with the same complaint one day. Feeling upset, Zhong Nanshan responded casually, "If you come here without seeing any result, you don't have to return in the future."

Seeing the expressions of disappointment and embarrassment on the patient's face, Zhong Nanshan realized that he had said something too offensive. He was fully aware of how significant a doctor's remarks were to a patient. A doctor's statement that "I don't know what to do anymore" was the heaviest blow to his patients.

When reflecting on the incident later, Zhong Nanshan pondered that if the patient had been well, how could he have come to him repeatedly? The patient trusted me, but I didn't trust him. From then on, Zhong

Nanshan made an oath never to make such a remark again.

Zhong Nanshan, a benevolent elder, is always as gentle as a spring drizzle, always looking easygoing and amiable. He had digested all the vicissitudes of his life. But he's also a courageous and upright man who doesn't hesitate to show his chivalry in the face of injustice.

Once, after seeing a patient, Zhong Nanshan asked that the patient be hospitalized. When the patient went through the formalities for admission, the Inpatient Department didn't take him in immediately because he didn't have enough deposits. When Zhong Nanshan got angry after learning about it and rushed to the counter to reason with the staff until the patient was hospitalized with admission paperwork completed. One of his female Ph.D. students commented, "If the admission procedures had gone awry that day, Dr. Zhong Nanshan would immediately get the patient admitted with his money."

Chapter Four

Setbacks Are a Man's Stepping Stone to Becoming Strong

With an empty suitcase and mental trauma, Zhong Nanshan looked at the gradually receding city of Beijing in a passenger car of a train heading to the south. He seemed to be melancholy, with infinite mixed feelings as he reflected on what had happened.... Gone were his youthful years with the tall buildings disappearing on the horizon. A large expanse of land came into view. As the green cornfields of the North China Plain turned backward outside the car window, his heart flew to his home in Guangzhou....

- 1 -

The place is where the Zhongshan Mountain rises, and the Yangtze River flows by. Boasting a beautiful landscape and bountiful talents, it has witnessed the rise and fall of dynasties.

The curtain of modern history was also lifted under the Zhongshan Mountain.

Returning from studying virology at the University of Cincinnati School of Medicine in the United States, Zhong Shifan chose this ancient and modern city to work as the director of pediatrics at the Nanjing Central Hospital at the southern foot of the Zhongshan Mountain.

Under the moonlit Zhongshan Mountain, he was reunited with Liao Yueqin, whom he had missed for a long time. Both natives of the Gulang Island, Xiamen City, Fujian Province, studied at the Union Medical College in Beijing, where Liao Yueqin had studied nursing and became a senior registered nurse. From then on, they started their faithful married life.

On October 20, 1936, Zhong Nanshan was born in Nanjing Central Hospital. Liao Yueqin asked her husband to name the baby. Thinking his son was born on the southern side of Zhongshan Mountain, he gave him the name Zhong Nanshan, which means "south of the Zhongshan Mountain."

Zhong Nanshan's birth coincided with troubled times. After his first birthday, China faced a national calamity: the Lugou Bridge Incident broke out, followed closely by the Battle of Shanghai. Nanjing became the Japanese Army's target of bombardment. Zhong Nanshan was in a dangerous situation a few months after he came into this world.

Air raids happened frequently and, sometimes, gave people no chance to find shelters. One day, after Zhong Shifan went to work, the siren rang immediately before the bombardment began, and there was no time for the residents to run into the mountain. Liao Yueqin and her mother rushed out of their home to observe the movement of the Japanese bombers. At that moment, a bomb hit the house and leveled it to the ground. Zhong Nanshan, who was still in it, was buried beneath the debris.

Liao Yueqin cried loudly. She and her mother removed the bricks and tiles, trying to dig Zhong Nanshan out. Her son was still lying in the cradle, covered with a thick layer of dirt. His head was dusty, and his face purple. Liao Yueqin hurriedly carried him out but found him unable to cry out for a long time.

Zhong Shifan and Liao Yueqin lost their home and almost their son, and their life in Nanjing became a nightmare. The couple had their first-hand understanding of the Chinese proverb, "An overturned nest leaves no egg unbroken."

After the Battle of Shanghai, the Nationalist government decided to relocate its central organs inland. The Zhong family began a life of drifting from place to place. They moved westward under the constant harassment of Japanese military planes. They sailed from Nanjing to Wuhan, traveled on land to Changshan, and finally arrived in Guiyang.

Zhong Nanshan has often heard his grandmother and parents talk about this calamity, but it isn't part of his memory. Neither did he remember the life of dispossession and wandering. Fortunately, both his parents were medical professionals, and their skills afforded the family a relatively better life than the average Chinese during the turbulent years. But with disaster victims everywhere, it would be lucky for the Zhong family to have a piece of fermented bean curd as a side dish for a meal.

The Zhong family settled in Guiyang, but the flame of war followed them before long. Their new home there suffered the same fate as theirs in Nanjing. It was bombed to ruins during an air raid in 1943. Luckily, the whole family had gone to a park, unwittingly keeping itself from harm's way. The furniture they had difficulty acquiring was buried in the rubble again, and even the precious medical books were burned. They were too saddened for tears.

The year following the victory against the Japanese aggressors, the Zhong family relocated to Guangzhou from Guiyang with the hospital. As Zhong Shifan was the hospital's head, the family rode in an ambulance and reached the destination after eight days and nights of a long journey. They had been battling lice and bed bugs along their way. The Zhong family had a luxury—DDT made in the USA. Sprayed over the body, it could repel mosquitos and bed bugs. But when its effect was spent, the pests would harass them again, so much so that they couldn't sleep, and Zhong Nanshan's two-year-old sister Qianjun began to cry nonstop before dawn.

After eight days and nights of the ordeal, the ambulance entered Guangzhou in the morning.

Zhong Nanshan saw the Pearl River and the skyscraping European-style Aiqun Hotel on the north bank. He felt an exotic atmosphere greeting him. He saw the gigantic steel Haizhu Bridge span the river and the red-roofed foreign houses on the Shamian island appear indistinctly among the banyan grove. He had no idea at the time that his Guangdong Institute of Respiratory Health (GIRH) would be established beside them, and he would have gone to and off of it for a few decades till today.

Zhong Nanshan still remembers his joy when he first saw Guangzhou, which wasn't as severely damaged as the other large cities like Guiyang in the war. Guangzhou looked like a paradise to those coming from those cities. Zhong Nanshan's bond with the city has since begun.

The Zhong family settled in a standalone building in a separate courtyard. Zhong Shifan served as the head of Guangzhou Central Hospital and held the concurrent posts of the director of the Pediatric Department and a professor of pediatrics with the Lingnan University Medical College. Later, after the institutional reorganization, he became the director of the Pediatric Department of Sun Yat-sen University of Medical Sciences. He devoted himself to academics and started research on the cultivation and isolation of the Japanese encephalitis virus from this time on.

Zhong Shifan's interest in studying viruses began during his studies in the US. The discipline of virology had just started. He studied virology and discovered that bacteria could protect the vitality of viruses during active reproduction. Many virologists in the US affirmed and praised his discovery, and his research paper was published in an authoritative journal of infectious diseases. Simultaneously, he also discovered that the Japanese encephalitis virus could be reproduced in and isolated from the fetus of mice. Therefore, in the 1950s, Zhong Shifan established the Pediatric Virus Laboratory of Zhongshan Medical College, the first batch of such clinic laboratories founded in China. In addition to researching viruses, he also trained graduate students in virology. His topic was culturing and studying the viruses in mouse embryos.

Without research funds, he bought laboratory mice with his salaries. Later, he did research in his study after he obtained an electromagnet. He wanted to cut the viral liquid with an electromagnetic field to trigger changes in the virus for the purpose of killing it.

If a visitor asked for the Zhong family's home address, the neighbors would tell him that he could trace the smell of mice to it.

After school, Zhong Nanshan would like to tease the little mice in his father's study. Zhong Shifan intentionally allowed his son to have more contact with the mice and become familiar with their habits, physiology, and functions. The experience would help drum up his interest in studying medicine.

When Father asked him to take care of the laboratory mice, Zhong Nanshan readily agreed and thus became a part-time feeder. He didn't care about the smell exuded from the mice cages and began exploring the fundamentals of medicine and some knowledge of treatment. Meanwhile, he increasingly enhanced his patience, sense of responsibility, and power of observation.

Zhong Nanshan grew into a happy teenager. Compared with Guiyang, Zhongzhou gave him a markedly different life experience: he could watch American and Hong Kong movies, eat various delicious fruits indigenous to South China, and enjoy many foreign luxuries unseen before, such as chocolates, sausages, bread, and more.... He was so obsessed with knight-errand movies that he wanted to fly like a chivalrous man with an umbrella as a parachute. One day, he jumped out of the window with a large umbrella when no one was at home. The umbrella in his hands turned inside-out as he fell to the ground unconscious from the third floor. He couldn't speak when he came to and remained immobile for an hour.

But his obsession never waned. He insisted on climbing down from the third floor and used a bamboo pole instead of an umbrella to aid him. Sometimes, he would clamber down the rain gutter downspout. He grew taller as fast as a bamboo shoot in spring. He was now a teen with a strong constitution. So, he thought of avenging himself on the children from wealthy families who pushed him around. He was determined to avenge his insult. He issued an open letter to the bully, challenging him to a duel in a grove.

Hearing about the duel, his "foe's" parents hurried to the Zhong family to tell on Zhong Nanshan. His father asked him if it was true. Zhong Nanshan had to admit his challenge now that he couldn't conceal it from his parents. His father wouldn't let him get his own way and forbade him to go out. The irritated Zhong Nanshan thought he would lose his credibility if he were chickened out of a fight he had initiated. He reasoned with his father only to be reprimanded and immured at home.

Zhong Nanshan hated studying and loved playing, thus repeating a school year.

Once, his teacher praised him for a true story he had written about his classmate, and this hard-earned compliment inspired him to feel that he could also become an excellent student.

His mother also encouraged him, saying that he would get a bicycle as a reward if he could study hard and pass the middle school entrance examination. Zhong Nanshan was exhilarated and had since become a conscientious student with increasingly better grades. Eventually, he succeeded in the exam and entered Nanling Middle School. His mother kept her promise by rewarding him with a bike.

Zhong Nanshan's killer instinct awakened. He no longer resigned himself to lagging behind others. His talent for sports, in particular, was suddenly brought into play. After participating in a contest, his performance got better each time. His competitive spirit became unprecedentedly high, and he gradually developed a character of admitting no defeat.

He initially participated in the Guangzhou Games, where he finished fourth in the 400-meter run. After the amateur training with the Guangdong Track And Field Team, he participated in the Guangdong provincial track and field competition and won second place in the 400-meter run. He also represented Guangdong in the national competition and won third place in the 400-meter race. He participated in the first National Games in 1959 as a college student and broke the national 400-meter hurdles record with a time of 54.4 seconds. The track and field competition vividly showed Zhong Nanshan's idiosyncratic mentality marked by his dissatisfaction with the status quo.

At the age of 19, Zhong Nanshan gave up the opportunity to become a professional athlete on the national team and was admitted to the Health Science Department of Beijing Medical College. Like his father, he chose a career as a medical professional devoted to treating patients for the rest of his life.

Beijing Medical College was where many top students from their previous schools assembled. Someone who had excelled before might become mediocre here because "There's always a taller mountain beyond the one seen nearby," as the saying goes. Zhong Nanshan's indomitable instinct kicked in among the superior students, and he was determined to catch up with them. He outperformed all his classmates the following year.

By now, Zhong Nanshan had become a handsome young man. Meanwhile, the gurgling girls had grown into gorgeous and charming young women. They were at the most romantic stage of human life when the desire for love first awakened. He had had a plain sailing from an adolescent in Guangzhou to a vigorous lad in Beijing. What would be better than flowers, applauses, friendships, and love affairs?

Zhong Nanshan got to know Li Shaofen, a member of the National Basketball Team. They trained and exercised together as they were from the same province and shared the same interest—one was a professional athlete and the other a student exceptionally skilled in sports. They soon got closer and fell in love while practicing hurdles and running and playing basketball together, and their affection bloomed to maturity on the playgrounds.

However, Zhong Nanshan's eagerness to excel was tested for the first time at college: he was eliminated in the National Games trials.

But following the first setback, another would have changed his life forever. Without his will as strong as iron, Zhong Nanshan's life would have been drastically different: he would have been so demoralized as to sink to the rock bottom of his life.

– 2 –

Zhong Nanshan worked as a school counselor and taught in the Department of Radiation Medicine of Beijing Medical College. But at the end of 1964, a year following his marriage, he had to leave his wife and go to the remote rural area in Rushan County of the Shandong Peninsula. He had to eat, live, and toil with the peasants there.

Newly restored to its administrative divisional status, Rushan County sits deep on the Yellow Sea, far from the inland. It reaches the southernmost of the Shandong Peninsula by the Yellow Sea, boasting a long coast and numerous beaches and islands, with the tall Rushan Mountain extending to the waters in the south. It is where the story featured in Feng Deying's novel *Snowthistle's Flowers* takes place.

In the heat of the "Four Cleanups Movement," or known as the "Socialist Education Movement (1963-1965), Zhong Nanshan found his once privileged intellectual background obsolete in the blink of an eye. He realized that he must align himself with the Party line to realize his career aspiration. He applied to join the CPC before leaving college. He pledged to get tempered in the countryside and stand the test of the "Four Cleanups Movement."

He was shocked by the stark impoverishment in the rural areas, where the peasants could only eat a meat dish once a year and wheat pastry twice a year. A year's grain ration could only feed a family for three months. Only a few households that paced it out could manage to make it last for four months. Even yams were rare food, treasured by each family. They had to stuff their hungry stomachs with Chinese scholar tree leaves when everything else edible was exhausted.

Zhong Nanshan stayed in a peasant's home, sleeping on a *kang* bed-stove of bricks or adobe blocks. The whole family crammed into the same bed at night. His *kang* bed-stove was solid and cold because it couldn't channel the cooking fire to warm it up. It was infested with lice, a situation worse than it had been in the inns of Guiyang and Guangzhou during his family's relocation. He felt itchy all over at first, but he became numb and could coexist with the parasitic bugs as time went by. The American DTT was but a luxury product of that remote part of the world.

Winter came, and the cold kept him from falling asleep. He had to kneel on the *kang* bed-stove wrapped in a cotton-padded jacket. Zhong Nanshan had to recoil himself into a ball as a tall man. He still trembled with cold after heaping anything he could find in the room over his body. His only hope was daybreak.

Gradually, he turned from a greenhorn to a veteran peasant as he stayed in the country long enough. He went to work early and returned late, engaging in manual labor ranging from repairing water conservatory facilities, raking and weeding the fields, to growing wheat, corn, and sweet potatoes. He had to attend meetings on socialist education. They were part of the movement of "Four Cleanups": cleansing people politically, economically, organizationally, and ideologically at large. Rural cadres were cleaned up regarding work points, accounts, granaries, and public property. Those who failed to come out clean had to make a sharp self-criticism in public. People would sleep on the floor spread roughly with wheat stalks during the meetings. Zhong Nanshan worked beyond and above to demonstrate his willingness to receive the socialist education. For example, if others carried one basket of dirt or manure, he would double the loads.

The villagers were friendly with Zhong Nanshan, treating him and others from Beijing as sent by Chairman Mao's cadres. They would share what they thought to be the best with him and greet him even when there was a distance from him as if he were one of their family members. Zhong Nanshan felt their unsophisticated affinity.

Lice bites took a toll. Zhong Nanshan suffered from unbearable itching and kept scratching himself until the skin of his ankles broke, infected, and festered. They swelled as big as small balloons, about seven to eight inches in diameter so that he couldn't put on his shoes because the strings became too short. The bottoms of his pants could no longer cover his swollen ankles. Exposed to the elements, they were frozen hard.

When work hours started, Zhong Nanshan had to bear the pain with clenched teeth and limped to the fields. He never stayed away from work even though knowing that his condition could lead to osteomyelitis, and he could become physically disabled if amputation were needed in the worst scenario. The thought scared Zhong Nanshan.

It would be psychologically unacceptable for a person who had broken the national 400-meter hurdles record to be crippled and even unable to walk. As a doctor, he was aware of his illness' severity. But staying away from work without reason would have more severe a consequence. His father used to be a Kuomintang member, and his political record was being closely investigated. Zhong Nanshan's current performance would affect the future of his life. In those years, the cost of a leg was nowhere near the loss of political trust. Without it, he would be a social outcast and an object of humiliation, even at the cost of his dignity. To Zhong Nanshan, who has such strong self-esteem, it would be such a calamity in his life that he would rather die than suffer it.

He endured the sufferings with the most incredible fortitude until the Spring Festival when everyone enjoyed a ten-day leave. The village's CPC Party branch secretary consented to Zhong Nanshan's request to return to Guangzhou for treatment.

Zhong Nanshan could cope with strange environments, lonely days, and monotonous and arduous life. But he couldn't help missing his wife. He had meant to go to Beijing to reunite with her, but returning to his home in Guangzhou would be better for his treatment. His parents were both medical professionals, and he needed to get treatment and heal in a short time. He wrote a letter to his father, telling him about his condition, and his father wrote back to urge him to hurry home for medication. His father said he had delayed for too long.

Though working so hard, Zhong Nanshan wasn't paid much, so he didn't have enough travel expenses. His parents' living conditions had deteriorated. Their reputation as renowned medical experts had made him proud, but they became "reactionary academic authorities" now. He didn't want to add to their woes. He forced himself to borrow some money from his friends, who, knowing his situation, gladly helped him.

Guangzhou was far away from Rushan County, Shandong Province. There was no train service between the two places, and even the public roads were poor. He would have to take a bus to climb Mount Mashi and Duoyuding and cross the Ru River. He would then have to leave Weihai and arrive in Laiyang to take the train and transit at Jinan. There were some more transits on the way before he could finally reach Guangzhou. A round trip would take a week, and the route wouldn't have given him enough time for his treatment. He couldn't afford to waste all his time on the way. Therefore, he chose the fastest itinerary: taking a train to Zhengzhou and flying to Guangzhou.

After a few days of treatment in Guangzhou, Zhong Nanshan had to return to Shandong without fully recovering from his wound. He limped on the train with some medicines. His mother saw him off with extreme reluctance as if some bad omen were lurking in the air. Zhong Nanshan looked back and found his mother petite, feeble, and lonesome. Both her children were far away from her, and she had to devote herself to her cancer hospital. Work became her whole life.

Zhong Nanshan changed plasters and took anti-inflammatory drugs per the doctor's instructions while nursing and treating himself. Before his wound was fully healed, he had to go out to work, and he still did the most challenging job he could find. When not working, he would treat sick peasants. He respected the old and loved the young, identifying with the villagers. They particularly complimented him for working while having his ankle problems. A year later, he was admitted to the CPC as its member.

Zhong Nanshan won the Party's recognition with his utmost forbearance. He thought the Party would trust him and firmly believed he would have a bright future despite his family background as long as he worked hard. But he couldn't have imagined a bigger disaster would be in store for him.

- 3 -

Two years later, Zhong Nanshan returned to Beijing, which had been on his mind for days and nights. But he couldn't be reunited with Li Shaofen because the latter had left the city a few months before.

Li Shaofen had spent her long days in loneliness when her husband was sent to the countryside. She wanted to return to Guangzhou to take care of her adoptive mother and her parents-in-law. She chose to retire from the national team at the height of her career and be transferred to the Guangdong Women's Basketball Team.

Knowing that they would be separated between such a long distance, Li Shaofen insisted on going back to Guangdong. The couple was in a big row, which they had through correspondence. Zhong Nanshan was deeply distressed because he liked Beijing and had chosen Beijing Medical College as his option for the college entrance examination, planning to have a career in the city. He deemed it the best platform to get ahead with his medical aspiration. But Li Shaofen wouldn't budge no matter how hard Zhong Nanshan tried to persuade her. She was resolute and argued that the future Zhong Nanshan was aspiring for was slim as he was still doing manual labor in the countryside. She hoped that he would come back to Guangdong like her.

Li Shaofen had her heydays. She was recruited into the National Basketball Team at 15 and served as one of the top players with overall skills. She could play center, forward, and guard. She was particularly good at the mid-range jump shot and boasted a high shot percentage. She had the habit of shooting from a long distance with both hands and would jump and shoot with one hand when she got to the middle or short distance. She was agile, decisive, accurate, and capable.

In 1958, she and her teammates defeated the European powerhouse Czechoslovakia. In 1963, at the opening ceremony of the first Emerging Power Games in Jakarta, Indonesia, she served as the flag bearer of the Chinese delegation, leading the team representing the collective event. At that time, the two camps, the East and the West, were at loggerheads in the international arena, and the Emerging Power Games was the most important sports meeting for the East camp. As the vice-captain of the Chinese Women's Basketball Team, Li Shaofen went out with the Chinese team and won the championship, attracting the world's attention.

The Chinese Women's Basketball Team won the championship in the four-nation basketball invitational tournament involving China, Hungary, France, and Romania. Subsequently, the Chinese team also won fourth place in the women's basketball competition of the 3rd International Youth Friendship Games.

Director Xie Jin used their basketball team as the prototype to shoot the movie Woman Basketball Player No. 5. The beautiful and lively basketball girls, their poignant love stories, and their amazing basketball skills deeply impressed and touched the Chinese. Their story and their images spread like a spring breeze throughout the country. People could see Li Shaofen in the role of the protagonist.

The French Basketball Club fancied Li Shaofen and wanted to keep her as a foreign player by paying a hefty transfer fee. Li Shaofen knew that the national team wouldn't let her go. Besides, she had just been married to Zhong Nanshan and was still in the honeymoon period. She couldn't tear her away from him as they had already been together less than being separated in different places.

But this time, she was determined to return to Guangzhou without any possibility of changing her mind. A woman taking courage in both hands, she was immune to Zhong Nanshan's persuasion and would put her idea into practice once having fastened upon it. She submitted her application and went through the formalities. She rejected the national team's offer to make her a coach and finished the paperwork quickly.

Zhong Nanshan was still alone back in Beijing. When missing his wife, he would take a walk on the basketball court and the playground where they had exercised and trained themselves. When depressed, he would play his clarinet. The pieces he played were mostly *On Night in Moscow's Suburb*, *Katyusha*, and *Troika*. The same melodies carried sounded a little bitter and sorrowful.

He recollected Li Shaofen's visit to the Soviet Union when she was 18 years old when she didn't know the world. She had only the basketball on her mind. Under the instruction of Soviet national-level meritorious coaches, the Chinese Women's Basketball Team's skills were significantly improved. The Soviet Union also left a deep impression on her. Many a time did she excitedly share with him what she saw and felt about Moscow with a fluctuating cadence as if she were chanting. Zhong Nanshan felt drawn to the Soviet Union. *How the Steel Was Tempered* by Nikolai Ostrovsky and *Far from Moscow* by Vasily Azhayev were among his favorite Soviet novels. The quote of Pavel Korchagin, the protagonist of *How the Steel Was Tempered*, has become his motto: "We must live our life to feel no tormenting regrets for wasted years and no burning shame for a mean and petty past." When he and his wife had been together, they had often talked about Soviet sports, literature, and music. But now, Zhong Nanshan had to be reticent and cherish the memory of everything in the past in solitude.

The college asked Zhong Nanshan to serve as a "Mao Zedong Thought" counselor. The unhappy past would vaporize like smoke once he was devoted to his work. Zhong Nanshan was getting his feet wet in the new post and slowly adjusting his mentality when a more violent storm swept the country a month later: the "Cultural Revolution" broke out, "reddening" the entire country overnight.

Classes were suspended in all the educational institutions, with big-character posters mounted on the walls of their campuses. Students suddenly turned into Red Guards, who subjected their teachers to humiliating and torturing public denunciation. They held them in the so-called "jet plane" or "home-made plane" position: the body was bent 90 degrees forward with both arms lifted into the sky while the Red Guards grabbed their hands and pressed them down hard by their necks or shoulders. Zhong Nanshan was classified as the descendants of the "Five Black Categories": landlords, rich peasants, counter-revolutionaries, bad influencers, and right-wingers, ordained to be enemies of the Revolution. His father was a member of the Kuomintang, and the Nanjing Central Hospital where his father worked was under Kuomintang's direct control. Therefore, Zhong Nanshan was labeled the "son of a bitch" of "a reactionary academic authority" and "a Kuomintang reactionary." He was also categorized as "a descendant of a Kuomintang reactionary and class enemy colluding with foreign countries." As a member of the "Five Black Categories," Zhong Nanshan must be reformed through forced labor.

Zhong Nanshan wouldn't accept the classification, arguing that his father was a patriot. After earning his MD from the University of Cincinnati School of Medicine, he chose to return to China. On the eve of Guangdong's liberation, Zhu Zhanggeng, deputy director of the Kuomintang Central Health Department, came to his home many times to talk his father into going to Taiwan. But his father didn't want to leave, saying that he must stay here because he was Chinese. His father handed over the $130,000 left by the Kuomintang to the government and the hospital's property inventory to the Military Control Commission. Zhong Nanshan did his best to explain that his family's class status might not be good, but he was a good person who could still work for a good cause.

Zhong Nanshan didn't object to continuing to do manual labor, which he regarded as an opportunity to prove he was pro-revolutionary. He worked harder, arriving at the worksite early and leaving it late without fearing tiredness and hardships. He only feared that others would treat him as an outcast.

However, a disaster occurred to his family, after all.

It was a sweltering summer. Zhong Nanshan felt edgy without rhyme or reason. A sense of sorrow and unease permeated the air.

One day, the grievous news came that his mother had plunged herself to death from a building.

Born in 1911, Zhong Nanshan's mother died at 55 that year. She was one of the three daughters of a merchant. Well-versed in English, she also had a talent for speaking and singing. Her smiling benign face flashed before Zhong Nanshan's mind's eye. She had always worn the plainest clothes except for the Chinese New Year when her garment would have a few floral patterns. All her lifetime, she had helped others and never criticized anyone directly. Though her family was tightly budgeted, she still loaned money to a classmate so that she could take a train to Beijing to go to college. She had bought Zhong Nanshan a bicycle to encourage him to gain self-confidence and love going to school....

His mother's suicide traumatized Zhong Nanshan. She had her part in establishing the Guangdong Cancer Hospital, where she was most responsible for her patients. Patients receiving chemotherapy are frail and prone to infections. Radical "Red Guards" of the "rebel faction" stormed into the wards to mount posters of Chairman Mao's quotations. Zhong Nanshan's mother adamantly tried to prevent the "rebels" from pasting the quotes to keep the premises from being septic. Enraged, the "rebels" incriminated and trussed her and dragged her out to a denunciation rally. Unable to bear the humiliation inflicted upon her by the "Red Guards" and the big-character posters, she jumped from the hospital building with grief and resentment.

Zhong Nanshan had visited his mother two years before, and he had never expected that it should have been the last time he could see her. He would have been more grieved and regretful if he hadn't returned home to treat the frostbite on his ankles. His otherwise healthy feet had suddenly swelled, which seemed to be a divine call for him to go back home. Now, he would never be able to see his mother again. He was extremely remorseful and heartbroken: mother and son were separated from life and death. But he couldn't even show his grief, let alone cry loudly. Otherwise, he would be seen as sympathetic to a class enemy and unable to make a clear distinction between what was politically right and wrong.

Zhong Nanshan found himself getting farther and farther from what he had studied. He had missed his internship due to participating in the National Games, and he finished his major only in three years. After graduation, he only worked briefly before being sent to the countryside. He returned to his college only to see it closed down soon. He and his classmates had to step out of the campus and march along the Red Army's Long March route to receive revolutionary education. When he finally came back to his college, he was assigned the job of an editor and a counselor. His aspiration for being a good doctor gradually faded into oblivion....

The "Cultural Revolution's" damage to his family didn't end. His father was also publicly denounced, expelled from the CPC, and forced to wash milk bottles in the hospital.

The "Cultural Revolution" didn't spare Li Shaofen and her family, either. She was sent to the rural area of Sanshui to do hard labor and stripped of the right to be briefed on any meeting. She and Zhong Nanshan had given birth to their son Zhong Weide by then.

Satisfied with Zhong Nanshan's performance, the college's Revolutionary Committee, an organ to replace the previous administration during the "Cultural Revolution," assigned him the most glorious job of tending the college's boiler. It was proof that he was politically qualified and trusted. The Party gave him a chance to serve the people and mingle with people of "red" (good) family backgrounds. Finally, he could chat freely with the working-class brothers and sons and daughters of poor and middle-class peasants.

The boiler room was much out of the way, and few people came here. Regarding it as a place to demonstrate his performance, he had to work hard whether people saw him or not. The colossal boiler had eight chambers that consumed a tremendous amount of coal, and he had to keep shoveling it into the compartments nonstop. Shoveling coal only tired him, but cleaning the chambers was no easy job. He had to remove the cinder while the boiler was still scorching. As he stirred the coal with a poker, sparks surged up with exceedingly high temperatures, which could scorch or burn him if he should make a wrong move.

After working for a week, Zhong Nanshan felt the job was too physically demanding. But he was fully aware that he couldn't afford to back down. It would put him in a more dangerous position if he, the son of a "dictatorship target," wouldn't lead in doing hard work.

But the blood donation drive came at the wrong time for him. Still, he voluntarily signed up in a hurry, though not many people did so. He didn't want to miss the chance to perform. Others donated 200ml while he doubled the amount. Others took their leave for a rest as required, but he forfeited his timeout. He donated blood during the day and came to work at night, thinking he was strong enough. But he hadn't expected that he could no longer be up to it due to malnutrition.

He knew his hands had no strength when he picked up the shovel, and they shivered when scooping the coal from the ground, and he felt dizzy when trying to throw it into the boiler's chambers. Instead of getting the fuel in, he hit himself with the tool. He fainted and collapsed before the boiler. Luckily, he fell far enough not to be burned to death.

A logistic staff member of the college came to get boiled water and found Zhong Nanshan lying unconscious on the ground. He called in the "Cow Demons and Snake Spirits," another name for the "Five Black Categories" elements. They helped him transport Zhong Nanshan to the hospital.

When he came to, he couldn't sleep at night anymore. He pondered a lot and thought of returning to Guangdong for the first time.

Fate was still as bitter as the freezing winter, of which he felt not the slightest warmth. He was sent to the countryside again, to a more frigid and barren place. He followed a medical team to the Kuancheng Manchu Autonomous County in Chengde City, Hebei Province. The rolling mountains in the distance offset the vast wilderness under the immense sky. The historical Liaoxi Prefecture was now covered with snow. His best friend was swept away by a torrent when they crossed a river, and his body had never been found.

The central government adjusted its policies in 1971 and called on the whole country to "carry out the revolution to promote production." Beijing Medical College began to transfer back some of its faculty and staff sent to the rural areas and place those outstanding professionals in the posts of teaching and researching. Zhong Nanshan cherished a strong desire to return to Beijing to engage in teaching and research. He wrote a lengthy application, reporting on his performance and thoughts over the years. Many colleagues returned to their previous positions, while Zhong Nanshan received no news. Zhong Nanshan almost had a nervous breakdown when he finally learned that his application was rejected due to his family class background.

As the saying goes, "Misfortunes love company." His wife, who had just returned to the basketball team, fell during a match and was diagnosed with a cerebral concussion. She had been the pillar of the family, taking care of the elderly and the young. The accident threw it into a predicament.

Zhong Nanshan would have cried his heart out. His ideal; career; aspiration; hope in the capital, Beijing; and the years of miseries he had endured—all became meaningless. He tasted his first defeat, which hit him like an onslaught of ice and snow in summer, freezing his heart to utter disillusion. He achieved nothing 11 years after his education and was worthless in society. Even his medical education was almost wasted together with his youth. It was time to say goodbye to Beijing. The thought of Guangdong caused him to feel he had owed too much to his family.

Separated in different parts of the country, the couple could only reunite once a year. But whether and when they could see each other was at the mercy of others. They didn't even have any correspondence in the meantime. Parting again after a brief meeting is the most painful human experience, which feels like heaven falling and earth cracking. Even the most stoic person can't hold back his tears when the time comes. Zhong Nanshan now felt solaced and joyful at the thought that he could finally reunite with his family, never to leave it again, especially since he could soon see his son. He looked forward to getting back as quickly as possible.

– 4 –

The Guangdong Sports Working Team planned to set up a representative basketball team. Hearing the news in Sanshui, Li Shaofen became interested in playing basketball again. Besides, it was also an opportunity to be transferred to the city from the countryside. He had to take care of a one-year-old son, two senile parents, and an in-law. Usually, she might be too old to return to the court at 34, but she was confident in her stamina.

The Sports Working Team was led by a Military Control Committee dispatched by the Guangdong Military Region. The committee, acting in the decisive and swift style of a military, quickly transferred her to the basketball team after discovering her eye-catching achievements as a talented basketball player.

But an accident happened during a competition. Li Shaofen fell hard on the court and suffered from a concussion. The commander-in-chief of the military region, a lover of talents, went to see her at her home. Seeing only a child and three elderly people under the roof, the commander asked Li Shaofen where her husband was. The latter told the former about Zhong Nanshan. Learning about the long-term separation, the commander commented in a raised voice of resonance, "How can that be?! What don't you have him transferred back?" He promised to call someone and get Zhong Nanshan back to Guangzhou immediately.

Local civilian governments dared not defy military orders. Beijing Medical College asked Zhong Nanshan to return to campus and get his paperwork done within a day. Zhong Nanshan left Beijing the following day.

With an empty suitcase and mental trauma, Zhong Nanshan looked at the gradually receding city of Beijing in a passenger car of a train heading to the south. He seemed to be melancholy, with infinite mixed feelings as he reflected on what had happened.... Gone were his youthful years with the tall buildings disappearing on the horizon. A large expanse of land came into view. As the green cornfields of the North China Plain turned backward outside the car window, his heart flew to his home in Guangzhou....

Zhong Nanshan looks much older than his actual age, thin, swarthy, with angular cheekbones. He looked exhausted in his clothes with patches upon patches. But there was still dauntlessness in his eyes—this was the wretched look he presented to his father and wife.

He and his father chatted for a long time in the evening. His father asked, "How old are you?" Zhong Nanshan answered, "Thirty-five." Father responded, "I see. Thirty-five. It's terrible."

Zhong Nanshan still remembers the remark his father made that night. He'll never forget it. It was filled with hope and frustration. Thirty-five became the watershed of Zhong Nanshan's life, like the national record of the 400-meter hurdles he had broken that year. But this time, he would make a final dash toward the finish line of his medical career. He refused to sink to degradation because he wasn't in desperate conditions. He still had his chance.

Zhong Nanshan began to work in the Fourth People's Hospital, a block away from his home. It was the predecessor of the First Affiliated Hospital of Guangzhou Medical College (now University). It was the smallest medical institution with the worse working conditions in Guangzhou. Zhong Nanshan had studied for three and a half years in a medical college without clinical experience. The administrator scratched his head when he tried to assign him to a specific department when he reported for duty.

Zhong Nanshan wanted to work as a chest surgeon in the Department of Surgery. The department director okayed his request, but the head of the Revolutionary Committee felt that Zhong Nanshan was too old to fit into the profession. He said he would be useless in any department without the slightest clinical experience. The head wanted to place him in the Medical Affairs Department as an office associate to do some office chores. Luckily, Zhong Nanshan had two friends in the Department of Internal Medicine. They implored the committee head and talked him into allowing Zhong Nanshan to work in that department.

Zhong Nanshan met his colleagues at the morning meeting on the first day he went to work in the Department of Internal Medicine. He introduced himself to his colleagues, "I used to work in the grassroots with little or no clinical experience. I'm bound to encounter difficulties. So, please feel free to give me your advice in case." He was a little nervous at the moment.

Stepping into the outpatient floor of the Department of Internal Medicine, Zhong Nanshan found everything old and shabby. The benches creaked when someone sat on them. He was a little disappointed again. *So, is this the place where I'll build my career? Are you going to learn internal medicine from scratch with others at 35?*

Zhong Nanshan worked in internal medicine for three months, and he found it unchallenging to prescribe prescriptions without almost doing anything else. *No, I must accomplish something!* He wanted to go to the emergency room, where he could encounter more problems and learn something solid despite the hard work.

He was transferred to the ER. But soon, an incident happened: a life was almost lost because he missed the chance for a timely diagnosis. His colleagues sneered, "Zhong Nanshan even has no common sense as he can't distinguish between hemoptysis (coughing up blood) and hematemesis (vomiting blood). How can he be a doctor and work in the ER?"

This incident made him feel too ashamed to show his face and dealt a severe blow to his self-esteem.

That day, the ER had received a call that a tuberculosis patient in Luogang, an eastern suburb of Guangzhou, was bleeding profusely and had to be admitted to the hospital immediately. Zhong Nanshan asked to go and see the patient. His eagerness persuaded You Suzhen, the ER director, to give him his consent.

Before Zhong Nanshan arrived, doctors from the local health center had preliminarily diagnosed and treated the patient. He had a history of pulmonary tuberculosis, and all his symptoms indicated massive bleeding due to pulmonary tuberculosis. Zhong Nanshan believed that he should be sent to a specialized hospital for treatment in this case. Seeing blood on the corner of the patient's mouth, he gave him regular hemostasis treatment before lifting him into an ambulance. It took him to the Tuberculosis Prevention and Control Center in Yuexiu District, Guangzhou City.

The patient vomited blood again on the way, and the blood color was black, to which Zhong Nanshan failed to pay attention. He rehydrated the patient and injected a hemostatic. The ambulance took three hours to cover 20 kilometers and arrive at the tuberculosis prevention and control center on bumpy roads in the suburbs in the rain. When Zhong Nanshan returned to the hospital, it was time to get off work. He explained how he had picked up the patient and his symptoms to the physician on duty and went home.

When he got to the hospital to work the following day, Zhong Nanshan saw his colleagues staring at him with odd looks. He sensed that something must have gone wrong. Entering the ER director's office, he saw him wearing a long face. The director emphasized, "The patient you picked up is hematemesis from the gastrointestinal tract. Pick him up right away."

Zhong Nanshan was dazed, knowing how grave the matter was. He rushed to the Tuberculosis prevention and control center and took the dying patient to the hospital in an ambulance with its siren blaring all the way. The patient vomited one mouthful of blood after another in the ER, and his blood pressure kept dropping until reaching nearly zero.

Zhong Nanshan dashed out to send for a surgeon because the patient needed an immediate operation. The operation was urgent, with blood transfused before opening the abdominal cavity and the stomach. A fishbone was found piercing into the small artery of the gastric mucosa and causing the bleeding....

While the patient's life was saved, Zhong Nanshan's face was lost. Only a doctor who doesn't have the basic medical knowledge can't tell hemoptysis from hematemesis. The former means the blood is coughed up, and its color should be bright red. The latter implies vomiting blood, whose color must be dark red.

After the patient was out of danger a few days later, Director You talked with Zhong Nanshan. He said, "Zhong Nanshan, the job in ER must be exhausting for you. How about working in a different unit, the outpatient department?"

Zhong Nanshan responded in haste, "No, I'm not tired, not at all." Director You forced a smile. Zhong Nanshan failed to get the transfer message from her insinuation, but she felt too embarrassing to say it explicitly. Since he didn't want to go, she worried about him every day, fearing that some patient might die in his hands. She never asked Zhong Nanshan to deal with a patient alone from that day on.

Zhong Nanshan wasn't afraid of being laughed at and began studying hard from practice. He asked Dr. Yu Zhen from the Department of Internal Medicine to be his tutor. She had been involved in rescuing the patient from Luogang. Zhong Nanshan would tag along when she examined, diagnosed, and treated her patients. He would do his homework and take notes after work. He learned from Dr. Yu like an elementary pupil for three months, during which the notes he had taken were enough to fill four thick notebooks. He also studied the cases in the ER closely. Most patients who needed rescue fell into several categories: cerebral hemorrhage, gastric bleeding, and respiratory or heart failure. He wanted to find out their regularities.

He studied hungrily. Every afternoon when there was a denunciation meeting or rally, he would borrow keys from a technician to sneak into the ECG or the X-ray room, where he would close the curtains and read and examine the ECGs and X-ray films as if they had enchanted him.

The level of Zhong Nanshan's medical skills soared. Since he was doing pretty well in the ER, he thought of transferring to the Department of Internal Medicine. The hospital had a quota of one doctor in this department. Zhong Nanshan's inclusion in it meant the exclusion of another key medical professional from it, and that person was Guo Nanshan. The director of the department wouldn't have him for anything. He told someone, "This Nanshan is different from the other Nanshan," meaning Zhong Nanshan's medical skills did not match the other's. This incident stimulated Zhong Nanshan to reflect upon himself. He blamed himself for not having done an excellent job than having a grudge against others for slighting him.

Zhong Nanshan lost weight: he was over ten kilograms thinner. He used to have a broad forehead, full cheeks, and a constantly beaming face with sparkling eyes. But now, both his cheeks and eyes were sunken, and his expressions solemn. He was pensive when walking. His otherwise tight white gown became loose and flowing, making him look like an ascetic Daoist monk.

That year, the central government paid attention to chronic bronchitis disease, for which there had been no effective treatment. State leaders called on the national medical system to carry out a mass campaign to prevent and treat chronic bronchitis. The Fourth People's Hospital of Guangzhou was also requested to participate in this campaign. Doctors "would rather see patients with coughing than breathing problems and shun the latter altogether." They generally balk at specializing in treating chronic bronchitis. On the one hand, the disease is difficult to cure. Patients are reluctant to see a doctor when their symptoms are mild, whereas a radical cure of the disease is impossible when early treatment is missed. On the other hand, doctors find it hard to make professional achievements in this area, thereby making their careers unpromising. However, in answer to the central government's call, the Revolutionary Committee demanded that the Fourth People's Hospital set up a designated department. Thus, the hospital established the Chronic Bronchitis Prevention Team.

A veteran professor surnamed Hou saw patients with chronic bronchitis in the hospital's Outpatient Clinic. The Revolutionary Committee asked that one more doctor be sent to the clinic to see chronic bronchitis patients. However, everyone refused to accept the assignment for various excuses. As a result, the committee had to appoint Zhong Nanshan, who had neither particular expertise nor professional knowledge, to the post.

Zhong Nanshan didn't want to go either because he dreamed of working as an internal medicine physician. The hospital had to force him by citing the Party discipline of individuals having to be subordinate to the organization. Odds had always been against Zhong Nanshan, but his tenacious character enabled him to eventually make the highest achievement in something so commonplace.

He has since dedicated himself to the field of respiratory diseases and constantly advanced the frontiers of medical science. And his dedication has become a lifetime until he has become one of the Top Ten National Science and Technology Talents, a member of the China Engineering Academy, President of the Chinese Medical Association, and Chairman of the Academic Committee of the Asia Pacific Respiratory Conference....

Initially, Zhong Nanshan could only perform physical examinations on patients almost every day. It was too tedious and leisurely a job for him to bear. In those days, patients with chronic bronchitis basked in the pale sun of South China in the corner, coughing up a mouthful of phlegm from time to time. With a disturbed state of mind, Zhong Nanshan walked back and forth by them.... It became a scene of the hospital at that time.

One day, a patient's sputum caught his attention. He gazed at it on the ground and found the substance of common sight exceedingly colorful in the sunlight. He went up and crouched down to observe it closely for a long time, and he even stirred it with a twig. Others thought he was looking for something he had lost.

After a long time, Zhong Nanshan discovered that each person's phlegm varied, and even the same person's could be different. Doctors in the outpatient clinic only asked a patient if he coughed or had sputum when he did so. But no one went into detail about what the patient's phlegm looked like. Perhaps there was a lot to study in the substance. He tried to understand the regularity of some patients' expectoration. He submitted his observation report to the Chronic Bronchitis Prevention and Treatment Team, leading the team to officially formulate a research and experiment plan, thus finding the breach in researching and treating respiratory diseases.

Once, he went to the countryside for research and collected sputum from the peasants. He rode a bicycle, and his colleague sat behind him. He reminded him not to lose the specimen he would use for research, treating it as something rare.

He had studied biophysics at Beijing Medical College and did biochemical experiments for a period. Therefore, he did a biochemical analysis of the patients' sputum, which was of different colors and forms: green, yellow, gray, foamy, viscous, or lumpy. He tried to find various components through the experiments and figure out appropriate therapies accordingly. This kind of chronic disease requires TCM treatment plans. So, he studied the TCM methods of holistically toning patients' five viscera and six bowels. During his studies, he became familiar with the TCM methods for treating respiratory diseases.

He carried out his research by integrating traditional Chinese and Western medicines. He analyzed cold and heat deficiency and excess and *zang-fu* (five viscera and six bowels) and figured out that chronic bronchitis mainly involved the three visceral organs of the lung, spleen, and kidney. Zhong Nanshan discovered three kinds of manifestation and types of deficiency of the three organs and the respective treatment methods, treating respiratory diseases by combing TCM's holistic approach and Western medicine's localized trait-treatment method. He complemented the treatment with the herbal medicine Zihua-Dujuan he had concocted. The so-called Zihua-Dujuan is the combination of Rhododendron amesiae Rehd. et Wils. and the embryonic meridian injection method.

Zhong Nanshan realized early on that the scope of research on chronic bronchitis was too narrow, and it should include emphysema, respiratory failure, and cor pulmonale. He conceived a grand plan: 1) a one-stop plan for chronic bronchitis research: one-stop for chronic bronchitis, emphysema, and cor pulmonale; 2) one-stop for experimental animal research and clinical research; 3) a one-stop service involving laboratories, wards, and outpatient service, and a chronic bronchitis medical base in a designated suburb.

In addition to studying sputum samples, the team also conducted experiments with mice. To study the visceral organs of the lungs, spleen, and kidneys, Zhong Nanshan looked for animals with similar human internal organs. He found out that hogs' internal organs were the closest to humans.

So, he bought a hog partly from his own pocket and partly from the hospital's budget. They set up a makeshift laboratory on the rooftop with limited space, so they moved their desks outside to make room for the animal.

Zhong Nanshan sometimes entered the lab at 6:00 a.m. and worked until 1:00 a.m. The team members often saw patients during the day and worked in the laboratory at night, and whoever had spare time would experiment on the pig. To find out the pathology, they anesthetized and intubated it. Then, they studied the physiological changes of its cor pulmonale, the changes of its histamine, its prostaglandins, and other mediators after hypoxia.

It became their ad hoc research institute, where the research on hogs yielded many results. They were highly praised by the experts at the National Conference on Respiratory Diseases four years later. Many of them were published as academic papers in national professional journals.

In 1978, the first National Science Conference was held in Beijing, and Zhong Nanshan attended it to represent Guangdong Province. The paper "Diagnosis and Treatment of Chronic Bronchitis by Integrated Traditional Chinese and Western Medicine," which he and Hou Shu had co-authored, was awarded the first prize at the National Science Conference of the State Science and Technology Commission.

As a result, a chronic bronchitis prevention and treatment team moved closer to becoming the formal Guangzhou Institute of Respiratory Health (GIRH). However, a severe lack of research equipment made it tremendously challenging for the team to surmount research difficulties.

Zhong Nanshan lobbied here and there for people, equipment, and location. He picked up cast-away apparatuses and learned to repair them. Take a spirometer, for example. It was left in a warehouse as scrapped equipment for many years. Zhong Nanshan dug it out and carried it to Shanghai to have it fixed by experts. He borrowed a gas analyzer from a college's basic laboratory and put a lot of effort into retrofitting it himself. He asked someone he knew in a machine tool factory to make a tee joint when he couldn't find one. The old-fashioned ventilator needed human attention and manual operation as it sometimes stopped working every other hour until it sounded abnormal. Then, everyone would know something went wrong and rush to repair it. They had to move their furniture out of the doctors' office to make room for experiments.

After work, the group crammed into one office to collect data or do experiments until midnight. They worked happily though they had no overtime pay and lacked funds. Zhong Nanshan often bought extra meals for his colleagues out of his pocket. He imbued everyone with his professionalism, ideals, and vigor.

The Guangzhou Institute of Respiratory Health (GIRH) was established in 1979.

That year, Zhong Nanshan passed the qualification examination for studying abroad. Fate suddenly awarded him a great opportunity.

Zhong Nanshan's life has been filled with ups and downs, and he has gone through many vicissitudes. But it is not difficult to find from him that his personal destiny is inextricably linked with that of the country. Reform and opening up changed the fate of a generation.

However, when he came to England full of expectations, only to see his enthusiasm dampened. A new setback awaited him: his advisor tried to drive him back to China. The contempt and insult the people in the foreign land inflicted upon him were more than he could withstand because it was also a national humiliation. That setback caused more mental trauma to him, a stranger in a strange land, than any other. He can't remain imperturbed at the mention of it even today.

Chapter Five

A Studying Tour in the UK

Zhong Nanshan was sleepless that night. He wondered why the Chinese were so looked down upon.... *Is it true that traditional Chinese medicine doesn't work? Our ancestors knew how to use ephedra to treat asthma 2,000 years ago, and ephedrine in the West wasn't extracted from Chinese ephedra until the 1940s. Li Shizhen of the Ming Dynasty already used mandala flowers to treat his patients....* The thought "I must have something to show for the Chinese" predominated Zhong Nanshan's mind.

– 1 –

The train chugged and chugged from sunrise to sunset and dusk to dawn, the continuous chuffing sounding like the ticking of a clock. Zhong Nanshan alternated from learning English to looking outside the window. It was the China Railway Express across Eurasia. The scenery along the way changed endlessly, from falling leaves in autumn to heavy snow flying in winter, from plains and mountains to rivers and lakes, from blue brick-and-tile *siheyuan* courtyards to red-roofed country houses, from Chinese scholar and birch trees to cedar, Chinese parasol, and maple trees. Mother Nature's magnificent scenery was so exciting that it gave him undescribable mixed feelings: he was sometimes thrilled, worried, or tired. The motherland's extraordinary trust was weighing the heaviest on his mind, which prompted him to make up his mind to learn something solid.

Zhong Nanshan took the qualification exam for studying abroad on a government scholarship in 1979. He scored 52.5 on the English test. The required minimum score for the subject was 45 that year, so he had thought his chance was slim. For two years, he unexpectedly got the opportunity to study at the Royal Infirmary of Edinburgh (University of Edinburgh Medical School) in the UK.

Zhong Nanshan was among the lucky bunch. China had just begun its reform and opening up, and many neglected tasks had to be tackled. It had just resumed the college entrance examination when it started to send students abroad. Zhong Nanshan was among the first batch of students sent to the UK. He couldn't conceal his joy, and he was even more excited than when he passed the exam and was enrolled in college. He was already 43 then. Although he was older than most of the students studying abroad with him, he felt he had returned to his youthful years. He took the qualification exam with great determination, and he had a strong desire to study advanced medical techniques overseas.

Zhong Nanshan's generation had been delayed for too long by the "Cultural Revolution." He couldn't wait to set off immediately. He first went to Gulang Island in Xiamen to visit his father, recuperating at his uncle's house, and bid him farewell. He returned to Guangzhou to pack up. He bought many items of daily necessity, considering that they might be expensive abroad. He also had two Wester suits tailor-made. The day to set out was October 20, coinciding with his birthday. He chose to take the train to save his expenses.

After nine long days of a train journey, he arrived in the UK via the Soviet Union, Poland, Germany, and the Netherlands. Together with him were another 15 Chinese students majoring in atomic energy, aviation, and mathematics.

The train entered Siberia in the Soviet Union from the Inner Mongolian grassland in China. A lake appeared outside the window with dark blue water. The landform sometimes lay flat with prairies of yellowed grass and sometimes rolled up and down, with the mountain ridges lengthy and sloping gently. It was feeling colder and colder, and snowflakes began to fly in the air.

They reached Moscow, and it was the most exciting moment for Zhong Nanshan. Here, it had his wife's sweat and his youthful dream. He took a fancy to the country because of his idol Pavel Korchagin. And it had been described by many Soviet novelists. He had cherished too many imaginations of this land for too long, and they had accompanied him through his adolescent and youthful years.

The train stopped in Moscow for half a day. After discussion, Zhong Nanshan and his fellow students decided to visit Lenin's Mausoleum on Red Square because it was a once-in-a-lifetime opportunity.

Red Square, where Lenin's Tomb sat, is paved with granite blocks. Surrounded by ancient European-style buildings on three sides, it has the Russian State Museum of History in the north, the onion-shaped St. Basil's Cathedral with its spire poking up high like a giant torch. Exiting the square there, one can see the Moscow River. In the east is the National Department Store, and on the west side is Kremlin, with three towers visible from the red wall. Lenin's Tomb is right under the Kremlin Palace's wall. It had a broad basement and a low-lying structure for the sarcophagus on the top. The tomb also features red granite walls and black dividing strips....

Everything was familiar and unfamiliar. Zhong Nanshan talked with the Russians in Russian. He came to the gate of the Kremlin and strolled by the Moscow River, imaging the historical events one by one, but none seemed real now.

Before the train entered Germany, the passengers were asked to get off to go through the security check. Zhong Nanshan and his fellow students had too much luggage. They even brought toilet paper to save money. Their luggage filled the racks and the space under their sleeping berths. They had to pull each piece down or off. Police dogs jumped into the car to sniff their baggage piece by piece.

The German police officers were searching for heroin smugglers. The students brought a lot of laundry detergent with them. The police mistook the white powder for drugs and immediately detained them, and dragged the large bags off the car. They tore open each of the detergent packages while questioning them in German. They dabbed the powder with their fingers and then squeezed, rubbed, and sniffed it. The train was about to leave. But none of the students could speak German. In desperation, Zhong Nanshan timidly said in English, "Detergent." The police officers understood, frowned, and let them get on the carriage.

After leaving Germany, they came to the Netherlands, a country on water. Windmills and herds of cows and sheep were everywhere on the plain. After crossing the English Channel by boat, they arrived in London on October 28, met the staff of the Chinese Embassy in London, and successfully arrived at the destination, Ealing College (present-day University of West London).

The students studying abroad would receive a three-month orientation in the college. Zhong Nanshan and a fellow student majoring in atomic energy stayed with an elderly English lady, eating together with her.

At Ealing College, their first task was to overcome the language barrier, a tough job for a 43-year-old. Zhong Nanshan had studied Russian at college and taught himself English, with his parents being his tutors. When learning English, he practiced listening to tapes repeatedly. He combined extensive listening with intensive practice and note-taking. After a few dozen notebooks, he found his listening gradually improved. After surmounting this critical obstacle in learning English, he felt he could deal with reading, speaking, and writing with less difficulty.

He wrote to his father in English, one letter a day. His father was pretty demanding regarding his English and would correct him each time, pointing out his mistakes and improper use of vocabulary and marking them neatly with red ink. His father would highlight his well-structured, smoothly written, or accurately expressive sentences and sometimes write down more idiomatic versions beside them. He then mailed the corrected letter and his reply to Zhong Nanshan. He kept doing so conscientiously throughout the two years of Zhong Nanshan's stay in the UK.

When Zhong Nanshan and I had a long talk, he told me that the most stressful time in his life hadn't been the SARS epidemic, but it was the predicament he faced while studying in the UK. When I asked why specifically, his face grew grave, which was rare, and he seemed emotional. It appeared that he still couldn't let go of a hidden mental trauma even after a few decades. He called what he had suffered the "British pride and prejudice." He particularly emphasized the words "mockery and insult." To use CNN anchor Jack Cafferty's comment, "It is arrogance and insult to the Chinese, not treating the Chinese as human beings."

"They didn't understand China and didn't realize that China also had its medicine. They see us as a primitive tribe venturing out of a jungle. A Brasilian doctor, unable to bear such discrimination, became so angry that he returned to his country. Although Brazil's medicine isn't backward, it's like from a primitive society in their eyes."

"But I couldn't go back to China because I would have been held accountable if I had done so. The motherland sent me there to study for two years. But before seeing anyone there, I received a notification demanding that I leave the UK in eight months. You can't imagine the pressure put on me, who had left China for the first time and found myself in a strange land."

Examining the path Zhong Nanshan has taken in his life, we can find that he has always risen courageously and become successful in adverse circumstances. Extraordinary pressure came in different stages of his life. When speaking of a person's success, he said, "People like to talk about intelligence and emotional quotients. But I want to add the quotient of withstanding setbacks." Today, we're building our country into an innovative one, and innovation means breaking conventions. To innovate, we're bound to encounter failures from time to time. Therefore, we must be able to withstand setbacks.

Not long after he arrived in London, Zhong Nanshan's advisor, Professor Franley, head of the Respiratory Department of the University of Edinburgh Medical School, replied to his letter. He wrote, "...according to our British law, your Chinese doctor's credentials are not recognized. Therefore, you can't diagnose or treat patients alone when trained in the hospital. You're allowed to make rounds of the wards or visit the laboratories as an observer only. Considering the situation, I think it would be too long for you to study with us for two years. Eight months would be the maximum, and any time beyond it would be inconvenient for you and us. You must contact the British Council as soon as possible and think of where to go after the eight months here...."

Zhong Nanshan felt deeply disappointed after receiving his advisor's admonishment before arriving at the university. He had sent an enthusiastic letter to the advisor when he was at Ealing College, and the advisor's reply came like snow in summer.

On January 6, 1980, it was freezing in Scotland, and snowflakes drifted in the air with sleet. It seemed much colder and gloomier here than in London. Zhong Nanshan will never forget this day. He traveled all the way north in the snow and sleet and plodded from England to the University of Edinburgh in Scotland. He finally located the Respiratory Department of the University of Edinburgh Medical School and found Professor Franley's secretary, Mrs. Alice. At 9.30 a.m., Mrs. Alice took him into Professor Franley's office....

Prof. Franley sat at the desk, looking a bit heavy with big eyes on his round face. His look was piercing, and Zhong Nanshan felt it press over with unveiled arrogance and condescension. He turned toward Zhong Nanshan and followed him as he entered the office with an odd gaze. He asked with a forbidden tone, "What're you here for?"

Zhong Nanshan responded with respect and modesty, "I'm here to research the respiratory system."

Prof. Franley's face was unusually expressive. It showed a fleeting smile as he spoke with lukewarmth, "You'd better visit the lab and make rounds of the wards before considering doing anything in a month."

The professor's remarks made Zhong Nanshan feel uneasy. He thought a lot: about how he had studied hard for the examination, competed with other candidates, and attended English-training workshops. He also thought of his two young children and his wife, who asked him not to worry and study abroad without care though she knew what was in store for her at home.

He had come by overcoming so many difficulties, only to be sent away by his advisor after a few minutes of talk. *I'm here to study advanced medicine, but does it mean I've come for nothing?* When saying goodbye to the professor, Zhong Nanshan felt his heart being hit by something, blood surging up, bringing an unspeakable depression to the top of his head and making him tense and breathless.

Zhong Nanshan was sleepless that night. He wondered why the Chinese were so looked down upon..... *Is it true that traditional Chinese medicine doesn't work? Our ancestors knew how to use ephedra to treat asthma 2,000 years ago, and ephedrine in the West wasn't extracted from Chinese ephedra until the 1940s. Li Shizhen of the Ming Dynasty already used mandala flowers to treat his patients.* These atropine drugs were also spread to the world from China.

The thought "I must have something to show for the Chinese" predominated Zhong Nanshan's mind. He was determined to prove his ability in the eight months before leaving the UK. He has been a man of righteous indignation with unyieldingness in his personality. *I won't let them discriminate against us Chinese!*

– 2 –

However, he had to start with the smallest details.

Discrimination was ubiquitous. When Zhong Nanshan went to the fiberoptic bronchoscopy room to observe a British doctor performing a fiberoptic bronchoscopic procedure, Director Stereo asked him, "Do you have equipment like this in your country?" Zhong Nanshan responded with modesty, "Yes." Dr. Stereo said with puffed-up pride while checking his patient, "I've done 300 cases like this." Zhong Nanshan had done 1,500, but he remained quiet, knowing that he wouldn't believe him even if he had told him.

One day, Zhong Nanshan was making rounds in the thoracic department when he met with a patient suffering from primary heart disease type II with respiratory failure and intractable edema. British doctors had given him a diuretic for a week, but the patient's edema had not disappeared, and his life was in jeopardy.

All the doctors with him in the ward all gave their opinions regarding the patient's condition, and many insisted on continuing to use common diuretics. Zhong Nanshan shared his thoughts. He had read the patient's case history, examined his tongue per TCM's syndrome differentiation theory, and found his tongue dry, dark red, and without coating. He concluded that the patient suffered metabolic alkalosis and suggested treating him with acid diuretics to promote pH balance and gradually reduce swelling.

Some doctors accused him of being arbitrary, saying that his diagnosis of the patient with alkaline poisoning based only on visuals was nonsensical. Some doctors argued that acid diuretics used rashly might cause the patient to suffer a breathing disorder or die.

Prof. Franley, however, was sunk in contemplation while glancing at Zhong Nanshan from time to time. He saw him as a persistent Chinese, and his gaze revealed his mixed feelings. He instructed the doctors to test the patient's blood. Sure enough, the result showed that he was suffering from metabolic alkalosis. Prof. Frankley said without hesitation, "Do per the Chinese doctor's treatment plan."

The patient was given an acid diuretic for three days running, and he was getting better. His symptom of metabolic alkalosis disappeared entirely on the fourth day. His edema was subsiding, and his ventilation was improving.

The incident changed the British doctors' minds, and they began to see Chinese doctors from a new perspective. Prof. Stereo said amiably to Zhong Nanshan, "It looks like China has done some solid research on respiratory failure diseases."

However, for Zhong Nanshan, what had happened was far from enough to make headway in the UK. He must remember his mission: he was here to study on behalf of his motherland. Not only would he prove the Chinese worth, but he must also stay on to learn more about his British colleagues' medical skills.

To this end, while making rounds of the wards and visiting various laboratories during the day, he buried himself in the reference room to study rudimentary medical knowledge. He looked for something worthwhile to him in the reference tools. He found a project done in a respiratory biology lab on the effect of carbon monoxide on oxygen transport in the blood. The project was related to his research on respiratory diseases, and it was also a research Prof. Franley hoped to do. He gave it a brief thought and felt it was an excellent opportunity. So, he decided to make the project successful.

He busied himself day and night for two weeks and finally came up with an experimental design for "the effect of carbon monoxide on blood oxygen transport." Prof. Franley was touched by this Chinese doctor's spirit of taking the initiative to do his work. After reading the design, Prof. Franley broke into a rare smile and said to Zhong Nanshan, "Great minds are alike. Go all out for it."

When Zhong Nanshan found an angle and was ready to put his heart and soul into the project, he discovered that the indispensable blood gas analyzer was broken and used for a year. The hospital had to wait for fund allocation before purchasing a new one. Zhong Nanshan needed nominal data from oxygen electrodes for his experiment, so he couldn't afford to wait for too long. Hard-pressed for time, he circled the device to see if he could fix it.

He drew 800 milliliters of blood from himself and tested and calibrated the instrument. After he had tried over 30 times, the device was finally ready to use. Mr. Walker, the laboratory director, was exceedingly happy, saying that Zhong Nanshan saved them 3,000 pounds. A doctor named Morgan asked him curiously if he had fixed a blood gas analyzer in China. Zhong Nanshan told him he hadn't seen such a device until he came to the University of Edinburgh Medical School. Dr. Morgan exclaimed, "Chinese doctors are incredible!"

More incredible was that Zhong Nanshan experimented on himself by inhaling carbon monoxide to get a complete curve. Zhong Nanshan always dares to struggle against tremendous odds at critical junctures. He's always been trusted with a mission in times of danger and gives no thought to his own safety. It was the case during the SARS epidemic and the COVI-19 pandemic.

He wants to devote himself to science, believing that a person must contribute to society instead of living for nothing. It was his father's instruction and most significant spiritual legacy. His father had just done so, helping his patients all his life. It has become their family's belief.

He had asked his colleagues from the hospital to inject carbon monoxide into his body and kept drawing blood for testing. When the carbon monoxide level in his blood reached 15%, the doctors and nurses shouted, "It's too dangerous!" "It's too risky!" They told him to stop. At this moment, Zhong Nanshan started to feel dizzy, as if he had smoked 50 to 60 cigarettes in a row.

Zhong Nanshan shook his head with a look of fortitude and determination. He couldn't give up halfway because he wanted to be successful and make his colleagues proud of him and the Chinese at large he represented. He continued to inhale carbon monoxide, and its concentration in hemoglobin rose to 16%, 17%, and 18% until 22% when the curve was displayed entirely. Zhong Nanshan felt the world spinning, and the experiment stopped. The doctors present were impressed by his dedication.

Zhong Nanshan worked more than 16 hours for more than three months to sort out the experimental data. He had only 6 pounds of living expenses per month. He couldn't take a bus or taxi because he had only enough for survival. So, he had to walk to the hospital from where he lived. He even learned to cut his hair to save money. He never bought a single piece of clothing but spent all the saved money on purchasing professional books. When he was too tired to sort out the data, he took a look at the letter that Prof. Franley had written to him when he set foot in England. The letter would help bestir himself again.

He finally completed his research project and made experimental observations on bronchial diseases. Soon, he found a new research project.

– 3 –

Winter had long been over in Edinburg, and with the late arrival of spring, everything came back to life again. The wind from the North Sea brought the fragrance of plants and flowers from the continent. The air over the bay occasionally carried the mixed smells of coffee and milk. Zhong Nanshan enjoyed the beautiful spring in the city. He could finally look at the world around him with calmness and gentleness and appreciate this exotic city's sensuous beauty.

Life in the spring season was like gushing spring water and became strips of waterfall hanging from the branches stripped of their leaves by freezing snow and ice. In Zhong Nanshan's eyes, the scenery of the British Isles had its unique charm full of exotic flavors. Hearing the sound of the Scottish bagpipes, he wanted to play his clarinet to express his feelings.

Mrs. Alice handed Prof. Franley's second letter to Zhong Nanshan. The letter stated that the Royal Air Force representatives and the chairman of the Scottish Medical Council would visit their laboratory next week. This visit would decide whether they could win considerable financial funding for constructing a laboratory building. Prof. Franley invited Zhong Nanshan to give a presentation on the influence of various factors on the hemoglobin dissociation curve.

An arrogant Englishman finally trusted a Chinese. His appreciation of Zhong Nanshan completely relieved the latter's stress. Zhong Nanshan was determined to do more and better.

Summer soon arrived, and Edinburg was basked in the brilliant sunshine with the sea breeze caressing it. On the afternoon of May 15, Prof. Franley came to the laboratory to observe Zhong Nanshan doing his research. Zhong Nanshan calmly demonstrated the experiment of the effect of carbon monoxide on the dissociation curve of hemoglobin.

Prof. Frankie obtained a formula for calculating the effect of carbon monoxide on the oxygen transport of hemoglobin with the method of mathematical derivation five years ago. He published the result in the *British Medical Journal* as a valuable paper.

Zhong Nanshan's experiment proved Prof. Franley's calculus formula and discovered its incompleteness. Zhong Nanshan maintained that Prof. Franley's derivation method only paid attention to the change in the position of the hemoglobin curve but ignored the difference in the shape of the hemoglobin curve, which was the most significant.

Stunned by the middle-aged Chinese doctor, Prof. Franley suddenly hugged Zhong Nanshan and exclaimed, "It's great! You've confirmed what I've been conceiving for many years, and you've made discoveries. I'll do my best to recommend you to the British Medical Research Association."

Then, looking into Zhong Nanshan's eyes, he said thoughtfully, "It seems like we've got an excellent prospect for cooperation. I hope you can stay in my laboratory for as long as possible.

Prof. Franley was the type of person who walked the talk. He recommended Zhong Nanshan to the British Medical Research Conference and organized a "beer symposium" for Zhong Nanshan one night to get the conference pass Zhong Nanshan's dissertation.

This form of academic meeting where attendees conduct discussions while drinking beer without the restraint of formality is widespread in Western academic circles. Zhong Nanshan felt a little nervous as it was the first time for him to have participated in such a symposium. This "beer symposium" would determine the fate of his dissertation and qualify or disqualify him for attending the British Medical Research Association conferences.

Prof. Franley meant the symposium to prepare Zhong Nanshan for participating in the British Medical Research Association's meetings. Zhong Nanshan gave his presentation in a relaxed atmosphere. He did so in front of his British counterparts in English for the first time but succeeded. His report won applause from all the medical professionals in respiratory, anesthesiology, and endocrinology. Many came up to congratulate him.

A doctor named Caffrey worked as Prof. Hanley's senior assistant. He was reticent and once responded to Zhong Nanshan's request to introduce Prof. Franley's research with silence. The only time they chatted briefly was in a café, where they ran into each other and exchanged a few words of greetings before he went away.

That evening, when Zhong Nanshan returned to the laboratory to sort out the experimental data acquired during the day, Dr. Caffrey made a special trip to the lab to congratulate Zhong Nanshan. He knocked on the door, and when it opened, he held out his hands to grasp Zhong Nanshan's and said excitedly, "Dr. Zhong, you're fantastic! Your presentation clarified some of my vague concepts with many of your discoveries. You'll have a bright future, and I sincerely congratulate you."

In September that year, Zhong Nanshan gave his research report to the British Medical Research Association meeting, immediately kicking up a great sensation. In October, he was invited to Vienna, the capital of Austria, to participate in the European Conference on Immunology. After listening to Zhong Nanshan's report, Professor David, director of the Department of Thoracic Medicine at St. Bartholomew's Hospital, Affiliated with the University of London, warmly invited him to collaborate with St. Bartholomew's Hospital in researching asthma disease mediators.

– 4 –

In the summer of 1981, Zhong Nanshan decided to end his research work in Edinburgh ahead of schedule and went to St. Bartholomew's Hospital to continue his new research. That day, he went to say goodbye to Prof. Franley, but the latter had gone to the United States for a meeting the day before. In the evening, he was invited to the professor's house and was about to ring the doorbell when the door opened, and Mrs. Franlee rushed to meet him.

Zhong Nanshan saw the great room full of people: the doctors and nurses from the Respiratory Department, the Anesthesiology Department, and the Radiology Department were all present. The table was spread with dishes and champagne. Zhong Nanshan was stunned, thinking that they were having a reception. He said embarrassedly to Mrs. Franley, "I'm sorry, but I came at the wrong time. Sorry for disturbing you."

Shaking Zhong Nanshan's hand, Mrs. Franley smiled, "Tonight's party is for you. Come in. Welcome on board!"

Smiles and laughs filled the house, like roses exuding their fragrance in summer to make people pleasant. The sincere display of friendship touched Zhong Nanshan. He had experienced the vicissitudes of life in his 16 months of stay in the UK. This evening, various mixed feelings churned in him. He bowed deeply to thank everyone.

In his hands, there was a Scottish painting given to him by Metheus, director of the Computer Room; a bracelet for his wife from Centro, deputy director of the Respiratory Department; and books and toys for his children from Prof. Franley's wife.... Everyone held their glasses up and toasted to Zhong Nanshan, celebrating his medical achievements.

Zhong Nanshan arrived in London and came to St. Bartholomew's Hospital in its East End to embark on his new research.

A month or so later, he suddenly received a call from the National Anesthesiology Academic Research Association inviting him to give a presentation. Why would the anesthesiology association ask him to share his ideas? He recalled that while studying the effect of artificial respiration on oxygen transport in the lungs in Edinburgh, he found that his results were the exact opposite of what Prof. Kerr of Anesthesiology, John Radcliffe Hospital, Oxford University, had concluded in a paper.

The professor was an anesthesiology authority in the UK, and the paper he had published five years before was well-known in the medical circles. Zhong Nanshan asked himself if he got it wrong.

Zhong Nanshan always takes academic matters seriously and dares to seek the truth. He repeated his experiment and tests several times and proved he was right. He didn't hesitate and wrote the paper "On the

Influence of Oxygen on Pulmonary Shunt in Patients with Respiratory Failure."

He had given a presentation on the paper to a small number of people in the Department of Anesthesiology, the University of Edinburgh Medical School, and immediately triggered a debate. Someone accused him of being audacious and arrogant. Only Prof. Truman, Director of the Department of Anesthesiology, fell into contemplation. He found it a valuable paper and felt he should recommend it to the National Society for Anaesthesia.

Zhong Nanshan got up early on September 6, 1981. He walked down the foggy street of London extremely excited. St. Bartholomew's Hospital is surrounded by ancient buildings of the 19th century. In the distance, St. Paul's Church's soaring tower highlighted the silhouette of its spire in the thick fog. This house of worship, designed and built with numerical concepts and geometric shape standards, vividly illustrates the rigor of the world-influencing Western civilization created with strict logic.

While pondering over it, he came to the train station. He had to rush 80 kilometers to Cambridge to attend an academic conference and challenge the authority of the British anesthesiologist. He wanted to bring something discovered by a Chinese there and tell the world the correct conclusion. He braced himself for a test in the form of a barrage of criticism.

All sorts of thoughts flashed through his mind. *Am I unaware of my limitations? But if I have the truth in my hands, why am I afraid of a debate? Isn't academic research a constant exploration of the truth? Whether he's an authority, science only recognizes truth but not idols.*

– 5 –

What moved him was that Prof. Truman arrived at Cambridge a day earlier and came to the station to pick him up. He showed Zhong Nanshan around the city with the intent to make him feel relaxed.

At the symposium convened in the afternoon, Prof. Truman sat in the audience, casting his look of trust and encouragement at him. Zhong Nanshan talked eloquently, with the self-confidence he had gained in England. He used slides to highlight the main arguments of Prof. Kerr's published paper and presented his contrary viewpoint based on his experiments. Finally, he projected the curve he had drawn for the oxygen pole correction to the screen, further proving the error of Prof. Kerr's theory.

The experts at the symposium were stunned by the presentation of this Chinese doctor. Silence reigned briefly before a commotion broke out. They exchanged opinions and discussed Zhong Nanshan's views among themselves. Then, three senior assistants of Prof. Kerr raised eight questions in a row. Zhong Nanshan, who came prepared, answered each by referring to his own experimental data and rigorous demonstration.

Per the meeting regulations, the standing committee members must raise their hands to vote yes or no to the publication of Zhong Nanshan's presented paper. When voting started, the audience quieted down. The standing committee members raised their hands high one by one. In front of science, none of them balked.

The conference host Prof. Lehn, Director of the Department of Anesthesiology of the British Clinical Research Center, gave his concluding remarks. He said, "We have also done experiments similar to Dr. Zhong's in our laboratory. Though we didn't have the time to sort out the data, we've roughly come to the same conclusion as Dr. Zhong has. I think this Chinese doctor's research is creative. I sincerely congratulate him on his success!"

As he stepped off the podium, Zhong Nanshan overheard several experts exclaiming, "He's from China!" "He's a Chinese physician!" At that moment, Zhong Nanshan felt proud of his motherland and himself, who has earned his due respect. He became emotional and felt tears swelling in his eyes. He thought he had come a long way! The two-year study in the UK was about to end, and he was confident that he hadn't wasted this precious time.

During the exceptional period of fighting against SARS, Zhong Nanshan once told reporters, "My middle school teacher said that people shouldn't simply live in reality. They must also live in ideals. If people do not have ideals, they'll focus on small things. If a person aspires, unpleasantries happening to them would be trivial compared with their ambitions." If a person doesn't have any ideals and goals, his various emotions would be wholly associated with material things. If he has pursuits, other considerations will become secondary. Then, he'll be highly tenacious, no matter what difficulties he encounters. He'll move forward despite any problem.

With his perseverance and honesty in pursuing the truth, those words best illustrate Zhong Nanshan's life of relentless fight against odds.

A person with ideals is often a person of noble character.

Chapter Six

A Man of Strict Moral Principles

Zhong Nanshan is the most typical representative of the intellectuals in Lingnan. They have a straightforward understanding of humanity and life and an unsophisticated love and dedication to their careers and lifestyles. Lingnan enjoys more men of strict moral principles because the land has had a long history of pragmatism.

A picture of Zhong Nanshan during the outbreak of the COVID-19 pandemic went viral. It was a screenshot of him being interviewed by a Xinhua News Agency reporter. He mentioned that the Wuhan citizens sang the national anthem, believing they could overcome the crisis because Wuhan was a heroic city. He said so as he suppressed his tears swelling in his eyes and pressed his lips into a thin line curving down. He hadn't shed tears during the most challenging times of the SARS epidemic, and this photo thoroughly reveals the two faces of Zhong Nanshan: indomitability and compassion.

If you explore Zhong Nanshan's inner spirit, you'll find the opposing duality of his character.

Doctors are believed to be kindhearted. A doctor must be a rigorous scholar with perseverance to scale new heights in medical science. Simultaneously, he's a man with true love. Zhong Nanshan is a perfect combination of rigor and passion. His character is the unity of dual opposites: wisdom and unsophistication, toughness and generosity, firmness and fragility, indomitability and compromise, dignity and amiability, impartiality and flexibility.... The first part of the duality is written on his unyielding face, whereas the second part is cherished deep in his heart.

Zhong Nanshan is the most typical representative of the intellectuals in Lingnan. They have a straightforward understanding of humanity and life and an unsophisticated love and dedication to their careers and lifestyles.

Lingnan enjoys more men of strict moral principles because the land has had a long history of pragmatism. Besides being practical, Zhong Nanshan is also principled, embodied by his stubborn and indomitable temperament. Character determines one's fate, which indeed bears the deep mark of his personality.

Zhong Nanshan's residence is in a renovated building of his hospital, with its exterior walls plastered with concrete and an elevator installed later. It has a small living space furnished with old-fashioned furniture and appliances: a bulky traditional sofa covered with a large cotton print fabric, an old-modeled air conditioner, ceiling fans, photo frames covering the walls, and a trophy cup on the table used to hold fruit. As the space is limited, his wife's decorative stuff has to be stowed away to make room for his. There is a long iron nail at the corner of the door frame. It is kept as memorabilia because it was used to hang the saline drip bottle when he was sick during the SARS epidemic. At first sight, his living quarters give a sense of history, or rather, time dislocation. It shows the residents' indifference to material life.

When the Zhong family gets together, they concentrate on medical treatment and academic pursuits instead of money in their conversations. Zhong Nanshan doesn't even have any idea about his salary.

He teaches his children to be dedicated and aspiring in the first place and be meticulous and honest when doing things. He tells them to base their viewpoints and research on facts and refrain from jumping to conclusions. He asks them to be confident in their observations. Zhong Nanshan bears in mind his father's expectations: a person must contribute to society instead of living for nothing. The sentence has become the Zhong family's faith.

Now that he's in his eighties, Zhong Nanshan has gradually understood his father, feeling that he has initially lived up to his expectations. But he isn't satisfied with his achievements. Two years ago, he said emotionally to his father in the photo, "Father, I still have two tasks to finish. Only when I complete them can I say I've met your requirements."

I don't know what his two tasks are and if he has completed them. I guess they must be closely related to his medical career. I've searched what he has been doing and found three ongoing projects: The first is to get the respiratory center completely set up. It's said to be very difficult and needs everyone's efforts to find a way to make it happen. The second is the anti-cancer drug he has been working on for three decades. He hopes to succeed, and it's said to be more than halfway to the goal. The third is to promote the early diagnosis and early treatment of chronic obstructive pulmonary disease and form a national and even worldwide treatment movement. Will his promised two tasks are included in the above three?

His participation in the fight against the COVID-19 pandemic alone will allow him to tell his father in the other world with pride: his son has met his requirements. He has dedicated his precious spiritual wealth and wisdom to the Chinese nation that has helped China and its people turn the corner in times of crisis.

Two characteristics mark Zhong Nanshan's home: many exercisers and books. The former includes a treadmill, a bicycle, chest expanders, a horizontal bar, and dumbbells. The exercise apparatuses and books fully reflect Zhong Nanshan's passions: medicine and sports, and they also give the family the greatest pride as a family of physicians and athletes. His father, Zhong Shifan, was an expert pediatrician, and his mother, Liao Yueqin, was a senior registered nurse. His son, Zhong Weide, has also inherited the family tradition and become a chief physician and doctoral advisor. His wife was a basketball star, served as Vice President of the Chinese Basketball Association, and went to a world competition in 1963 as an associate captain of the Chinese Women's Basketball Team. His daughter Zhong Weiyue is an excellent butterfly swimmer, breaking the world record in short-course swimming and winning the 100-meter butterfly championship at the World Short-course Championships in 1999. His son Zhong Weide is also a key player in his hospital's basketball team. Zhong Nanshan himself broke the national record for the 400-meter hurdles with 54.4 seconds in the first National Games and won the Beijing decathlon runner-up in 1961. The family characteristics account for Zhong Nanshan's stamina in the fight against the COVID-19 pandemic at such an advanced age. This physical and mental strength has enabled him to travel here and there with brisk footsteps.

A calligraphy scroll hanging on the Zhong family's condo wall read, "Dare to be a doctor; dare to speak up." The motto mirrors the condo's residents' strength of character. Zhong Nanshan practiced it during the SARS epidemic and the COVID-19 pandemic 17 years later. So, time can't wear away the moral character because it's his nature and the Zhong family's tradition of "speaking the truth and doing practical things" that Zhong Nanshan has upheld in his life.

Zhong Nanshan is 84 as of the time this book is being written. He has been pursuing his goal all his life without wasting his existence. He still works till very late every day, even having no rest on the two-day weekends, when he always arranges work meetings. He has never taken a vacation and gone on a tour with his wife. He isn't simply biting the bullet; he's enjoying what he's doing: curing his patients and releasing them from the hospital.

He finds his life's value and pleasure in his patients' delight.

Looking back at Zhong Nanshan's life, we can find the setbacks and tribulations he has suffered far exceeding those experienced by the average Chinese. They have enabled him to march toward success step by step. Setbacks are disastrous to losers, but they're mere topics of conversation for successful people or those of a strong character.

COVID-19's rage is subsiding, and the pandemic is passing in China, with most provinces seeing zero confirmed cases. The various provinces' medical teams supporting Hubei have completed their tasks and are leaving one by one. The light in the tunnel is visible, and a new phase has begun to "prevent the novel coronavirus from re-entering China from abroad and resurging within the China's territory...

After going through all this, the Chinese deeply feel that it's the luck of this era for China to have someone like Zhong Nanshan.

Afterword

Zhong Nanshan is worth writing about. Alive, he's already a historical figure. It's the writer's responsibility to record him and do an excellent job of documenting him. His actions will become the spiritual wealth of our nation, and his existence is the luck of our time! He'll also be a memory of an era!

2020, the year of the Rat, will be a sorrowful chapter in Chinese and world history. The sorrows will always flow in the long river of humanity.

This year, the Chinese people were preparing for the Chinese New Year when a few people got sick in Wuhan unexpectedly. The news media hemmed and hawed as they reported their cases veiledly until their sickness turned into a matter of grave consequences. A demon sneaking out of Pandora's box soon loomed over the entire land of China, forcing the Chinese to stay at home. Villages and cities were locked down everywhere, and their residents were isolated. The demon seized China and the world, getting every Chinese and global household into its clutches. A scene that can only happen in fantasy stories became a reality during the Chinese New Year season.

I was in Guangzhou to celebrate the Chinese New Year in 2020. We had relatives coming far away from Hunan to reunite with us. We were dining out on the second day and had reservations at Bingsheng for lunch and Toudantang for dinner. Both were restaurants serving authentic dishes. The Toudantang Restaurant had to entertain its guests in batches with good business. We had reserved our table for the second batch. On the afternoon of the day before New Year's Eve, we had to hurry there to pay the deposit and order the dishes to be cooked and served during our gathering. As soon as we stepped out of our residence, my wife and I felt the tenseness of the atmosphere: people's body temperature was gauged at the entrance of the subway station, and everyone wore their face masks and remained quiet. It was the day Wuhan was locked down. Seeing the situation, my wife was a bit panicky, asking me if we should return to get our car. Considering the difficulty in parking downtown, I decided we take the subway train anyway.

We hadn't purchased face masks because I thought Wuhan was remote, albeit the epidemic's severity there. We hadn't been scared by the SARS epidemic breaking out in Guangzhou. We had gone through our daily routines without wearing any masks. Those who did so were few on the Guangzhou streets in those days. We even jeered at the Beijing residents for their cowardness by covering their faces. I remember Li Guowen being adequately protected when he arrived in Guangzhou from Beijing. Seeing very few Cantonese wearing masks and everyone staying cool, he had been so embarrassed that he took his off immediately. *But why, this time, do we behave as if we were confronting a formidable enemy?* I thought it would have been like the SARS epidemic if the worst scenario had happened. *Why bother now since we didn't purchase any protective gear during the SARS period?*

All kinds of news came flooding when we returned home. We canceled the restaurant reservation in the evening per my daughter's suggestion. The restaurant promptly met our request and even told us that they could understand our action. From that moment on, we refrained from stepping out of our condominium. Our daughter would gauge our body temperature several times a day with a touchless forehead thermometer. The reading of my temperature fluctuated, and my daughter would yell with alarm. I thought she must have read too many fantasy books and watched too many horror movies. I wondered why this outbreak was worse than SARS.

One or two occasional passers-by would evoke suspicion and mixed feelings on the street below the condo buildings. The only person we saw every day was the street cleaner working quietly. The world was so quiet that only wind and rain could be heard. A cat might blurt out a mew on the top roof at midnight, and the shrill sounded so sad that it caused the residents to shudder with fear. It was Guangzhou's CBD, where the Tee Mall was located. It would have been bustling and hustling every day, not to mention on New Year's Day. *So, is the situation more severe than the SARS epidemic?*

I called my father on New Year's Eve, and he told me no villagers set off fireworks. They had vied to do so before and illuminated the sky red. By convention, children in my hometown would say "Happy New Year" and ask for candies and fruits from door to door, lanterns in hand, as soon as night falls. But not a single kid stepped out of his house this year.

The whole village would turn out to extend New Year greetings to their neighbors, particularly the elderly, after getting up on New Year's Day. There would be a constant stream of people in the alleys and on the streets. But not a soul could be seen this year, with each road empty and every door closed. The road leading into the village was blocked before long.

On the sixth day of the New Year season, my native village celebrated the 60th anniversary of its founding. It was the first time they had ever thought of having such a ceremony, for which they had been preparing for half a year. They had collected old photos and invited the best flower-drum drama troupe in the area. The villagers loved the opera so much that they had built a stage with their own funds and put on a show themselves at the onset of China's reform and opening up. But the organizer had been detained the following day. However, they would go all out to celebrate the event this time. Unfortunately, this pandemic forced it to be canceled. My childhood friend called and told me that he had to shout out a "Happy New Year" to his uncle outside his courtyard and left. Neither did his uncle dare to open the door, nor did he have the guts to enter the house.

The Qu Yuan Administrative District was locked down, the roads to all the villages were blocked, and everyone hemmed themselves in, which was a scene rarely seen during the war years. The enemy was invisible, existing only in people's imagination, but people were all surrendering to it as it spread the sense of crisis everywhere.

One night, I drove out just for driving's sake. I crossed the Liede Bridge after passing by the Canton Tower (the Guangzhou TV Astronomical and Sightseeing Tower), drove through the Zhujiang New Town CBD, and entered the Five Goats New Town after arriving at the far bank of the Zhu River in the north. From there, I turned to the Guangzhou Bridge. I saw brilliant lights everywhere but little traffic and very few pedestrians. No one except me was enjoying such a splendid night view. I was the only one to stop and go at traffic lights on several occasions. Only a few 24-hour marts and fast-food chains were still open. A lone hotel in the Five Goats New Town had its lights on with one or two clerks working while there wasn't a single customer. All the buses were empty, and so were the bus stations, but the drivers insisted on stopping at each. The night scene felt exotic, magic, sad, expansive, and luxurious. I had the feeling of the brightest confusion and the most extravagant sorrow. I couldn't help tuning my car radio to listen to a piece of music. I thought of Gabriel Garcia Marquez's novel *Love in the Time of Cholera*. I had read it years before, but the thought of it now gave me a different sensation.

The pandemic situation was getting worse and worse. The novel coronavirus is highly contagious, and no drugs can cure it. The only way to avoid a large-scale spread is to discover the virus and get the infected quarantined as early as possible. It was a people's war. Various regions have launched a first-level response to major public health emergencies.

We don't feel it is a war because there's no gunfire. But think about it: even the outbreak of a large-scale war couldn't affect the 1.4 billion Chinese people's daily life to such a degree. The lifestyle and behavior of almost everyone in every Chinese family have fundamentally changed in this COVID-19 pandemic. To say that China has entered a state of war is not a hyperbole; it is a fact.

In the time of globalization, sinologists and translators are the most concerned about my safety. Fiori Picco sent me a message asking me where I was and how I was doing. She told me that she watched the news every day. Fiori had meant to come to China and bought the plane ticket already, but the Ministry of Foreign Affairs of Italy wouldn't allow her to fly over because all flights had been canceled. She hoped that I would keep her posted so she would know I was okay.

Hao Mutian (Martina Hasse) from Germany left a WeChat message, telling me she was worried about the danger of COVID-19. She said she had learned from her search result that my hometown Miluo was less than 300 kilometers away from Wuhan and asked after my loved ones. A Russian named Rodionov sent me a message saying that the novel coronavirus was terrifying, according to the news. He asked after my family and me several times. Natasha, his colleague at the Saint Petersburg State University, also sent me a message asking after me at the same time.

An Indian poet, Priyadarsi Mukherji, sent me the number of deaths from the epidemic in China in a few days, firmly believing that China would be reborn like a phoenix from ashes. Szekeres Klara from Hungary, Meng Na (Elham Sadat Mirzania) from Iran, Anna Gustafsson Chen and Eva Margareta Ekeroth from Sweden, Liliana Arsovska from Mexico, and Mira Ahmed and Hassanein Fahmy Hussein from Egypt—all sent wished me a happy New Year. Most of them have translated my works.

I had never expected that the situation would be reversed a month later. It was my turn to ask after those people and feel worried about them. COVID-19 had become a pandemic breaking out globally.

Shockingly, the pandemic deteriorated rapidly in a matter of ten days. By March 19, the number of confirmed cases of COVID-19 in foreign countries had reached 163,037, which was twice the number of confirmed cases in China, and the number of deaths had reached 6,792, which was doubled the number of deaths in China. The confirmed cases, having doubled in four days, would accelerate at lightning speed to exceed the scale of the crisis in China. Due to differences in cultures, concepts, lifestyles, and political systems, the world, especially the West, may see an astronomical number of people infected by such a powerful and hidden virus. The "epicenter" will oscillate between some countries and regions so that few or even no countries can be spared!

Brescia, the hometown of Italian sinologist Fiori Picco, is only 80 kilometers from Lombardy, the worst-hit region in Italy. Her March new book reading events were canceled at the city hall and bookstores. It's her novel about local Chinese. Lombardy was locked down, followed by several northern provinces, and the streets of Milan and Venice were empty.

Soon afterward, the whole of Italy was under lockdown. Brescia quickly became the place with the most confirmed cases. Fiori Picco's family was in isolation at home. She was worried about her aged parents and young child. She received countless messages showing concern for her and felt even more at a loss. She felt her stress increase sharply.

The pandemic in Italy has gone sharply downhill. On March 19, the number of confirmed cases of COVID-19 reached 41,035, with 5,322 new cases and 427 deaths that day! The cumulative death toll was 3,405, and the daily number of confirmed cases, peak death toll, and cumulative death toll surpassed China. The severity of the outbreak far exceeded that of Wuhan. The hospital morgue was full of corpses, so churches had to be requisitioned to keep the ever-increasing bodies and bury them every half hour. Giorgio Valoti, mayor of Cene, Lombardy, and Vittorio Gregotti, father of modern architecture, both succumbed to the pandemic. Antonio Decaro, mayor of Bari, burst into tears as he walked on the empty street during a curfew.

On the evening of March 12, the Chinese anti-pandemic expert team arrived in Rome with 31 tons of medical supplies. The Chinese national anthem rang out on the streets of Rome.

The global pandemic first broke out in Daegu and Gyeongsang-bukdo, South Korea, and the South Korean government designated them as special disastrous zones. Italy and Iran followed them soon. The pandemic also went out of control in Europe, which had been calm until now. The number of confirmed cases in Spain, Germany, and France increased rapidly, and Norway, Denmark, and Sweden in northern Europe also saw the disease quickly spread. The US issued a travel ban on Europe. The pandemic worsened in Japan, Malaysia, Singapore, the Philippines, and other Asian countries. The number of confirmed cases accelerated in the US, threatening a quick spread and making people panicky. The pandemic had hit over 100 countries.

Italy, Spain, the Czech Republic, France, Belgium, and Jordan placed their cities under lockdown nationwide. A few dozen countries, including Japan, Korea, Italy, Hungary, USA, Spain, Poland, Hungary, Switzerland, and Portugal, declared a state of emergency, with some closing their borders and suspending personnel exchanges. French President Emmanuel Macron called COVID-19 France's worst health crisis in nearly a century, declaring the country into a "state of war."

Meng Na's Iran faced a severe pandemic outbreak and became the hardest-hit country in the Middle East. It went out of control in a few days. A thousand and forty-six new cases were added on March 19, bringing the number of confirmed cases to 18,407. More than a dozen senior officials, including First Vice President Eshaq Jahangiri, were infected with COVID-19, and Nasser Shabani, a senior commander of Iran's Islamic Revolutionary Guard Corps, died of it. The Iranian army was dispatched to empty all the shops, streets, and markets. The government decided to screen all its citizens. Checkpoints were set up at all entrances and exits from Tehran to other places, and most gas stations were closed. Biodefense drills would be carried out across the country. In the early morning of February 29, Chinese medical staff arrived at Meng Na's hometown with medical supplies, and the death rate in Iran began to decline.

Meng Na was in Toronto, Canada, and I asked her to stay for a while and not return to Iran yet. She told me she also lived in isolation and continued in her message, "This novel coronavirus is showing the level of each nation's civilization and wisdom."

Hao Mutian's hometown in Germany was also in the grip of the pandemic. Confirmed cases suddenly rose and caused panic throughout the country. She said she was translating at home without venturing out. She was needed to provide interpretation service at a court in a few days and told me that she would wear a mask then.

On March 16, Germany closed the borders of France, Austria, Switzerland, Luxembourg, and Denmark and banned the export of masks, gloves, protective clothing, and other materials. Germany seized the pandemic-prevention materials imported by Italy and Switzerland, causing disputes. On March 19, Germany reported 2,094 new confirmed cases, bringing the total to 15,320. Chancellor Angela Merkel made a rare televised speech, calling the fight against COVID-19 a historical task and the biggest challenge Germany had faced since World War II. Hao Mutian told me that the Leipzig Book Fair had been canceled, and so had the exhibition in Hannover. We were worried that the Frankfurt Book Fair would also be canceled. The German edition of my novel *Rain and Snow in 2019* would have been debuted at a symposium during this international book fair in October. Organizers of the event, Christina Werum-Wang, Director of the Confucius Institute at the University of Frankfurt, and Dorothee, President of the German East Asia Publishing House, discussed the arrangement of the event with me, and we were all very anxious....

After confirmed cases increased rapidly, Sweden decided to stop case counting and narrow the scope of testing. It claimed that it was impossible to prevent the spread of COVID-19 in Sweden and that limited resources would be used for high-risk groups such as medical staff and hospitalized patients. In the face of the pandemic, the UK government intended to do nothing but let the Britons develop immunity on their own. Its actions shocked the world!

I immediately wrote to Anna Gustafsson Chen and Eva Margareta Ekeroth in Sweden. Anna Gustafsson Chen wrote back to tell me that her country's decision was correct. She said Sweden couldn't test a million people. Everyone with fever or cough should stay at home instead of going to the hospital to infect other patients, doctors, and nurses. Those with acute conditions were exceptions, of course. The government didn't want the virus to spread so quickly as to overwhelm the medical system. Almost everyone who could work remotely now stayed at home. She estimated that 60 to 70 percent of the Swedish would be infected, but most wouldn't suffer from severe illness. She and her husband were both translators and lived like hermits. They were working hard on their translations without having to worry too much. Of the two children, the elder one could work at home, while the younger one worked in a restaurant, exposed to some dangers.

Eva Margareta Ekeroth confirmed that it was the case: Sweden adopted the same policy as the UK. The elderly and high-risk patients were protected, while others were expected to acquire immunity naturally. It was a gamble like playing Russian roulette. Each Sweden had to take precautions individually. She thanked me for the anti-pandemic experience I shared with her and said they had to resign themselves to luck besides being cautious.

No reporters could be seen at the regular press conferences held by the World Health Organization (WHO) in Geneva. Starting from March 13, it would only hold press briefings online. Only the speaker and one or two staff members were in the empty hall. Tedros Adhanom Ghebreyesus, Director-General of WHO, announced on the same day that the number of confirmed cases and deaths of COVID-19 reported in Europe continued to increase, thus becoming the "epicenter" of the "COVID-19 pandemic." By then, the pandemic had reached a "tragic point" worldwide.

China had dispatched medical staff from Guangdong, Sichuan, Shanghai, and Jiangsu to Iraq, Italy, Iran, and Pakistan. It had also established a joint prevention and control mechanism with South Korea and provided emergency medical relief supplies to more countries.

Overseas Chinese trying to return to China made it difficult to find a plane ticket, and the ticket price of some flights had soared dozens of times. The number of imported cases exceeded China's, and the focus had shifted from fighting the pandemic at home to preventing it from being imported from overseas. Once used to battle against the SARS epidemic, the Xiaotangshan Hospital in Beijing had to be reopened.

Humanity faces a global crisis that hasn't been encountered in a century. Death, economic collapse, humanitarian crisis, human sense of decency, personal privacy, state surveillance, isolated nationalism, and globalization will be challenged. As the pandemic deteriorates, it will lead to many disasters, including riots, conflicts, and wars.... Significant changes will happen to the world, its situation, and its setup. In a word, the world we live in will never be the same.

Every day after I got up, the first thing I did was read the pandemic news report column. I had paid attention to domestic news before shifting it to what was going on overseas. Initially, I had been touched to tears by many moving deeds and worried about the constantly developing pandemic. As infections surged exponentially, a "barrier lake" effect threatened Wuhan. Only then did I realize that the pandemic could be more damaging than a war. The number of confirmed patients increased at a rate of over 3,000 per day for several days running, from 291 on the 26th of the twelfth lunar month to 68,586 on the 22nd of the first lunar month, with 1,666 deaths. The inflection point that I had expected to occur on the 15th of the first lunar month failed to do so that day, which told me that the pandemic was much worse than the SARS epidemic. As I was writing this book, the number of confirmed infections had exceeded 80,000, and the death toll had been over 3,000. It was a tragic disaster! My worries had given way to sorrows. The pandemic has taught me a lesson: People always underrate a catastrophe at the onset and watch it develop and transform like in a dream from impossible to possible until it goes out of control.

I was helpless, sad, moved, and anxious.... I wanted to write something but was hesitant. I suddenly understood the many intellectuals who gave up their writing career to join the army. How helpless I felt! What was the use of scholars in the face of a calamity?

Mu Tao, editor-in-chief of *Belles-Lettres*, called me, saying that their magazine would publish a special issue featuring the fight against COVI-19. He expected me to contribute an article. But I wasn't in the mood to write any essays. However, I didn't have the heart to turn his request down right away. I waited till the next day to tell him that I felt too stressed to write anything. Two days later, Han Chunyan, the editor-in-chief of *Contemporary Writers Review*, requested me to contribute to her publication. I had to say I would give it a try.

After I calmed down, I gave the request a second thought. I felt I couldn't be worried without doing anything in a disastrous pandemic. Recording a historical event and providing comfort and encouragement were extremely necessary. It was something worth doing. Therefore, I called the two editors and told them I would write something for them. Before I finished "The Pandemic of 2020," the Guangdong Writers Association asked me to write something about Zhong Nanshan because I interviewed and wrote a lot about him after the SARS epidemic and knew him pretty well. Therefore, I agreed to write another article about Zhong Nanshan and his fight against COVID-19. He is an intellectual that I admire. Unlike the so-called "public intellectuals," he lives a real life without singing his own praises. Working quietly, he has done what many can't in our time.

After its publication on the first page of the *Guangming Daily* and the magazine *Belles-Lettres*, the article I wrote based on my interview with Zhong Nanshan evoked such a considerable repercussion that *Xinhua Digest* and *Essays (Overseas Edition)* reprinted it. The Guangdong Writers Association and the Publicity Department of the Jiangmen Municipal Party Committee, where I worked temporarily, asked me to mine the resources and write more about Zhong Nanshan. Meanwhile, many publishers and publications also requested contributions. So, I buried myself in writing for over a month, during which I slept only five to six hours a day. I dared not waste a single second. At the same time, I had been in hotline contact with Mr. Su Yueming, Zhong Nanshan's assistant. He had been with Zhong Nanshan all the time, seldom letting him out of his sight. I consulted Mr. Su while writing, and he provided a lot of details and got essential questions confirmed and answered by Zhong Nanshan. Huang Qinghui, secretary of the Guangdong Institute of Respiratory Health (GIRH)'s CPC Committee, and Zhang Zhimin, director of the Department of Traditional Chinese Medicine of the First Affiliated Hospital of Guangzhou Medical University, gave me the help I needed.

After finishing the book manuscript, I interviewed two experts in Beijing: Gao Fu, academician of the Chinese Academy of Sciences and director of the Chinese Center for Disease Control and Prevention, and

Zeng Guang, the chief epidemiologist of the Chinese Center for Disease Control and Prevention. I went to the office of the Central Steering Group in Wuhan and interviewed Jiao Yahui, the supervisor of the National Health Commission's Bureau of Medical Administration. She made a phone call in Beijing to Zhong Nanshan and the other five experts, asking them to rush to Wuhan the same day. I interviewed Zhang Jixian in the ward of the Hubei Provincial Hospital of Integrated Chinese and Western Medicine (HPHICWM) and visited the COVID-19 patients whom she had first discovered and reported to the higher authorities. All their family members had recovered, and they were happy when they talked about their treatment. I also interviewed Zhang Dingyu, director of the Wuhan Jinyintan Hospital. I went to the Wuhan Central Hospital, where Li Wenliang had worked before his death, and visited the Huanan Seafood Wholesale Market and the Huoshenshan and Leishenshan hospitals. I also went to the Baibuting community, where the "Ten-Thousand-Household Banquet" had been held and had in-depth contact with 40 to 50 people from all walks of life in Wuhan. I was given a nucleic acid test before leaving Wuhan. As a result, I revised the manuscript repeatedly and made a follow-up revision even after its publication in *Harvest*, a prestigious bi-monthly literary magazine.

Zhong Nanshan is worth writing about. Alive, he's already a historical figure. It's the writer's responsibility to record him and do an excellent job of documenting him. His actions will become the spiritual wealth of our nation, and his existence is the luck of our time! He'll also be a memory of an era!

I'm not a creator of gods, and I don't want to deify anyone. Humans are humans: They all have emotions, desires, and flaws. I only write about them as ordinary people who can be compared: some are of loft character and worth others' respect, whereas others are mean, seeking personal gain shamelessly, and, what's worse, many are in power. Because of this, the emergence of Zhong Nanshan is all the more precious.

The SARS epidemic and the COVID-19 pandemic occurred when he was advanced in age, and both have been so sinister. Each time, he marched toward the battlefields without hesitance. Seeing him working so hard at the age of 84, I felt ashamed and uneasy while watching TV. Such an old man's enlistment itself is worth reassessing.

What progress have we made, and what scenarios and tragedies remain the same during the 17 years between the SARS outbreak and the COVID-19 pandemic? How can we ensure that such happenings will no longer repeat themselves in a few years? Can we do better or worse without Zhong Nanshan?

The TV special of him shedding tears as he talked about Li Wenliang reminds me of his bitter experience 17 years ago. He was empathetic with Li Wenliang, but his situation was far more challenging than Li Wenliang's. As an editor of the *Yangcheng Evening News*, I witnessed a lot of what had happened to him. Therefore, I can write about him without even interviewing him. I still remember vividly the stern faces of those who criticized him. I felt his pressure at that time, one that others may feel too much to withstand.

After 17 long years, a similar tragedy happened again! I put the incident of Li Wenliang and Zhong Nanshan's challenging time during the SARS outbreak together. Time can separate two events, but I can omit the time difference in writing and let the two incidents come tete-a-tete. Only then can we see the truth of time and history.

It's gratifying that our country is more powerful, our people are more united, their patriotism and national cohesion are at an all-time high, and their sense of mission has never been stronger. Governments and social forces at all levels were quickly stimulated and mobilized in the face of the disaster. The rapid action, the unity of top leaders and grassroots organizations, and the unity of the officials and the people have come together to form a formidable force. Once the central government issues an order, the Chinese act immediately, regardless of their regions and ages. They'll work by the hour to implement the policies of the highest decision-makers at the most basic grassroots level of Chinese society. China's robust emergency response capability, especially its institutional advantages highlighted in the face of crises, has been vividly exhibited, thus shocking the world with overawing power. It's where the national strength and hope lie and an essential guarantee for China's rise. China's governance capacity and its national characteristics and cohesion are more evident when compared to how foreign countries have responded to and coped with the pandemic. As Meng Na, an Iranian sinologist, states, "This COVID-19 shows the level of each nation's civilization and wisdom." It has been a test indeed.

In retrospect of a painful lesson we've learned, we must focus on the Huanan Seafood Wholesale Market, where the novel coronavirus first appeared, and on the suspicious wild animals such as bamboo rats, badgers, pangolins, bats, civet cats. We must also pay attention to the ambiguous rhetoric and the loss of precious time at the beginning of the novel coronavirus outbreak.... We've got a lot to reflect upon, from our lifestyle to the nature of our civilization. We need to reexamine and think hard about our worldview, values, way of social development, and our relationship with nature, animals, and plants.

With the advancement of science and technology, our self-confidence is growing. We think humanity has evolved from its backward lifestyle into a modern civilization. We even begin to despise our past and dismiss it as archaic. We no longer pray to gods and spirits in the face of death because we trust the omnipotence of modern medicine. We think we've got nature, society, and even our future under control. The illusion and severely uncoordinated efforts resulting from the rapid development have laid trouble for the future. The pandemic reflects the crises of civilization, modernity, and globalization.

Our contempt for nature has developed to a point where we can fix all animals except humans into gourmet dishes, depriving them of their life's value, dignity, and the divinity they enjoyed in the world before. After routing the beasts threatening their lives, humans have begun to lay their hands on smaller and weaker animals, catching them to savor their taste. It's understandable for primitive homo sapiens to hunt down wild animals to fill their hungry stomachs. Their number was so small that they had no way to drive all the species to extinction. However, we have had the power and means to capture and destroy all the wild creatures today. We no longer need to kill them to sustain our lives, but we still slaughter them.

The wild lives on one globe aren't enough to satisfy our greed. Unfortunately, we have only the Earth to live in, which is also the fate of humanity. The irreversible destruction and damage human beings have caused to the Earth have created crises or even catastrophes threatening the survival of human beings. We find viruses more likely to transmit from insects and animals to humans by destroying our living environment. Dangerous infectious diseases may not have increased much for thousands of years. But we've been hit by the West Nile virus, the Japanese encephalitis, the AIDS, the Hantavirus, the Hendra virus, the Henipavirus, the Rift Valley fever virus, the Marburg virus, the Lassa fever, the Zika virus, the Chikungunya virus, the SARS, the Ebola virus, the MERS, and the SARS-CoV-2 virus in the past few decades alone.... These many viruses that have appeared may spearhead countless large-scale infectious epidemics or pandemics. These newly discovered viruses often break out repeatedly and mutate rapidly. Human technology and dense urban populations have contributed significantly to their spread, which is also accelerated by the rapid worldwide flow of people and commodities facilitated by modern means of transportation. Nowadays, very few places on the globe are not infected.

SARS and COVID-19 belong to the microbiological world. They are from the Pandora's box we've opened of our own accord. The novel coronavirus is a virus that humans haven't seen since the Spanish flu in 1918. Unlike other viruses, it combines contagion and lethality. We've experienced the Ebola and the Henipavirus and are researching many others. They're highly lethal, and some studies have put Ebola's death rate at 80%. But they're nowhere near as contagious as the novel coronavirus so that they won't spread worldwide. Will something like novel-novel coronavirus or even novel-novel-novel coronavirus appear after the SARS-CoV-2 virus? It's by no means alarmist talk.

The world of microorganisms is so tiny that it's invisible, but it's also an infinite world comparable to the universe. Scientists have found 200 million viruses in a drop of water in a cave hundreds of meters deep in a desert, isolated from the world for several ten-million years. There are also viruses in the lake water more than 1,000 meters deep under the Antarctic ice cap. About 174 kinds of viruses can be found in a person's lungs. Viruses are very active in the Earth's ecosystems, moving their DNA from one species to another, altering biological evolution, regulating life's survival, and even affecting the Earth's climate, soil, oceans, and freshwater. For thousands of years, the genetic codes of viruses and humans have been integrated. For example, the sequences in the long DNA chain of humans are derived from ancient viruses. The number of bacteria and viruses in our body far exceeds that of our cells. They can be ten times more, and some are even necessary to maintain our life. If viruses were birds, a human body would be a vast forest in which they perch.

We could have avoided some disasters if we showed respect for life, revered all creatures and objects as having volition, and sought a wholesome life in harmony with our natural environment.

Like it or not, bacteria and viruses are always with us as they share this planet with us. Viruses existed on Earth before the birth of human beings. We can never destroy them because they enjoy a symbiotic relationship with humans and make up the history of humanity's struggle against plagues. We always illusorily think that we are outside such history and it's none of our business. In fact, infectious diseases have never stopped. Instead, they happen once every few years, with large-scale plagues breaking out often, only that we're reluctant to face and pay attention to them. Our selective amnesia makes viral diseases run more rampant.

In 430 BC, the ancient Greek historian Thucydides recorded a terrible plague that lasted for three years. The plague broke out in the Middle East in the 6th century, and the Black Death in the 14th century reduced Europe's population by a third. The plague continued from the Jin Dynasty when it broke out in its capital Bianjing (Kaifeng) to the bubonic plague hitting North China in the Wanli era (1563-1620) and from the Qianlong era (1711-1799), when people treated dead rats as man-eating tigers, to the Tongzhi (1856-1875) and Guangxu (1871-1908) eras. The world has experienced seven significant cholera outbreaks in the past two centuries. It has also seen smallpox, malaria, leprosy, diphtheria, dysentery, typhoid, scarlet fever, typhus, paratyphoid, meningococcal meningitis, dengue fever, yellow fever, whooping cough, measles, and enteritis popping up almost everywhere.

In the past century, the epidemics in China included the bubonic plague breaking out in Guangdong and Hong Kong in 1894. The bubonic plague had been endemic to Yunnan. It became prevalent in Yingkou, Northeast China, five years later. The pneumonic plague transmitted from marmots to humans broke out in the northeast in 1910 and spread along the railway, killing 50,000 people. Cholera was prevalent in northern Thailand in 1919 and entered China two years later. It went on shore at the Chaozhou-Shantou area, advanced along the coastal cities, and spread to inland China.

The latest epidemics included the meningitis outbreak during the "Cultural Revolution" (1966-1976), the hepatitis A outbreak in Shanghai and the hepatitis E outbreak in Xinjiang 32 years ago, the SARS that erupted 17 years ago, and today's COVID-17. If we take a city as an example, infectious diseases occurred in Shanghai almost every year before the 1930s. We can't comprehend the gravity without experiencing it. A pandemic can kill 10,000 people a day and a total of 100 million eventually. Some pandemics can last as long as three centuries.

As COVID-19 is raging among us, repeating the same tragedy in history, we still can't do anything more than our ancestors did. We still have to wear facial masks without knowing how much harm the pandemic will do to humans. Fortunately, humanity has avoided one disaster after another and keeps going. But we often easily forget our painful historical lessons! Our future generations will probably forget we are suffering today in a few decades. Now that we've forgotten Wu Liande, the public health scientist who guided the Chinese in their fight against an epidemic a hundred years ago, will the future generations also forget Zhong Nanshan? That year, Wu Liande dissected some corpses, found Yersinia pestis, and confirmed it as a pneumonic plague. He took such measures as isolation, wearing masks, burning dead bodies, mobilizing the army to lock cities down, and cutting off traffic. How similar were they to the measures we're taking today! Zhong Nanshan served as the 23rd president of the Chinese Medical Association, and Wu Liande was the first one. He died only 60 years ago.

We must ask ourselves whether we should persist in conducting inhuman germ warfare research. How rational are humans armed with biological and chemical weapons? Humans may have never been so savage while claiming to be highly civilized. Can we ponder the significance of viruses to the Earth? How can we take care of our beautiful planet if we humans blindly embrace a more bizarre new lifestyle according to our logic regardless of other creatures?

Unavoidably, viruses could find themselves in humans during their genesis, and they can also profoundly impact and reshape their future and civilization.

The manuscript was finalized in Jiangmen City, Guangdong Province, on March 20, 2020

Appendix

A Biographical Timeline of Zhong Nanshan's Life

On October 20, 1936, Zhong Nanshan was born in Nanjing.

In November 1937, Zhong Nanshan moved to Guiyang with his parents.

From 1942 to 1945, Zhong Nanshan went to elementary school in Guiyang, Guizhou Province.

In January 1946, Zhong Nanshan relocated to Guangzhou with his parents.

In 1949, Zhong Nanshan entered the Private Secondary School Affiliated to Lingnan University (renamed the Affiliated Middle School of South China Normal College in 1952, now the Affiliated Middle School of South China Normal University) (junior high)

In 1952, Zhong Nanshan was admitted to the Affiliated High School (senior) of South China Normal College (now South China Normal University).

In 1955, Zhong Nanshan was admitted to the Medical Department of Beijing Medical College (renamed Beijing Medical University in 1985, merged with Peking University in 2000, and renamed Peking University Medical Department).

He participated in the Guangdong Provincial Track and Field Competition, won the runner-up in the men's 400-meter competition, and broke the record in Guangdong Province. Then, he represented Guangdong Province to participate in the National Track and Field Games in Shanghai and won third place in the men's 400-meter event.

In 1956, Zhong Nanshan was received by Premier Zhou Enlai as one of the merit college students in Beijing.

In 1958, Zhong Shanshan won the 400-meter race championship in the Beijing University Games.

In 1958, Zhong Nanshan was selected to participate in the Beijing Sports Training Team in preparation for the First National Games of the People's Republic of China.

In September 1959, Zhong Nanshan broke the national record in the men's 400m middle hurdles in the preliminaries of the First National Games of the People's Republic of China.

In 1960, Zhong Nanshan graduated from Beijing Medical College (now Peking University Medical School) and stayed at the school as a counselor.

From July 1960 to August 1971, Zhong Nanshan served as a teaching assistant in the Radiation Medicine Teaching And Research Group of Beijing Medical College (now Peking University School of Medicine).

December 31, 1963: He married Li Shaofen.

From 1964 to 1966: He was sent to Rushan, Shandong Province, to participate in the "Four Cleanups Movement."

In March 1966, Zhong Nanshan joined the Communist Party of China (CPC).

In 1968, Zhong Nanshan became a boiler man at the college, and his son, Zhong Weide, was born.

In 1969, Zhong Nanshan was sent to the countryside in Huancheng, Hebei Province, with the medical team.

In 1971, Zhong Nanshan was transferred back to Guangzhou from Beijing and served as a doctor in the Fourth People's Hospital of Guangzhou (now the First Affiliated Hospital of Guangzhou Medical College)

In 1974, Zhong Nanshan joined the Chronic Bronchitis Prevention and Treatment Group of Guangzhou Fourth People's Hospital.

In 1978, the First National Science Conference convened in Beijing. His co-authored paper "Diagnosis and Treatment of Chronic Bronchitis by Integrated Traditional Chinese and Western Medicine" was awarded the First Prize for the National Science Conference Achievements by the State Science and Technology Commission.

In 1979, after its establishment, he served as the deputy director of the Guangzhou Institute of Respiratory Diseases (under the First Affiliated Hospital of Guangzhou Medical University).

In September 1979, Zhong Nanshan passed the examination to study abroad with state funds. In October, he went to the University of Edinburgh Medical School to pursue advanced studies.

In 1980, his "GD Micro Peak Expiratory Flow Monitor" project won the Guangdong Science and Technology Progress Award's third prize.

In April 1981, Zhong Nanshan went to the Respiratory Department of the St. Bartholomew's Hospital to study. In September, he attended a British Anesthesiology Academic Research Association's symposium at Cambridge University. The association voted in favor of his paper

"On the Influence of Oxygen on Pulmonary Shunt in Patients with Respiratory Failure." He published seven academic papers during his studies and returned to China after completing his studies in November.

In 1982, his "Research on Genetically Modified Factors" project won the Guangzhou Science and Technology Achievement Award's first prize.

From January 1983 to December 1986, Zhong Nanshan served as an associate professor at Guangzhou Medical College (now Guangzhou Medical University) and was designated as a healthcare doctor for the central leadership in 1985.

In 1984, Zhong Nanshan served as the director of Guangzhou Institute of Respiratory Health and was awarded the title of "China's First Batch of National-level Expert with Outstanding Contributions."

In 1985, Zhong Nanshan became a special member of the Fellow of the American College of Chest Physicians (FCCP).

In 1986, Zhong Nanshan served as a professor and master's tutor at the Department of Respiratory Medicine of Guangzhou Medical College.

From January 1987 to March 1993, Zhong Nanshan served as the president of the First Affiliated Hospital of Guangzhou Medical College (renamed the First Affiliated Hospital of Guangzhou Medical University in 2013).

In 1987, Zhong Nanshan became a Cambridge International Celebrity Biography Center member.

In 1988, the American Thoracic Society awarded Zhong Nanshan "Special Membership."

In 1989, Zhong Nanshan proposed a correction formula for basic energy consumption in Chinese patients with COPD for the first time in China.

In 1990, the National Health Commission of the PRC appraised him as an "Excellent Returned Overseas Student."

In 1991, Zhong Nanshan proposed the new concept of "hidden asthma" for the first time

From June 1992 to July 1994, Zhong Nanshan served as secretary of the Party Committee of Guangzhou Medical College.

From July 1992 to September 2002, Zhong Nanshan served as the president of Guangzhou Medical College.

In 1992, Zhong Nanshan served as an executive member of the WHO's Global Alliance for Chronic Respiratory Diseases (GARD). He was elected a member of the Guangzhou Municipal Committee of the CPC and awarded the title of "Model Worker" in the national health system.

In 1993, Zhong Nanshan was elected a member of the 8th National Committee of the Chinese People's Political Consultative Conference and served as an advisor to doctoral candidates. The Guangdong Provincial People's Government issued an order to commend him.

In 1994, Zhong Nanshan participated in formulating the "Global Asthma Prevention and Control Strategy" for the UN's WHO as the only Chinese scientist representative. His "Asthma and Airway Hyperreactivity" project won the National Science and Technology Progress Third Prize from the Chinese Ministry of Health.

In 1995, Zhong Nanshan was appraised as a "National Advanced Worker" ("National Model Worker") and won the National May 1st Labor Medal. In August, he began to serve as a professor and doctoral tutor at the Department of Respiratory Medicine, Peking University Medical School.

From October 1995 to October 1996, Zhong Nanshan was a visiting scholar at McGill University, Montreal, Canada.

In April 1996, Zhong Nanshan was elected an academician of the Medical and Health Engineering Department of the Chinese Academy of Engineering.

In 1997, Zhong Nanshan was elected the representative of the 15th National Congress of the CPC and awarded the title of "Model CPC Member" by the Guangzhou Municipal CPC Committee.

In 1998, Zhong Nanshan served as a member of the Ninth National Committee of the Chinese People's Political Consultative Conference and deputy director of the Medical and Health Engineering Department of the Chinese Academy of Engineering.

In 1999, Zhong Nanshan was named one of the six outstanding alumni of Beijing Medical University and served as the chairman of the Guangzhou Association for Science and Technology.

In 2000, Zhong Nanshan served as chairman of the Chinese Society of Respiratory Diseases.

In 2002, Zhong Nanshan served as the Guangdong Association for Science and Technology's vice chairman.

In 2003, the SARS epidemic broke out, and medical workers represented by Zhong Nanshan fought against it and won the long-term battle.

He was elected an advanced national worker, won the National May 1st Labor Medal, the "Chinese Physician Award" of the Chinese Medical Doctor Association, an Advanced Individual in the National Health System's Fight against SARS, a National Outstanding Scientific and Technological Worker in the Prevention and Treatment of SARS, and a National Outstanding CPC Member. He was elected a member of the 10th National Committee of the Chinese People's Political Consultative Conference and served as WHO's global medical consultant for chronic respiratory diseases.

He was awarded the only Special Merit by the Guangdong Provincial CPC Committee and the Provincial Government and served as the Guangdong Provincial Expert Group leader for the Prevention and Treatment of SARS.

He was awarded the honorary title of "Anti-SARS Hero" by the Guangzhou Municipal People's Government. He was appraised as an Outstanding CPC Member in Guangzhou, an Advanced Worker in Constructing Guangzhou's Spiritual Civilization, an "Anti-SARS Model" in Guangzhou, and an Advanced Anti-SARS Individual in Guangzhou City.

He won the China Medical Foundation's "Huayuan Medical Ethics Award," the "The China Comment Award for Innovative Ideological and Political Work," and the Ho Leung Ho Lee Science and the Technology Progress Award (Medical Pharmacy Award). He served as a medical consultant to the UN WHO's Chronic Respiratory Diseases and a Pandemic Influenza Topics Team member.

The paper "Atypical Pathogens Emerging in Guangdong," which Zhong Nanshan co-authored with his research team, was published in *The Lancet*, an authoritative international journal of clinical medicine.

In 2004, Zhong Nanshan was named one of the "2003 Persons Who Touched China" and awarded the "Bethune Medal," the highest honor in China's domestic health system, and the "Chinese Doctor Award" by the Chinese Medical Doctor Association. He won the 6th National Book Award's special prize, the Guangdong Provincial Science and Technology Special Award, and the Guangzhou Medical College Award for Outstanding Contribution. He was appraised as one of the "National Top Ten Outstanding Overseas Chinese" by the Overseas Chinese Affairs Office of the State Council, an Outstanding Teacher in Nanyue (South Guangdong), and one of the "Top Ten Models in Constructing Guangzhou's Spiritual Civilization.

In 2005, Zhong Nanshan was elected the 23rd President of the Chinese Medical Association and awarded the titles of "National Model Worker," "Model CPC Member of Guangdong Province," "Excellent CPC Member of the Guangzhou Education System," and "Excellent CPC Member of Guangzhou Medical College." His article "Interpretation of Acute Infectious SARS—Prevention and Countermeasures" won The First Outstanding Book Award for Popular Science Works in Guangdong Province and the Guangdong Province Science and Technology Individual Special Award. He became a Fellow of the Royal College of Physicians of Ireland (FRCPIRE).

In 2006, Zhong Nanshan won the "Chinese Respiratory Physician Award" and the "Wu Yang Award" (for special contribution). He was named a "Model of Constructing Guangzhou's Spiritual Civilization."

In 2007, Zhong Nanshan was awarded the "National Moral Model (Dedication and Contribution)" Award, one of the "National Top Ten Scientific and Technological Talents," and an honorary doctorate by the University of Edinburgh, UK. He served as the State Key Laboratory of Respiratory Diseases director and the "Image Ambassador of the Volunteers in Guangzhou."

In 2008, Zhong Nanshan was elected as the 11th National People's Congress representative. He won the Guangdong Provincial Science and Technology Outstanding Contribution Award and the Guangzhou Xinqiao Returning Home Entrepreneurship Honorary Award. He became a lifetime honorary member of the European Respiratory Society (ERS) and was selected "A Person Touching Guangdong on the 30th Anniversary of Reform and Opening Up."

His project "Experiments on Animals Using siRNA Strategy to Develop Specific Drugs for the Prevention and Treatment of SARS" won the Guangdong Science and Technology Award's second prize. His project

"Research on Etiological Diagnosis, Pathogenesis, and Treatment of Chronic Cough" won the Guangzhou Science and Technology Progress Award. His "SARS Coronavirus Inactivated Vaccine and Related Research" project won the Guangzhou Science and Technology Progress Award's second prize.

In 2009, Zhong Nanshan was elected the representative of the 11th National People's Congress, won the 5th National Famous College Teachers Award, and was named one of the "100 People Who Touched China since the Founding of PRC." He was hired as Honorary Dean of Guiyang Medical College and Honorary President of Guizhou Medical University and served as a permanent member of the Executive Committee of the WHO's Global Alliance Against Chronic Respiratory Diseases (GARD) and chairman of the Academic Committee of the Asia Pacific Annual Respiratory Conference (APRS).

The paper "Effect of Carbocisteine on Acute Exacerbation of Chronic Obstructive Pulmonary Disease (PEACE Study): A Randomised Placebo-Controlled Study" won first place in The Lancet's Readers' Poll for "Best Paper." Twenty-two hospitals in China contributed to the article under Zhong Nanshan's leadership and coordination.

The project "Creating a Model for Training General Medicine Talents with Combined Skills in Prevention and Treatment and Promoting the Sustainable Development of Community Health Services" won China's National Teaching Achievement Award's second prize.

In 2010, Zhong Nanshan was named one of China's "Top Ten National Outstanding Scientific and Technological Workers" and received an honorary doctorate from the Macau University of Science and Technology.

In 2011, Zhong Nanshan became a member of the Royal Medical College of Edinburgh and a Ph.D. of Science from the University of Birmingham.

In 2013, Zhong Nanshan was elected a deputy to the 12th National People's Congress. He served as the Guangzhou Institute of Respiratory Health director and leader of the H7N9 Prevention and Control Expert Group in Guangdong Province. He published a series of studies on H7N9 in the *New England Journal of Medicine*, making significant contributions to H7N9's prevention and control.

In 2014, Zhong Nanshan was awarded an honorary doctorate of Science by the Chinese University of Hong Kong.

In 2015, Zhong Nanshan successfully cured the first H5N6 patient in Guangzhou.

In June 2016, Zhong Nanshan won the "Achievement Award," the highest of the 11th Guanghua Engineering Science and Technology Awards, the second prize of the National Science and Technology Progress Award, and the title of "Hong Kong University Centennial Outstanding Chinese Scholar."

In 2017, Zhong Nanshan's study proving that using tiotropium, a long-acting bronchodilator, in patients with early COPD in the asymptomatic or mildly symptomatic stage could produce significant clinical effects was published in the *New England Journal of Medicine*. It created a sensation in the world's field of respiratory diseases. The American Thoracic Society granted him the "Giant in Respiratory Medicine" award.

In 2018, Zhong Nanshan was selected as one of the "100 Outstanding Persons Contributing to the Reform and Opening-up." The CPC Central Committee and the State Council awarded him the title of "Reform Pioneer" and issued him the "Reform Pioneer Medal." He was awarded the title of a "Significant Promoter of Constructing a Public Health Emergency Response System."

In 2019, Zhong Nanshan was awarded the title of "The Most Beautiful Fighter" at "The Most Beautiful Fighter" Commendation Conference on the 70th anniversary of the founding of the PRC. He was listed as one of the "70 Returned Overseas Chinese in the Past 70 Years" jointly issued by the Center for China and Globalization (CCG) (a Think Tank of Globalization) and the China International Talents Committee.

On January 20, 2020, the National Health Commission's Team of Senior Experts held a press conference with Zhong Nanshan serving as the expert team leader. The next day, he became the leader of a research expert group of the Mechanism for Joint Prevention and Control of COVID-19 established by the Ministry of Science and Technology.

www.ingramcontent.com/pod-product-compliance
Lightning Source LLC
Chambersburg PA
CBHW040314170426
43195CB00021B/2966